CW00555519

## Useful Websites for Finding Australian Ancestors

| | |
|---|---|
| Ancestry.com (Australia) | www.ancestry.com.au |
| Archives Office of Tasmania | www.archives.tas.gov.au |
| Australian Cemeteries Index | www.ozgenonline.com/aust_cemeteries |
| Australasian Federation of Family History Organisations | www.affho.org |
| Australian Institute of Aboriginal and Torres Strait Islander Studies | www.aiatsis.gov.au/library/family_history_tracing |
| Australian Libraries Gateway | www.nla.gov.au/libraries |
| Australian War Memorial | www.awm.gov.au |
| Commonwealth War Graves Commission | www.cwgc.org |
| National Archives of Australia | www.naa.gov.au |
| National Library of Australia | www.nla.gov.au |
| NSW Registry of Births, Deaths & Marriages | www.bdm.nsw.gov.au |
| Picture Australia | www.pictureaustralia.org |
| Public Record Office Victoria | www.prov.vic.gov.au |
| The Ryerson Index to Contemporary Death Notices and Obituaries in Australian Newspapers | www.ryersonindex.org |
| Queensland State Archives | www.archives.qld.gov.au |
| Queensland Births, Deaths & Marriages | www.justice.qld.gov.au/16.htm |
| Society of Australian Genealogists | www.sag.org.au |
| State Records Authority of New South Wales | www.records.nsw.gov.au |
| State Records of South Australia | www.archives.sa.gov.au |
| State Records Office of Western Australia | www.sro.wa.gov.au |
| Victorian Births, Deaths & Marriages | online.justice.vic.gov.au/ots/home |
| Web Sites for Genealogists | www.coraweb.com.au |
| Western Australian Births, Deaths & Marriages | www.bdm.dotag.wa.gov.au |
| World Vital Records | www.worldvitalrecords.com.au |
| World War 2 Nominal Roll | www.ww2roll.gov.au |

## Second Australian Edition
# Tracing Your Family History Online For Dummies®

Cheat Sheet

## Useful Websites for Finding Overseas Ancestors

| | |
|---|---|
| Access to Archives (A2A) | www.nationalarchives.gov.uk/a2a |
| Ancestry.com (US) | www.ancestry.com |
| Ancestry (UK & Ireland) | www.ancestry.co.uk |
| Cyndi's List of Genealogy Sites on the Web | www.cyndislist.com |
| Families in British India Society | www.fibis.org |
| FamilySearch | www.familysearch.org |
| Federation of East European Family History Societies | www.feefhs.org |
| Federation of Family History Societies (UK) | www.ffhs.org.uk |
| Find My Past | www.findmypast.com |
| FreeBMD | www.freebmd.org.uk |
| Genes Reunited | www.genesreunited.com |
| GENUKI: UK and Ireland Genealogy | www.genuki.org.uk |
| Guild of One-Name Studies | www.one-name.org |
| Library and Archives Canada | www.collectionscanada.gc.ca/index-e.html |
| National Archives of Ireland | www.nationalarchives.ie |
| National Archives (UK) | www.nationalarchives.gov.uk |
| New England Historic Genealogy Society | www.newenglandancestors.org |
| Origins Network | www.origins.net |
| Public Record Office of Northern Ireland | www.proni.gov.uk |
| RootsWeb | www.rootsweb.ancestry.com |
| ScotlandsPeople | www.scotlandspeople.gov.uk |
| Scottish Association of Family History Societies | www.safhs.org.uk |
| Scottish Genealogy Society | www.scotsgenealogy.com |
| Society of Genealogists (UK) | www.sog.org.uk |
| The Statue of Liberty–Ellis Island | www.ellisisland.org |

## For Dummies®: Bestselling Book Series for Beginners

Second Australian Edition

# *Tracing Your Family History Online*

FOR

# DUMMIES®

*Second Australian Edition*

*Tracing Your Family History Online*

FOR

DUMMIES®

**by the Society of Australian Genealogists**
**and Matthew L. Helm and April Leigh Helm**

**WILEY**

Wiley Publishing Australia Pty Ltd

**Tracing Your Family History Online For Dummies®**

Second Australian edition published by
**Wiley Publishing Australia Pty Ltd**
42 McDougall Street
Milton, Qld 4064
www.dummies.com

Authorised adaptation of *Genealogy Online For Dummies*, 3rd Edition (978-1-74031-071-0).
Original English language edition text and art copyright © 2001 Wiley Publishing, Inc. This edition published by
arrangement with the original publisher, Wiley Publishing, Inc., Indianapolis, Indiana, USA.

The moral rights of the authors have been asserted.

National Library of Australia
Cataloguing-in-Publication data

| | |
|---|---|
| Author: | Society of Australian Genealogists. |
| Title: | Tracing Your Family History Online For Dummies/Society of Australian Genealogists, Matthew L. Helm and April Leigh Helm. |
| Edition: | 2nd Australian ed. |
| ISBN: | 978 0 7314 0909 9 (pbk.) |
| Notes: | Includes index. |
| Subjects: | Genealogy. Computer network resources. |
| Other Authors/ Contributors: | Helm, Matthew L. and Helm, April Leigh. |
| Dewey Number: | 929.10285 |

Cover image: sozaijiten/Datacraft

Typeset by diacriTech, Chennai, India

Printed in China by
Printplus Limited

10 9 8 7 6 5 4 3 2 1

# About the Authors

**Heather Garnsey** is the Executive Officer for the **Society of Australian Genealogists** (also known as SAG). She prepared this work on behalf of the Society.

SAG, founded in Sydney in 1932, helps thousands of Australians to trace their family histories each year. It maintains an extensive genealogy library at its Sydney offices and regularly runs courses and workshops around the country on all aspects of Australian and overseas genealogy, including specific genealogy software programs and internet sites. SAG has published early muster and census lists of New South Wales, monumental inscriptions for Sydney's main cemeteries and databases of early Australian resources. SAG works to promote the tracing and preservation of family histories throughout Australia and encourages genealogists to place a copy of their research papers or published family history in its collection. SAG is online at www.sag.org.au.

Heather is a Fellow and Diplomate of the Society, regularly lectures on genealogy both in Australia and overseas, and writes a monthly genealogy column for one of Australia's leading internet magazines.

**Matthew L. Helm** is the Executive Vice President and Chief Technology Officer for FamilyToolbox.net, Inc. He's the creator and maintainer of the award-winning Helm's Genealogy Toolbox (www.genealogytoolbox.com), Helm/Helms Family Research Page and a variety of other websites. Matthew speaks at national genealogical conventions and lectures to genealogical and historical societies. Matthew holds an AB in History and an MS in Library and Information Science from the University of Illinois at Urbana-Champaign.

**April Leigh Helm** is the President of FamilyToolbox.net, Inc. She lectures on genealogy and other topics for various conferences and groups. She holds a BS in Journalism and an EdM in Higher Education Administration from the University of Illinois at Urbana-Champaign.

Together, the Helms have co-authored several books in addition to the five US editions of *Genealogy Online For Dummies*. They include *Family Tree Maker For Dummies, Your Official America Online Guide to Genealogy Online* and *Get Your Degree Online*.

# *Dedication*

Heather, on behalf of the Society of Australian Genealogists, dedicates this second Australian edition to all of SAG's members who have begun to paddle, but are yet to confidently surf, the World Wide Web.

## Publisher's Acknowledgments

We're proud of this book; please send us your comments through our online registration form located at http://dummies.custhelp.com.

Some of the people who helped bring this book to market include the following:

*Acquisitions, Editorial and Media Development*

**Project Editor:** Caroline Hunter, Burrumundi Pty Ltd

**Acquisitions Editors:** Charlotte Duff, Bronwyn Duhigg

**Technical reviewer (Chapter 12):** Carole Riley

**Editorial Manager:** Gabrielle Packman

*Production*

**Graphics:** Wiley Art Studio

**Cartoons:** Glenn Lumsden

**Proofreader:** Pamela Dunne

**Indexer:** Don Jordan, Antipodes Indexing

The authors and publisher would like to thank the following copyright holders, organisations and individuals for their permission to reproduce copyright material in this book.

• Generations Network: **page 41** AncestryIreland.com. Reproduced by permission • Genealogy.com: **page 63** reproduced by permission • RootsWeb.com: **pages 66, 67, 69** and **182** reproduced by permission; **pages 164, 165, 167, 168, 199** and **201** Family Tree Maker is a registered trademark of The Generations Network, Inc. • Jon Baker: **page 44** • Roy Andrews: **page 46** • The Guild of One-Name Studies: **page 47** • Vance G. Wingfield: **page 48** • Church of Jesus Christ of Latter Day Saints: **page 53** FamilySearch.org © by Intellectual Reserve, Inc. Use by permission • © Cyndi Howells: **page 57** • Cornwall Online Parish Clerks: **page 61** © John Simm/Cornwall Online Parish Clerks • Sydney DPS: **page 76** Ryerson Index • Geoscience Australia: **pages 78** and **79** © Commonwealth of Australia — Geoscience Australia. This material is copyright Commonwealth of Australia. Other than the Coat of Arms and departmental logo, you may reproduce, distribute, adapt and otherwise freely deal with this material for all purposes (retaining this notice) without charge on the condition that you include the acknowledgement 'copyright Commonwealth of Australia (year of publication) and (title of the source)' on all uses. You may not sub-licence this material or use it in a misleading context. While every effort has been made to ensure accuracy, the Commonwealth does not accept any responsibility for the accuracy, completeness or currency of this material, and will not be liable for any loss or damage arising from use of, or reliance on, the material. Nothing in this licence affects the operation of any applicable exception or limitation contained in the *Copyright Act 1968*. • © NSW Registry of Births Deaths & Marriages: **page 95** • © State Records Authority of NSW: **pages 101** and **106** • AIATSIS: **page 118** © Australian Institute of Aboriginal and Torres Strait Islander Studies' Family History Unit • Find My Past Ltd: **page 131** www.findmypast.com • General Register Office for Scotland: **page 139** reproduced by permission of General Register Office for Scotland • © Albox Australia Pty Ltd: **page 155** • Commonwealth Copyright Administration: **page 154** 'Caring for Your Wartime Memorabilia', Department of Veterans' Affairs online book © Commonwealth of Australia reproduced by permission • © Kapitol SA: **page 181** • Dashper Family website: **page 186** www.dashper.net.nz • The Ballarat and District Genealogical Society: **page 188** • © Sorenson Molecular Genealogy Foundation: **page 193**

Every effort has been made to trace the ownership of copyright material. Information that will enable the publisher to rectify any error or omission in subsequent editions will be welcome. In such cases, please contact the Permissions Section of John Wiley & Sons Australia, Ltd.

# Contents at a Glance

# Table of Contents

# Introduction

. . . . . . . . . . . . . . . . . . . . . . . . . . . . . . . . . . . . . . . . . .

*T*hanks to the internet, the world of genealogy has undergone a tremendous amount of change over the past ten years. The quantity and quality of research material that's available online has grown dramatically, and almost all researchers now use the internet to trace their family histories and to keep in contact with each other. This means that some of the fundamental ways that family history research is conducted have changed. To keep up with these changes, we wrote this book.

To be a genealogist these days you don't have to travel hundreds of kilometres to find information about an elusive ancestor or wait weeks for details of records to arrive in the mail from overseas. Increasingly, you can be an 'armchair genealogist' — remaining in the comfort of your home as you research around Australia and overseas. Research that previously required hours of painstaking study in an archive can now be conducted over the internet, and since more and more records are being digitised and indexed, the number of websites catering for genealogists is growing daily.

If you have an interest in genealogy, a wealth of information is at your fingertips. You can correspond with family members who live in far-off lands. You can research the history of a particular area and find images of historical documents without setting foot outside your home. You can discover resources that you never suspected were available in the pursuit of your family history. And you can do all of it using your computer and the internet.

## About This Book

Having so many resources available on the internet is great, but you have to be careful not to overload yourself with information and get so frustrated that your interest in genealogy becomes a burden. The number of genealogy-related websites is so huge that you can easily become overwhelmed. This is where we come in to help you.

Of course, you're probably asking yourself how this book differs from the many other genealogy books on the shelf. For example, some books tell you only the traditional methods of genealogical research — which have you travelling hundreds of kilometres to visit archive repositories, and contain chapter after chapter of information about the records and what they contain. Other books that do cover online genealogy tend to group resources by topic, simply listing all the archival websites, all the research sites and which sites contain census information. But these books don't explain *how* to approach your research and integrate the many online resources to achieve your genealogical goal. As genealogists, we understand that researchers don't conduct searches by trying, for example, an alphabetical listing of all the government archive sites to see whether any of these sites contain details of their ancestors.

Also, some books become too computer heavy — giving you lots of overkill about the ins and outs of each kind of internet resource — and neglecting to help you with basic research techniques online and offline that you need to successfully meet your goal. We don't want you to have a bad experience online. So rather than focus on just one thing — genealogy or online resources — we try to balance the act. In this book, we show you how to integrate genealogical research with the use of online resources so that you can learn to effectively and efficiently use your computer and the internet in your family research.

What are the requirements for becoming a genealogist? Well, do you have a mirror nearby? If so, go to the mirror and look at yourself. Now say out loud, 'I declare myself a genealogist'. There you go. It's official — you're a genealogist, and it's time to start pulling together the jigsaw puzzle that is your family history.

Seriously, tracing your family history online requires no formal qualifications. You simply need an interest in your ancestry and a willingness to devote the rest of your life to pursuing information and documents. And access to a computer and the internet, of course.

# Foolish Assumptions

In writing this book, we made a few assumptions. If you fit one of these assumptions, this book is for you:

- ✔ You've done at least a little genealogical groundwork, and now you're ready to use the internet to pursue (and better prepare yourself for) your family history research both online and off.

- ✔ You have at least a little computer experience, are interested in pursuing your family tree and want to know where and how to start.

- ✔ You have a little experience in genealogy and some experience with computers, but you want to learn how to put them together.

Of course, you can have a lot of computer experience and be a novice to genealogy or to online genealogy and still benefit from this book. In this case, you may still want to skim some of the basic sections on computers and the internet.

# How to Use This Book

We know that you may not read this book in order from cover to cover. But don't worry, you're not hurting our feelings by skipping through the sections looking only for the information that you're interested in at that particular moment! In fact, we've tried to write this book to accommodate you. Each section within each chapter can stand alone as a separate entity, so you can pick up the book and flip directly to a section that deals with what you want to know. If we think something relevant in another section can supplement your knowledge on the particular topic, we provide a note or reference telling you the other place(s) we think you should look. However, we've tried very hard to do this referencing in a manner that isn't obnoxious to those of you who choose to read the book from cover to cover. We hope we've succeeded in accommodating both types of readers!

We use a couple of conventions in this book to make it easier for you to follow a set of specific instructions. Commands for menus appear with arrows between each selection. (For example, the command Format ⇨ Tree Format tells you to choose Tree Format from the Format menu.) Also, if you need to type something, the explanation uses **bold type** to indicate what you need to type.

# How This Book Is Organised

To help you get a better picture of what this book has to offer, we explain a little about how we organised it and what you can expect to find in each part.

## Part I: Getting Your Act Together

You need to have a good foundation before starting your online genealogical research. This part explores the fundamental family information that you need to collect first, how to form an online research plan, and how to start searching the internet for information about ancestors and geographic locations.

## Part II: Finding the Elusive Records

Searching online for a specialised type of record or for information about ancestors in government records both here and overseas can be challenging, even for the most skilled genealogist. For this reason, Part II examines resources that are available online to help you find those elusive ancestors.

## Part III: Keeping Your Ancestors in Line: Organising and Presenting Your Findings

What you do with the information that you find is just as important as finding it in the first place. So, in this part, we look at how to store and organise your documents and photographs, as well as how to store research results in a genealogical database. We also give you methods of retrieving that information through reports that can help you with your future research.

## Part IV: Share and Share Alike

One of the most important aspects of genealogical research is using a coordinated effort to achieve success. This part takes a look at what goes into this effort, including using all available online resources, cooperating with other researchers, coordinating with groups and societies, and sharing the fruits of your research with the online community.

## Part V: The Part of Tens

Ah, the infamous Part of Tens (infamous because every *For Dummies* book has one of these sections with profound advice or lists of things to do). Here you find a series of quick-reference chapters that give you useful genealogical hints and reminders. We include a list of online database sites we think you should know about, a list of websites we think every beginner to genealogy should visit, hints to keep your online research sailing smoothly and some tips for creating your own genealogical website.

## Appendixes

As you read this book (or skip from chapter to chapter, section to section, looking over only those parts that interest you), you may have additional questions in some areas. That's why we include the appendixes. Appendix A provides definitions of many terms that you're likely to encounter in your genealogical research. Appendix B gives you an overview of the software that we include on the CD-ROM that accompanies this book, as well as basic instructions for installing and using it.

In Appendix C, we present the *Tracing Your Family History Online* Internet Directory. We can't possibly list every website out there you may want to visit during your research, so in this directory we've gathered together some of the main ones that we think are helpful and interesting. You can find sites for everything — surnames, government records, geographic-specific research and genealogical gateways. For each site that we identify, we provide the name, URL (Uniform Resource Locator) and a brief overview of what the site has to offer.

We want you to be able to see immediately whether a site in the directory has a particular type of information or service of interest to you. For this reason, we created some mini-icons — or, if you prefer, *micons* (see Appendix C for details).

# Icons Used in This Book

To help you get the most out of this book, we include some icons that tell you at a glance whether a section or paragraph has important information of a particular kind.

Here you can find concepts or terms that are unique to genealogy.

Here, we refer you to other books or materials in case you'd like additional information.

This icon points out software that's included on the CD-ROM.

This icon marks important genealogical stuff, so don't forget it.

This icon signals a website that has a search engine you can use to look for content within the site.

When you see this icon, you know we're offering advice or shortcuts to make your researching easier.

We walk you step by step through an example of something.

Look out! This is something tricky or unusual to watch for.

# *Where to Go from Here*

Depending on where you're reading this introduction, your next step is one of two possibilities:

- ✔ If you're in the bookstore, you need to go to the front counter and pay for this book so that you can take it home and use it. (Many bookstores are pretty understanding about your sitting and reading through parts of books — that's why they provide the comfortable chairs, right? But we're not sure they would look highly upon you whipping out your laptop computer, firing up your wireless internet access and proceeding to go through this entire book right there in the store. Then again, we could be mistaken — so use your best judgement based on your knowledge of the bookstore in which you're standing.)

- ✔ If you've already bought the book and you're at home (or wherever), you can go ahead and start reading, following the steps for the online activities in the book as they come along.

# Part I
# Getting Your Act Together

'Researching my family history on the net
is so much easier now I've learnt to
spell "genealogy" correctly.'

# In this part ...

**S**o you wanna be an online genealogist? Well, you need to prepare yourself for that first online research trip by finding out about the basics of genealogy and how to form a research plan. When you're ready to take the online plunge, we help you find worthwhile surname and area-specific resources on the internet.

# Chapter 1

# You Gotta Have Groundwork

*W*ouldn't you know it — one of the most successful keys to researching your family history online doesn't even include turning on the computer. That's right, we said, 'doesn't include the computer'! You may ask yourself, 'How can people writing a book about tracing your family history online say that?' Well, our experience is that you need to know a few details about your family *before* you try to find all those great nuggets of information online. Don't worry, we get to the internet soon. But first you have some homework to do, and the place to do that really is at home!

Before we begin, we want to make one very important disclaimer. As you venture into online genealogy, keep in mind that you can't complete your entire genealogy by using only online resources. To trace your family history properly, you still need to visit libraries and archives, and sift through dusty old books and manuscripts, or use microfiche and microfilm. Why? Because many crucial records simply haven't been converted into electronic format. In fact, you should think of online research methods as only one of many tools that you can use to gather the information you need for a complete picture of your ancestors.

In this chapter, we outline several resources that you can use for information before you begin your online genealogical research. We also provide some websites that can assist you in accessing these resources.

# Starting Your Research with What You Already Know

Sometimes, beginning genealogists start their search by trying to find out whether they're related to someone of the same name who lived 200 years ago, or to discover the identity of their families' first arrivals in this country. Such a strategy often becomes frustrating because either they can't find any information or they find something that they assume is true, only to discover later that the information doesn't apply to their family branch. To avoid this mess, we recommend that you conduct your genealogical research one step at a time — and that you begin your family history journey with yourself.

## Making a few notes about yourself — the autobiographical sketch

You already know a great deal about yourself — probably more than anyone else knows about you. (Unless you're married. Then your spouse knows more about you, right?) You probably know your birth date, place of birth, parents' names and where you've lived. (We recognise that not everyone knows all this information; adoption or other extenuating circumstances may require you to do the best that you can with what you know until you discover additional information about yourself.) So, sit down at that computer, open your word processor and create an autobiographical sketch. Or if you prefer, grab a piece of paper and write down those details instead.

You can approach the sketch in several ways. Sometimes, the easiest method is to begin with current events and work back through your life. For instance, first note the basics: Your current occupation, residence and activities. Then move back to your last residence, occupation and so on until you arrive at your birth date. Make sure that you include milestones like children's birth dates, marriage date(s) and other significant events in your life. If you prefer, you can cover your life by beginning with your birth and working forward to the present. Either way is fine, as long as all the important events are listed in the sketch.

## Finding primary sources

Although you may know a lot about yourself, someone else may have difficulty discovering these facts about you if they were to research you at some point in the future. This is where primary sources come in handy.

*Primary sources* are documents, oral accounts (if the account is made soon after the actual event and witnessed by the person who created the account), photographs or any other items created at the time of a certain event's occurrence.

For example, a primary source for your birth date is your birth certificate. Typically, a birth certificate is prepared within a few days of the actual event and is based on information given by an actual witness to the birth. Because of this, the information (like the time, date and parents' names) is usually a reliable first-hand account of the event — unless, of course, someone lied about the parents' names. However, even if a record was prepared near the time of an event, this doesn't mean that every fact provided on the record is correct. Cases arise where typographical errors occurred or incorrect information was provided to the creator of the record. So it's always a good idea to try to find other primary records that can corroborate the information found in any record.

*Secondary sources* are documents, oral accounts and so on created some length of time after an event or for which information is supplied by someone who wasn't an eyewitness to the event.

Secondary sources don't have the degree of reliability or surety of primary sources. Often, secondary source information, such as that found on death certificates, is provided by an individual's children or descendants, who may or may not know the exact date or place of birth. So, backing up your secondary sources with reliable primary sources is always a good idea.

Some records may be considered both primary and secondary sources. For example, a death certificate contains both primary and secondary source information. The primary source information is the date of death and cause of death. These facts are primary because the certificate is prepared around the time of death and the information is usually provided by a medical professional who certifies the death. The secondary source information on the death certificate includes the birth date and place of birth of the deceased individual. These details are secondary because the certificate is issued at a time significantly later than the birth — assuming that the birth and death dates are at least a few years apart.

You can familiarise yourself with primary sources by collecting some information for your own autobiographical profile. Try to match up primary sources for each event in the sketch — for example, birth and marriage certificates or land and property records. For more information on finding these types of documents, see the appropriate sections later in this chapter. If you can't locate primary source documents for each event in your life, don't fret! Your autobiographical sketch can serve as a primary source document because you write it about yourself.

For additional information on primary and secondary sources, see the *Online Information Literary Tutorial* at the Queensland University of Technology Library (`pilot.library.qut.edu.au/module1`).

# Chatting with Grandad and Aunty Elsie: Interviewing Family Members

After you complete your autobiographical sketch, interviewing family members to collect information about them and other relatives is a great next step. Collect the same type of information about their lives that you provided about your own. Your parents, brothers, sisters, grandparents, aunts, uncles and cousins are all good candidates for information about your family's most recent generations.

Talking to relatives provides you with leads that you can use later to find primary sources. For more information on primary sources, see 'Finding primary sources' in the preceding section. You can complete family interviews in person or through a questionnaire — although we strongly recommend that you conduct them in person. For an example of a covering letter to send your family, go to this website: `www.genealogy.com/00000059.html`.

There's no easy way to say this, so please excuse us for being blunt — your family members won't live forever, so begin interviewing your relatives as soon as possible, depending on their ages and health. If a family member passes away before you arrange to interview him or her, you may miss the opportunity of a lifetime to learn more about his or her personal experiences and knowledge of previous generations.

Here are a few tips to remember as you plan a family interview:

- ✓ **Prepare a list of questions that you want to ask:** Knowing what you want to achieve during the discussion helps you get started and keeps your interview focused. (See the sidebar 'Good interviewing questions' for some ideas.)

- ✓ **Take a digital (or video) recorder to the interview:** Make sure that you get permission from each participant before you start recording, because even though your relatives may be very happy to share their knowledge with you, they may not like the idea of being recorded — or, if they're uncomfortable with the experience, they may clam up and not tell you everything they know. For example, Cousin Lou may know very well that Aunt Jane disappeared to the country for a few months in her late teens because she was 'in the family way', but certainly doesn't want to be the one to go on record about it. While capturing each

TIP

# Good interviewing questions

Before you conduct an interview with a family member, pull together a set of questions to guide the discussion. Your planning makes the difference between an interview in which your relative stays focused, or a question-and-answer session that invites bouncing from one unrelated topic to another. Here are some examples of questions that you may want to ask:

- What is your full name and do you know why you were given that name?

- Where were you born and when? Do you remember any stories that your parents told you about the event?

- Where did you go to school? Did you finish school? If not, why not? (Remember to ask about all levels of schooling.)

- What are the names of your brothers and sisters? What were they like?

- When you were a child, who was the oldest person in your family?

- Did any relatives (other than your immediate family) live with you?

- Do you remember who your neighbours were when you were a child?

- Did your family have any traditions or celebrate any special holidays?

- When did you leave home? Where did you live?

- What occupations have you had? Did you have any special training?

- How did you meet your spouse?

- When and where did you get married? Did you go on a honeymoon? Where?

- When were your children born? Do you have any stories about their births?

- Where and when were your parents born? What are their full names? What did they look like? What were their occupations?

- Did your parents tell you how they met?

- Do you remember your grandparents? What did they look like? Do you recall any stories about them?

- Did you hear any stories about your great-grandparents? Did you ever meet your great-grandparents?

- Have any items (stories, traditions or heirlooms) been handed down through several generations of your family?

- Were any of your family involved in either of the World Wars? What do you know about their service?

- Do you know who in the family originally immigrated to this country? Where did they come from? Why did they leave their native land?

You can probably think of more questions that are likely to draw responses from your family. During the interview, stay flexible. Explore specific family events, share family legends and ask for photographs that illustrate the events you discuss.

interviewee's stories can play an important role in your family history research, you have to weigh up whether the opportunity to be able to replay what was said word by word is as important as ensuring that the family member you're interviewing is as relaxed as possible and sharing with you all he or she knows.

✔ **Use photographs and documents to help your family members recall events:** These items open doors and prod your interviewees' memories, especially if the photos are of them in their youth. Ask whether they can identify other people in the photos, whether they remember why a particular photo was taken and where. Sometimes, their stories may contradict information you already have, but it's important to let them tell you what they remember. And don't forget to ask them whether they have photographs or other items of interest — you don't want to spend a couple of hours chatting with a family member only to hear on your way out the door: 'What a shame we didn't get time to look at the suitcase of photos I've got tucked away under the bed in the back room.' Which brings us to our next point . . .

✔ **Try to limit your interviews to two hours or less:** You don't want to be overwhelmed with information, and you don't want the interviewee to get worn out by your visit. Within two hours, you can collect a lot of information to guide your research. Remember, you can always do another interview if you want more information. (Actually, we strongly encourage you to do subsequent interviews — often the first interview stimulates memories for the individual that you can cover during a later interview.)

# Looking for Love Letters, School Reports and Other Important Documents

Are you, or have you ever been, accused of being a hoarder? You know what we mean — someone who keeps every little scrap of paper 'just in case'. If you are, then you're probably well suited for genealogy. In fact, if you're lucky, you descend from a long line of hoarders who saved all those scraps from the past and put them in boxes in the garage or attic. If you dig through these treasures you're sure to find things that can further your genealogical research. For example, envelopes full of old driver's licences, war ration cards, letters, receipts, school report cards and vaccination certificates. Some of these items may contain original signatures and many can help you to work out where a particular family member was on a specific date.

When you go through old family files, look for things that can serve as primary sources for facts that you want to verify. For more information on primary sources, see 'Finding primary sources' earlier in this chapter. Look for documents to verify addresses, occupations, church membership and military service. Here's a list of some specific things to look for:

- ✔ Baptismal certificates and other church records
- ✔ Books given as gifts that have inscriptions inside the front cover
- ✔ Copies of vital records (such as birth, marriage and death certificates, and divorce decrees)
- ✔ Diaries
- ✔ Family bibles
- ✔ Family letters
- ✔ Legal documents (such as mortgages, titles and deeds)
- ✔ Membership cards
- ✔ Naturalisation (citizenship) records
- ✔ Obituaries and newspaper articles
- ✔ Occupational or personnel records
- ✔ School reports
- ✔ Wills

For a list of items to look for around the home to help you with your family history research, see *Finding Information at Home* at www.genealogy.com/00000027.html.

# Dusting Off the Old Photo Albums

A picture is worth a thousand words — so the saying goes. That's certainly true in genealogy. Photographs are among the most treasured documents for genealogists. Pictures show how your ancestors looked and what conditions they lived in. And sometimes, the back of the photo is more important than the picture itself, because it may include crucial information, such as names, dates and descriptions of places that help identify who's in the photograph.

Photographs are also useful as memory-joggers for your family members (see also 'Chatting with Grandad and Aunty Elsie: Interviewing Family Members' earlier in this chapter). Pictures can help others recollect the past and bring up long-forgotten memories. Just be forewarned — sometimes the memories are good, and sometimes they're not so good! Although you may stimulate thoughts of some great moments long ago, you may also open a can of worms when you ask your grandmother about a particular person in a picture. On the plus side, in the end she may give you the lowdown on not only that person but every single individual in the family who has ever made her angry — this can provide a lot of genealogical leads.

You may run into several different types of photographs in your research. Knowing when certain kinds of photographs were produced can help you associate a time frame with a picture. Examples include

- **Albumen prints:** These were produced on a thin piece of paper that was coated with albumen and silver nitrate. They were usually mounted on cardboard. These prints were used between 1858 and 1905 and were the types of photographs found in cartes-de-visite and cabinet photographs.

- **Ambrotypes:** Ambrotypes used a much shorter exposure time and were popular in Australia between 1855 and 1865. Some were still being produced as late as 1880.

- **Cabinet photographs:** Cabinet photographs are a larger version of the carte-de-visite and were introduced in 1866 — although they weren't widely used until 1880. They were not produced after 1905. A cabinet photograph often has the photographer's name and studio address on the front or back of the card, making it easier to determine the date it was taken.

- **Cartes-de-visite:** Carte-de-visite prints are one of the most common formats found in family albums. They were introduced into Australia in 1859. Cartes-de-visite from the 1860s usually have square corners, and after 1870 were mounted on a thicker board.

- **Daguerreotypes:** Daguerreotype photos were taken from 1839 to 1860. They required a long exposure time and were taken on silver-plated copper. The photographic image appears to change from a positive to a negative when tilted.

- **Glass-plate negatives:** These were used between 1848 and 1930. They were made from light-sensitive silver bromide immersed in gelatine.

- **Platinum prints:** Platinum prints have a matte surface that appears embedded in the paper. The images were often highlighted with artistic chalk. They were produced from the 1890s to the 1930s.

- **Stereographic cards:** Stereographic cards were very popular between 1855 and 1865, and 1895 and 1910. They were often paired or mounted on a curve to produce a three-dimensional effect when used with a special viewer.

- **Tintypes:** These were often postage-stamp sized, making them difficult to date because there was rarely room to write inscriptions on the back of them. They were introduced in 1858 but most would date between 1880 and 1890.

For online resources that can help you identify different types of photographs to determine when a picture was taken, see Chapter 6. Also, when you deal with photographs, keep in mind that too much light or humidity can easily destroy them. For more information on preserving photographs, see Chapter 8.

# Getting the Framework Right: The Importance of Vital Records

Vital records are among the first sets of primary sources typically used by genealogists (for more on primary sources, see 'Finding primary sources' earlier in this chapter). *Vital records* include birth, marriage, divorce and death records. These records contain key and usually reliable information because they were produced near the time that the event occurred and a witness to the actual event provided the information. In Australia, vital records are called *BDM records* (birth, death and marriage records) or *civil registrations*.

Overseas, local governments tend to maintain vital records, although in some countries central databases have been created. In Australia, vital records are maintained by the states and territories, so in order to get hold of a copy of a record, you need to determine in which state or territory a birth, marriage, divorce or death took place. For information on where to find details online, see Chapter 5.

The states and territories have different methods and laws regarding civil registration records — their indexes, the date range for public access to records and the information contained on certificates all vary. Yes, Australia's state registries are moving towards a uniform approach to registration and access to vital record information, but for now, be aware that differences apply.

Don't expect open access to birth, marriage, divorce and death records. The older a record, the better your chances, but for privacy and security reasons you won't be able to obtain a civil registration certificate relating to any person who's still alive. For example, an 1870 marriage certificate is quite easy to obtain, but getting a copy of a 1970 marriage certificate is a different story — unless it's your own.

# Birth records

*Birth records* are helpful primary sources for verifying — at a minimum — the date of birth, birthplace and names of an individual's parents. Depending on the information requirements for a particular birth certificate, you may also discover the birthplace of the individual's parents, their ages, occupations, addresses at the time of the birth, the date of marriage of the parents, whether the mother had given birth previously, and the names and ages of any previous children. Sometimes, instead of a birth certificate, you may find another record in the family's possession that verifies the existence of the birth record. For example, among family papers you may find copies of birth extracts — a summarised version of a birth certificate. In the past, these were often adequate for children to prove how old they were to start school, or for someone to obtain a driver's licence or join a sports club. However, they're no substitute for the full record. They normally just state the person's name, and the date and place of birth.

The further back in time you go, the less formal the record of a birth is. Although you may be accustomed to providing copies of your birth record to numerous government departments and organisations to prove who you are, your ancestors certainly didn't have to. In fact, before modern record-keeping, a birth record may have been no more than a handwritten entry in a register book, giving brief details. Always be specific when citing a birth record in your genealogical notes — include any numbers that you find on the record and where it is located so that it can readily be tracked down again.

# Death records

*Death records* are excellent resources for verifying the date of a person's death, but are the least reliable of the vital records for other details, such as birth date, birthplace and so forth, because the person who died is not supplying the information and those that are tend not to have been witnesses to the earlier events in the deceased's life.

Early death records may contain only the date of death, the cause and the deceased's place of residence. However, more recent death certificates in some Australian states and territories tell you not only the date and place of death, and the deceased's place of residence and age at death, but also the spouse's name, when and where they married, how many children they had and the age of each child at the time of the person's death, as well as information about the deceased's parents, when the deceased came to Australia (if not born here) and how long ago. In other words, clues to three generations in one family!

Always check the name of the informant on a death certificate for clues to the accuracy of information. For example, don't assume a son-in-law knows where his wife's father was born and when. Also, be wary that the deceased's age may have been rounded up or down — when asked by the clerk, the informant may have guessed and said, 'Oh, he's about 60'. So, although '60' is recorded as the age on the certificate, the person could actually have been 58 or 63.

## Marriage records

*Marriage records* come in several forms. Early marriage records may include

- **Marriage banns:** Proclamations made to a church congregation on the three successive Sundays prior to a marriage taking place.

- **Marriage bonds:** Financial guarantees that a marriage was going to take place. These are commonly found in early English records.

- **Marriage licences:** Documents granting permission to marry, without the need to publicise the fact in front of a church congregation by calling banns.

- **Marriage records or certificates:** Documents certifying the union of two people.

- **Permissions to marry:** Documents granting a convict permission to marry, based on good behaviour. (Believe it or not, when Australia was a penal settlement, being allowed to marry was also known as an 'indulgence' — a reward for being a well-behaved convict. Sometimes, a convict may have applied for a permission to marry a number of times, to different people, before the authorities finally agreed.)

These records contain — at a minimum — the name of both the bride and bridegroom and the location of the marriage. They may also provide details of their ages, places of birth, occupations, parents' names and marital status (which can lead you to previous marriages). Names and signatures of witnesses, who are often related to either the bride or bridegroom, can also be found. In fact, a marriage certificate may be the only place where you can find an ancestor's original signature, although in cases where he or she could not write, an X was indicated in its place.

Don't assume that if you find a marriage licence, a bann or a permission for a convict to marry that the event actually took place. Just as they do today, people in the past got cold feet too, and backed out of marriages at the last minute.

## Divorce records

Until the 1870s, it was almost impossible for the average person to obtain a divorce. Even then, there was no such thing as a 'no fault divorce' — there had to be a guilty party, determined by a court case. Not surprisingly, many families hid the fact that there had been a divorce in the family.

Even today, *divorce records* are still often restricted, although you can find cases written up in newspapers, especially if the couple was well known in an area. These articles can give you a great deal of information about both parties and the circumstances of the divorce. Likewise, divorce records themselves contain many important facts, including the age of the petitioners, their places of birth, addresses, occupations, the names and ages of their children, any property they owned and the grounds for the divorce.

If you do dig up divorce records, be sensitive about how you use the information — especially if previous generations had closed ranks and decided not to let the information pass down the line. Descendants of a branch of the family may not like you to broadcast the fact that your grandfather's brother was found guilty of beating his wife when he'd had too much to drink and that she had successfully divorced him.

# Perhaps They Were Convicts?

A few decades ago, most Australians kept quiet about their convict connections. These days, however, family historians are much more open about finding a convict among their ancestors, and in many cases find records that survive detailing many different aspects of the convict's life. In fact, it's easier to trace a convict in the early years of Australian settlement than a free person, because the authorities had to keep a tight rein on prisoners — and they had to feed them, clothe them, house them and employ them. This created a whole bureaucracy, which ensures that many records of the day-to-day lives of convicts are available today for researchers to use.

Many different resources are available to help you to trace your convict ancestry. These include convicts' sentence and transportation records to the colony; when and where they worked or to whom they were assigned after arrival; what rewards they received for good behaviour during their sentence; whether they married; whether they were eventually freed; whether they received a grant of land; and when they died.

Convict records account for thousands of individuals. For example, more than 160,000 people were transported from overseas to New South Wales — Australia's first penal settlement. They were sent to the colony for various crimes, ranging from minor burglary to murder. Some received a sentence of seven years, others 14 years and many were transported for life.

Did your ancestors unwittingly leave you some clues that they had convict origins? Obviously the year and place of their arrival in Australia is important: If they came to New South Wales before about 1820, there's a strong chance they were convicts. Another good clue is if one of your ancestors was a young, single male who needed the Governor's permission to marry. Early records of the colonies regularly recorded the ship and year of arrival as a way of identifying one person from another, and if you're lucky enough to find this information in, say, a hospital admission register, it may quickly point to whether your ancestor arrived on board a convict ship.

Not all of Australia's early settlements accepted convicts, and those that did operated at different times. For example, New South Wales took in convicts from 1788 to 1842, but Western Australia accepted convicts up until 1868. These penal colony dates can provide you with vital clues as to whether or not you have convict ancestors. For an overview of the convict system, see the *Basics on Convicts to NSW* page under the Helping You tab at the Society of Australian Genealogists website at www.sag.org.au.

Because convict research is now so popular, many individual historians, groups and government agencies have made records available online. These may be transcribed listings or records describing events in more detail. We cover using the internet to search for convict ancestors in more detail in Chapter 5.

# They Couldn't Have Swum: Locating Shipping Records

Tracking down an ancestor's ship and arrival date is at the top of most family historian wish lists — even for experienced genealogists. It can also give you new leads to research, so that you can go on and find where the person or family originated.

Finding ancestors in early immigration records can be challenging, however, especially if they arrived as free settlers in the 1800s. If they were convicts, their records may be easy to locate; but if their passage was unassisted, their arrival may have gone undocumented.

# *Not all shipping records are equal*

Don't let your hopes get too high and expect to be able to trace the year, ship and place of arrival for every one of your ancestors. Unfortunately, the records that are available vary enormously, and this means the amount and type of information that you find may be patchy, too.

Besides being shipped out as a convict, there are three other ways people could have made it to Australia before 1901, which we tell you about in the following sections.

### *Free passengers*

Many people paid their own passage to one of the Australian colonies. The better-off were able to travel as cabin passengers, often accompanied by servants or governesses to care for their children on the voyage. However, many could only just scrape together the money they needed for the voyage and travelled as steerage passengers, sharing living space for the three-month voyage with several hundred others in the bowels of the ship. These steerage passengers were often young, single men or families with small children determined to make a better life for themselves, risking a long voyage to a country they knew little about. This form of travel to Australia was especially common when the gold rushes began in the 1850s.

Because free passengers paid their own way the authorities weren't terribly interested in them. In fact, once they started to flood into colonies like New South Wales and Victoria in search of gold, the authorities sometimes stopped collecting their names and just counted heads! This means you may never be able to determine exactly the name of the ship on which your great-grandfather travelled to Australia.

### *Bounty or assisted immigration*

By the 1820s, the colonial masters had a problem — their new society was way out of balance, because they had more males than females in the convict system. In order to populate the country they desperately needed to attract young, single women to Australia, and encourage families with small children to make a new life here. They came up with inducements, offering to pay people's passages for them — either with a form of financial assistance or by offering a 'bounty' per head to shipping companies to select suitable applicants and bring them out. The authorities set specific qualifications though, in terms of health, age and occupation, which required record-keeping. This means that today you're likely to have better luck tracking down information about ancestors who came out as bounty or assisted immigrants than free passengers.

### Marines and crew

In the early years, the penal colonies needed marines (or soldiers) to manage the prisoners, and many of these chose to stay on after their period of service was over. Others worked their way to the colonies on board ships, either taking a one-way passage or 'jumping' ship once here. These 'illegal' immigrants are obviously hard to find in records because they didn't want to be located in the colony. They covered their tracks by changing their names or giving false information about how they'd got here in the first place. So trying to track down these ancestors' records can be a very frustrating business.

# Researching shipping records

The good news is that because shipping records are so integral to family history research in this country, much effort has been made to copy them, maintain them and sometimes even to index them. In fact, many of these records are online.

Like vital records, shipping records were maintained on a colonial or state basis until Australia became a federation in 1901, and even then the records continued to be maintained individually in some places. In New South Wales, for example, the state authorities maintained responsibility for shipping records right up until 1922 when the Commonwealth government took over that role.

The websites of state and territory archives provide information about shipping records they hold. Some have online indexes that you can check, although in other cases the records are on microfilm, microfiche or CD-ROM. To locate these archives, see the section 'Visiting Libraries, Archives and Historical Societies' later in this chapter, or the *Tracing Your Family History Online* Internet Directory in Appendix C at the end of this book. We also discuss shipping records in more detail in Chapter 5.

If you're looking for an ancestor's arrival records, an important step is to determine his or her first port of entry — or try several if you're not sure. Why? You could spend years searching unindexed shipping records in one state without knowing that your relative actually arrived in another state. For example, an ancestor may have first arrived in Victoria, but then decided to go to Queensland. Or, perhaps a family arrived in Adelaide, then made for the goldfields in Victoria. Don't assume your ancestors arrived in the colony in which they later settled.

# Marching to a Different Drummer: Searching for Military Records

If your ancestors were involved in any of the major international military campaigns, you may be able to locate their *service records*. These records often provide rich, personal information about ancestors, as well as helping you to understand the part they played in the conflicts.

Service records chronicle the military careers of the individuals involved in military campaigns. They often contain details of when and where individuals enlisted, how old they were, their physical appearance and state of health, occupation, birthplace and details of their discharge from service. Information on where they served, wounds or illness they experienced and promotions or decorations they received may also be listed.

Two major websites chronicle the role of Australians involved in past conflicts:

- ✔ The Australian War Memorial website (`www.awm.gov.au`) has online databases detailing personnel records, honours, awards and commemorations, as well as historical information and resources about the role of Australian troops in peace-keeping efforts.

- ✔ The Commonwealth War Graves Commission website (`www.cwgc.org`) can help you locate an ancestor's final resting place overseas. As well as giving information on the person's burial place, details of enlistment and next of kin are available.

For further advice on records relating to military service in Australia, check out the website of the National Archives of Australia (`www.naa.gov.au`). We also discuss military records in more detail in Chapter 5.

# Coming to Your Census

Finding genealogical records in your relatives' attics can take you only so far in the pursuit of your ancestors. Although vital records (see the section 'Getting the Framework Right: The Importance of Vital Records' earlier in this chapter for more details) can fill in some of the gaps, eventually you need a set of records that provides information on your ancestors that was taken at regular intervals. This type of record is called a *census record*.

Early census records provide more than just a record of an individual's name, age and address. Some also record each person's place of birth, occupation, relationship to others in the household and state of health. Census records are valuable in that they can tell you where ancestors were living on a particular date.

Many countries have been conducting a regular census (every ten years) since 1901, but also have other collections that go as far back as the late 1700s. For example, the United States has census records from 1790 and the United Kingdom has records from 1801. Both countries have long preserved their census collections, and when released from privacy restrictions many have been made available to the public — after 72 years in the United States and after 100 years in the United Kingdom.

To control the population in the penal settlements of Australia, the authorities regularly took head counts. Sometimes these were for census records. A census collector — usually a police constable — knocked on every door and filled out a form to report who lived there, how old they were, what ship they arrived on, and whether they were a free settler, a convict and so on. In other cases the authorities organised a *muster*, whereby all the people in a particular area had to turn up, or muster, at a particular place on a given day and provide their details to the authorities.

Lists of convicts were taken from the arrival of the First Fleet in 1788. Musters were prepared as early as 1795. Throughout the first 50 years of the colony various records were collected, but name-identified census records do not survive later than 1841. Since then census records have been collected regularly, but have been destroyed in accordance with Australia's privacy laws. To this day Australia still deliberately destroys its census records, although in the 2001 census 53 per cent of the population directed that their returns were to be retained for 100 years and then made available to researchers after genealogists mounted a campaign to have them retained.

 A useful guide to muster and census records for the penal settlement of New South Wales can be found at the State Records Authority of New South Wales site (www.records.nsw.gov.au). We cover census and muster records in more detail in Chapter 5, where we also discuss searching census records abroad.

# The Importance of Knowing Where Your Family Lived

In the past, the success of an individual was measured by ownership of land. The more land your ancestors possessed, the more powerful and wealthy they were. This concept often encouraged people to migrate to new countries in the search for land.

Land records may tell you where your ancestor lived prior to purchasing the land, and the names of his or her spouse, children, grandchildren, parents or siblings. However, to effectively use land records, you need to have a good idea of where your ancestors lived and possess a little background information on the history of the areas in which they lived. Old land records can include leases and tenancies.

In early Australia, land was first given to people to encourage them to settle and open up the country. For example, ex-convicts, military personnel, women and free settlers were all eligible to receive *free grants* of land in New South Wales up to 1825. After that date a fee was payable, even though the transaction was still called a *grant*. These early records of land grants are held in each state and territory government's archives. For example, see the *Land Grants 1788–1856* page at the State Records Authority of New South Wales website at www.records.nsw.gov.au.

In New South Wales, records of land traded between private individuals are held by the Department of Lands (www.lands.nsw.gov.au). These records detail not only the names and occupations of purchasers, but also how much they paid, what they called their property, what improvements were made on it and much more.

Each state and territory has its own government department responsible for the administration of land. Using land records can be quite complex and you need some knowledge of the local area, parish names and county boundaries. However, online guides and websites can help you. For example, check out the listings for land records at Cora Num's gateway site at www.coraweb.com.au for further information on land records in the state or territory of specific interest to your research.

# Visiting Libraries, Archives and Historical Societies

Collecting additional information on the area where your ancestors lived may inspire you to search for information in both public and private libraries. Public libraries often have city directories and phone books, past issues of newspapers (good for obituary hunting) and old map collections. Libraries usually also have extensive collections of local history books that can give you a flavour of what life was like for your ancestors in that area. For a list of libraries with online catalogues, see the Libraries Australia website (www.nla.gov.au/apps/libraries).

Archives are another place to find good information, and throughout this book we often point you to resources in online archives (usually in state records). Australia's main archive, the National Archives of Australia (www.naa.gov.au) covers Commonwealth government records (see Chapter 14 for more details). Archives at state and local government levels are represented by the following websites:

- ✔ **New South Wales:** State Records Authority of New South Wales at www.records.nsw.gov.au

- ✔ **Northern Territory:** Northern Territory Archives Service at www.nt.gov.au/nreta/ntas

- ✔ **Queensland:** Queensland State Archives at www.archives.qld.gov.au

- ✔ **South Australia:** State Records of South Australia at www.archives.sa.gov.au

- ✔ **Tasmania:** Archives Office of Tasmania at www.archives.tas.gov.au

- ✔ **Victoria:** Public Record Office Victoria at www.prov.vic.gov.au

- ✔ **Western Australia:** State Records Office of Western Australia at www.sro.wa.gov.au

The Australian Society of Archivists (www.archivists.org.au) maintains an online directory of Australian archival institutions that outlines each institution's major holdings and includes address and contact details, along with links to a website, if available.

A third place to find additional information is at an historical society. Generally, historical societies have collections of maps, documents and local history books pertaining to the area in which the society is located. Also, they are repositories for collections of papers of people who lived in the community. You may find references to your ancestors in these collections, especially if the person whose personal documents are in the collection wrote a letter or transacted some business with your ancestor.

You can find links to historical societies at the Royal Australian Historical Society (www.rahs.org.au) or by visiting Cora Num's *Family History and Historical Societies* page (www.coraweb.com.au).

# Discovering Family History Centres

FamilySearch (www.familysearch.org), the official research site of The Church of Jesus Christ of Latter-day Saints (LDS), is a treasure trove of online databases and resources for family historians everywhere (see also Chapters 3 and 15). If you can't find records or information about some of your ancestors in its databases, you're likely to find other resources in its Family History Library catalogue, which lists more than 2.2 million rolls of microfilm, more than half a million microfiche, and hundreds of thousands of books and CD-ROMs available at the Family History Library.

The LDS Family History Library is in Salt Lake City in the United States, but you don't have to visit the Library to access records listed in the catalogue (although, if you ever get the chance, we highly recommend you do). Instead, you can visit one of its many Australian Family History Centres, where you can order in and view many of the records the LDS has on microfilm. Work has also begun to transfer many records that were previously only available on microfilm into digitised images available online.

To find the centre nearest to you, consult your local telephone directory, or go to the FamilySearch website (www.familysearch.org), click on the Library tab on the home page and then the Family History Centres link. By the way, you don't need to be a member of the LDS Church to use a local Family History Centre; the resources it maintains are available to everyone.

# Chapter 2

# Planning for Genealogical Success

· · · · · · · · · · · · · · · · · · · · · · · · · · · · · · · · · · · · · · ·

· · · · · · · · · · · · · · · · · · · · · · · · · · · · · · · · · · · · · · ·

*I*t wouldn't be a normal day at the Society of Australian Genealogists if we didn't receive at least one email message saying something like 'I'm looking for information about the Smith family. My great-grandfather, John Smith, is believed to have come to Australia sometime last century'. Although we'd love to have an all-encompassing library that contains everyone's genealogy, we regret to tell you that we don't. Likewise, we don't have the time to research everyone's emails; all we can do is point you to resources that may help. The fact is, as much as we'd love to help each individual who contacts us, we receive far too many emails every day to be able to do that. Our solution to this problem is this book!

If you're a novice genealogist, you may not know where and how to start your research because you're unsure of the standard process. This is where we come in to help. This chapter covers some of the basic things to keep in mind when you begin your research journey and offers a number of tips on what you can do when you hit brick walls along the way.

When you start out, you discover very quickly that an organised genealogist is a successful genealogist. Just diving into a new resource and extracting everything you can find on the name you're looking for may be fun for a while, but it won't take you too far — whether you're online or at the library. You need to be organised in your approach, have a research goal in mind and keep your records in order. Elsewhere in this book we cover some of the ways you can do this, but in this chapter we concentrate on the planning stage — an essential step in the process to becoming a successful genealogist.

Your family wasn't created in a day and you won't be able to trace its history after one night's research on the internet. This chapter shows you why having a methodical and well thought-out approach to your research ensures the greatest success.

# Introducing the Online Family Tree Research Cycle

No book on research would be complete without some sort of model to follow, so we provide one called the *Online Family Tree Research Cycle*. Sounds impressive, doesn't it? If you're researching the Walker family line, you'd call it the Walker Online Family Tree Research Cycle; if you're tracking the Thompson family, you'd call it the Thompson Online Family Tree Research Cycle. Figure 2-1 shows the five phases of the cycle: planning, collecting, researching, consolidating and distilling.

Sticking with the family tree analogy here, we liken the cycle to the steps you take to plant and sustain a tree:

- ✔ **Planning:** The first step in planting a tree is figuring out what kind of tree you want and then finding a good place in your backyard for the tree to grow. This step in the cycle is the *planning* phase. Select a family that you know enough about to begin a search and then think about the resources you want to use to find the information that you're looking for.

- ✔ **Collecting:** After you plan the location for the tree, you go to a nursery and pick out a suitable sapling and other necessary materials to ensure that the tree's roots take hold. The second phase of the cycle, *collecting*, is the same — you collect information on the family that you're researching by conducting interviews in person, over the phone or through email, and by finding documents tucked away in the spare bedroom, or even in sheds, attics and garages.

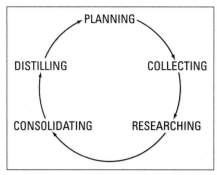

**Figure 2-1:**
The Online
Family Tree
Research
Cycle.

✔ **Researching:** The next step is to actually plant the tree. You dig a hole, place the tree in it and then cover the roots. Similarly, you spend the *researching* phase of the cycle digging for clues, finding information that can support your family tree and obtaining documentation. You can use traditional and technological tools to dig — tools like libraries, archives, your computer and the internet.

✔ **Consolidating:** You've planted the tree and covered its roots. However, to make sure that the tree grows, you should mulch around it and provide the nourishment the tree needs to survive. The *consolidating* phase of the cycle is similar in that you take the information you find and place it into your computer-based genealogical database or your filing system. These systems protect your findings by keeping them in a centralised location and provide an environment in which you can see the fruits of your labour.

✔ **Distilling:** After your tree has taken root and begins to grow, you need to prune the old growth, allowing new growth to appear. Similarly, the *distilling* phase is where you use your computer-based genealogical database to generate reports showing the current state of your research. You can use these reports to prune from your database those individuals you've proven don't fit into your family lines — and perhaps find room for new genealogical growth by finding clues to other lines you need to follow up.

Using this model makes researching a lot easier and more fulfilling. However, this model is merely a guide. Feel free to use whatever methods work best for you — as long as those methods make it possible for someone else to verify your research (through sources you cite and so on).

## Planning your research

You may have heard that the internet puts the world at your fingertips. Discovering all the wonderful online resources that exist makes you feel like a kid in a lolly shop. You click around from site to site with wide eyes, amazed by what you see, tempted to record everything for your genealogy — whether it relates to one of your family lines or not.

Because of the immense wealth of information available to you, putting together a research plan *before* you go online is very important — it can save you a lot of time and frustration by keeping you focused. Tens of thousands of genealogical sites are on the internet. If you don't have a good idea of exactly what you're looking for before you go online, you can readily lose your way. And getting lost is even easier when you see a name that looks familiar and start following its links, only to discover hours later (when you finally get around to pulling out the genealogical notes you already have) that you've been tracking the wrong person and family line.

Now that we've convinced you that you need a research plan, you're probably wondering what a research plan is. Basically, a *research plan* is a commonsense approach to looking for information about your ancestors online. A research plan entails knowing what you're looking for and what your priorities are for finding information.

If you're the kind of person who likes detailed organisation (like lists and steps that you can follow to the tee), you can write your research plan on paper or keep it on your computer. If you're the kind of person who knows exactly what you want and need at all times, and you have an excellent memory of where you leave off when doing projects, your research plan can exist solely in your mind. In other words, your research plan can be as formal or informal as you like — as long as it helps you plot what you're looking for.

For example, say you're interested in finding some information on your great-grandmother. Here are some steps you can take to form a research plan:

1. **Write down what you already know about the person you want to research.**

   In this case, include details like your great-grandmother's dates and places of birth, marriage and death; spouse's name; children's names; and any other details you think may help you distinguish your ancestor from other individuals. Of course, all you may know at this time is your great-grandmother's name.

2. **Conduct a search using a genealogically focused search engine to get an overview of what's available.**

   Visit sites like RootsWeb (www.rootsweb.ancestry.com) to search for information by name and location. Using your great-grandmother's name and the names of some of the locations where she lived provides you with search results that give you an idea of what kind of resources are available. (Chapters 3 and 4 go into more detail about searching for this type of information.) You may want to make a list of the websites that you find on a sheet of paper or in your word processor.

3. **Prioritise the resources that you want to use.**

   Your search on a genealogically focused search engine may turn up several different types of resources, such as newsgroups, mailing lists and websites. We recommend that you prioritise which resources you plan to use first. You may want to visit a website that specifically names your great-grandmother prior to signing up for a mailing list for all researchers interested in the same surname. (For more on using these resources, take a look at Chapter 3.)

**4. Schedule time to use the various resources that you identify.**

Genealogy is truly a lifelong pursuit and, as such, you can't download every bit of information and documentation that you need in the one go. Because researching your genealogy requires time and effort on your part, we recommend that you schedule time to work on specific parts of your research. (Scheduling time is especially useful if you're paying by the hour for your internet connection.) You don't need to narrow this down to within five minutes, but deciding before you begin whether a specific search is worth five hours or 30 minutes of research time helps you to focus.

## Collecting useful information

After you generate your research plan, you may need to fill in a few details like dates and locations of births, marriages and deaths. You can collect this information by interviewing family members and by looking through family documents and photographs (see Chapter 1 for tips on interviewing relatives and using family documents and photographs). You may also need to look up a few things in an atlas or a gazetteer (a geographical dictionary) if you aren't sure where certain locations are. (Chapter 4 provides more information on online gazetteers.)

For a list of things that may be useful to collect, see Chapter 1. In the meantime, here are a few online resources that identify items to collect for your genealogy:

- **Ancestry.com:** *First Steps — Memories* at `www.ancestry.com/learn/start/memories.htm`

- **Family History Research Course:** *Where Do I Start* and *Organising Your Family History Research* at `www.ulladulla.info/fhc/intro.html`

- **Genealogy.com:** *A Trip Down Memory Lane* at `www.genealogy.com/00000025.html`

You can find a variety of online resources listed in the Internet Directory in Appendix C.

## Researching: Through the brick wall and beyond

Of course, researching your family history online is the topic of this entire book, so you can find the necessary resources to do a great deal of your online research in these pages.

A time will undoubtedly come when you run into what genealogists affectionately call the proverbial brick wall. A *brick wall* is when you think you have exhausted every possible way of finding an ancestor.

The most important thing you can do is to keep the faith — don't give up! Websites change frequently (especially as more people begin sharing their information online), so although you may not find exactly what you need today, you may find it next week at a site you've visited several times before or at a new site altogether.

Fortunately, others have shared their experiences of getting through a brick wall by posting suggestions online. Check out the following pages:

- *Brick Walls from A–Z* at `www.rootdig.com/adn/brickwall_a_z.html`
- *Sources of Genealogical Information* at `www.rootsweb.ancestry.com/~genepool/sources.htm`

## Consolidating your information in a genealogical database

After you get rolling on your research, you often find so much information that it feels as if you don't have enough time to put it all into your genealogical database.

A *genealogical database* is a software program that allows you to enter, organise, store and use all sorts of genealogical information on your computer.

Make sure that you set aside some time to regularly update your database with the information that you've recently gathered. This process of putting your information together in one central place, which we call *consolidating*, helps you gain a perspective on the work that you've completed and provides a place for you to store all those nuggets you'll need when you begin researching again. By storing your information in a database, you can always refer to it for a quick answer the next time you try to remember where you found a reference to a marriage certificate for your great-great-grandparents.

See Chapter 9 for more details on setting up and organising your database.

## *Distilling the information you gather*

The final step in the cycle is distilling the information you gather into a report, a chart or a detailed research log that you can use to find additional genealogical leads. Frequently, you can complete the distillation process by producing a report from your genealogical database. Most genealogical software programs allow you to generate reports in a variety of formats. For example, you can pull up a pedigree chart or an outline of descendants from information you've entered in the database about each ancestor. You can use these reports to see what holes still exist in your research, and you can add these missing pieces to the planning phase for your next research effort (starting the whole cycle over again).

Another advantage to genealogical reports is having the information readily available so that you can toggle back to look at the report while researching online, which can help you stay focused. (*Toggling* means flipping back and forth between open programs on your computer. For example, in Windows you press Alt + Tab to toggle, or you can click the appropriate task-bar item on the toolbar at the bottom of the screen. On a Macintosh, you can use the Application Switcher in the upper-right corner of the screen.) Of course, if you prefer, printing copies of the reports and keeping them next to the computer while you're researching on the internet serves the same purpose.

# *Enjoying Your Genealogical Journey*

When you set off on your annual holiday to the Gold Coast or wherever, you don't just jump in the car and start driving. Before you head off you think about the route you want to take and plan your trip accordingly. When you reach unfamiliar territory on the way, you may like to stop and have a bit of a look around: The best kind of holiday is one that isn't so rushed that everything is a blur a week later, but rather one where you really do get time to 'enjoy smelling the roses'.

Researching your family history online is like this, too. Jumping straight in and trying to research back to Adam and Eve in a single night simply isn't practical. And just as you may discover a few dodgy traders ready to take advantage of the unsuspecting tourist, so too in genealogy you find some who are happy to take advantage of people just beginning their family history adventures.

Not everything you find on the internet for genealogy is going to be free. However, stop and consider carefully whether you need to spend money to obtain the information you need. Is this material available on another site free of charge, or can you get the basics online and then visit a genealogical society or library to help you further for little or no charge? Don't assume that the first website you find is the only one that has the information you need: Shop around.

## To pay or not to pay? Why 'pay to view' websites can be good value

Now we know that people like to get something for nothing, so now is probably as good a time as any to challenge your attitude towards paying for services over the internet.

As you become more familiar with family history resources online you find that the majority of smaller sites provide free access to records, whereas the very large sites ask you to subscribe or pay a one-off fee for information. Usually, the free sites are individual or small-enterprise efforts posted by dedicated family history researchers willing to share their results with others. They often make space for advertisers and want to promote their own work and interests along the way. The big sites that charge for information tend to be run by large companies and government organisations. They usually spend many thousands of dollars digitising original pages, indexing official records and making the material available online, so it's only reasonable that they receive some return to maintain their databases and continue to expand their online resources.

Your first reaction may be to shy away from commercial websites and refuse to pay for genealogy services over the internet. However, shelling out US$35 for a month's access to one of the large US commercial sites or paying £5 to download some specific details from an English site run by a government organisation can be a very good investment if it gives you new research leads or unearths the precise information you're looking for.

If you do decide to sign up with an internet site that requires an online payment, though, be wary about the following:

✔ Be careful to whom you give your credit card details online or you could be in for a nasty shock when your bill arrives. If you're asked to enter your credit card details, check first whether the site is safe. The data you enter should be encrypted so that it cannot be intercepted by a third party.

✔ Check the fine print if a site asks you to pay to subscribe. Sometimes, sites are very easy to subscribe to (for either a set time or specific information), but very difficult to shake off — once the site has your details it bombards you with emails enticing you to pay for its services again.

✔ Think carefully about websites that offer you a free 14-day trial but insist that you provide your credit card details upfront — for security or ID purposes. After the 14 days have expired, you may automatically become a paying customer, and you may find that contacting the site's owners to stop these payments or to get your money back isn't easy. Make sure that you know exactly what you have to do to 'opt out' *before* you sign up.

Our advice: Before you hand over your credit card details check out just how relevant the information on the site is to you, and make sure it isn't available somewhere else for free. Don't forget, the free version may be in a printed format at your local library or family history society: By paying for the material online, all you're doing is paying for a digitised version of the printed book.

Some people are highly critical of these commercial sites, with many complaining that you have to pay to access public records such as shipping lists and census returns. That isn't true. You can still research this information the 'old' way — travelling to the repository that holds those records and spending hours trawling through microfilms looking for details of your specific family. Chances are, to access these records you may end up spending more on travel costs and accommodation than you would have done if you'd stayed at home and taken out a subscription to the site that has indexed and digitised those records.

Check whether your local family history society or public library has corporate subscriptions to at least one or two of the major 'pay to view' sites. If it does, you should be able to access the sites without having to pay your own subscription. However, note that most history societies and libraries require you to physically visit their library to take advantage of the corporate subscription.

## *Verifying information: Don't believe everything you read*

We can't emphasise enough the importance of verifying all the information you put into your family tree. How you do that is a topic we talk about in more detail in Chapter 3. But for now just remember that a 'fact' you take from someone else's research that you find on the internet isn't worth much unless that person has provided the documentation to back up that information.

For example, if you go online to find where your great-grandmother is buried and discover her name among a list of cemetery transcriptions that someone has posted on the internet, by all means add the place of burial into your genealogical database. However, be sure to note where you found the information — and include the website address as your source — so that you know you still have to prove you really have found your great-grandmother's place of burial. Until you're able to verify the information from another source — such as her death certificate — you can't be certain that she's actually buried there.

## *Avoiding having too many ancestor irons in the research fire*

Take your time and don't be in a big hurry. Keep things simple and look for one piece of information at a time. If you try to do too much too fast, you risk getting confused, having no success and getting frustrated with the internet. This result isn't very encouraging and certainly doesn't make you feel like jumping back into your research, which would be a shame because you can find a lot of valuable research help online.

Your aim (most likely) is to trace a family history that spans many generations and goes back several hundred years. Remember, Rome wasn't built in a day, and even the most computer-savvy family historians can't track down their ancestors overnight. It all takes time, but planning and learning to use the internet effectively certainly let you get there much more quickly.

# Chapter 3

# What's in a Name?

*A*s a genealogist, you may experience sleepless nights trying to figure out all the important things in life — the maiden name of your great-grandmother, whether your grandfather's brother actually was a bigamist and whether your great-great-grandmother really did hide Peter Lalor under her camp bed during the Eureka Stockade. Okay, so you may not have sleepless nights, but you undoubtedly spend a significant amount of time thinking about and trying to find resources that can give you the answers to some crucial questions.

In the past, finding information on individual ancestors online was compared with finding a needle in a haystack. You browsed through lists of links in the hope of finding a site that contained a nugget of information to aid your search. Well, looking for your ancestors online has become easier than ever. Nowadays, you can use search engines and online databases to pinpoint information on your ancestors, so a lot of the hard work has already been done for you.

In this chapter we help you with your first online search by covering the basics of a search for an ancestor by name, presenting some handy surname resource sites and showing you how to use several different internet resources to successfully find information on your family.

# Selecting a Person to Begin Your Search

Selecting a person sounds easy, doesn't it? Just select your great-great-great-grandfather's name and you're off to the races. But what if his name was John Smith? You may encounter thousands of sites with information on John Smith — unless you know some facts about the John Smith you're looking for, you may have a frustrating time online.

## Trying a unique name

The first time you research online, try to start with a person whose name is, for lack of a better term, unique or not common. By this, we mean a person with a surname that doesn't take up ten pages in your local phone book, but is common enough that you can find some information on it the first time you conduct a search. Consider any variations in spelling that your ancestor's name may have. Often, you can find more information on the mainstream spelling of a surname than on one of its more rare variants. For example, if you're researching someone with the surname Helme, you may have better luck finding information under the spellings Helm or Helms. If your family members immigrated to Australia from a country such as Germany or Italy, they may have anglicised their surname. *Anglicising* a name was sometimes done so that the name could be easily pronounced in English, or sometimes the surname was simply misspelled and the new version adopted by the family — the German name Braun, for example, may have become Brown in Australian records.

To find various spellings of the surname, you may need to dig through some family records or look at a site such as *The Table of Common Surname Variations & Surname Misspellings* (www.ingeneas.com/alternate.html). This Canadian site offers a good grounding on the variations you can expect to find for many surnames.

Right from the start, Australia's colonies were multicultural — people from many nationalities and with different regional accents mixed together. Even a Yorkshireman stating his surname to a compatriot Cornishman on arrival in the colony was liable to have that surname written down incorrectly, as the clerk would have written down his interpretation of the name he heard, and a Cornishman and a Yorkshireman have very different English accents.

## Narrowing your starting point

If you aren't sure how popular a name is, try typing the name into Telstra's White Pages® online telephone directory (www.whitepages.com.au) and see how many hits you get for each state and territory. You can do the same in other online telephone directories almost anywhere else in the world using Infobel's world telephone directories (www.infobel.com/en/world).

Some special sites also let you see a surname's distribution across a country. For example, the Hamrick Software surname distribution site (www.hamrick.com/names) lets you see the distribution of the 50,000 most common surnames found in the US census and telephone books from 1850 to 1990. The *1890 Surname Distribution in Ireland* page (www. ancestryireland.com/database.php?filename=db_mathesons) at the Ulster Historical Foundation website, shown in Figure 3-1, may give you some useful leads for Ireland. Other sources for the British Isles can be found at the Ancestry Learning Centre (www.ancestry.co.uk/learn/facts/default.aspx) where you can see the distribution of a surname in the 1891 English and Welsh census.

Typing a surname and selecting a country in the FamilySearch website's search page (www.familysearch.org) also quickly shows you the popularity of a name in a particular region (see also the 'FamilySearch' section later in this chapter for more details about using the website).

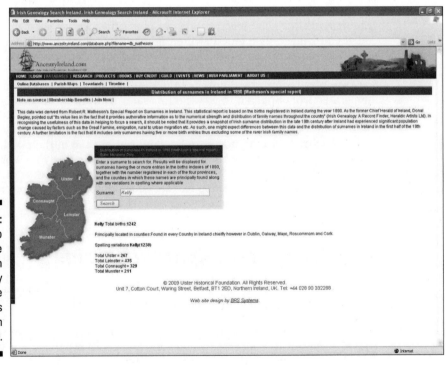

**Figure 3-1:**
A map showing the distribution of the Kelly surname across Ireland in 1890.

You can purchase software programs that automatically plot the distribution of a surname on maps for you. For example, GenMap UK (www.archersoftware.co.uk/genmap01.htm) covers the whole of the British Isles.

A good reason to check out the distribution of a surname is that you can use the information to identify potential geographic areas where you can look for your family later in your research. For example, say you find some listings of people with the surname that interests you in Perth and Melbourne. Later on, if you hit a brick wall and can't find additional information online about a particular individual or surname, you know that you can start looking at records in Western Australia and Victoria for more clues about the particular branch of the family to determine whether they belong to the family you're tracing, and if so, when they moved to the area.

## Using a person you know about

In addition to picking a person you're likely to have success researching, you want to start with a person you know something about. If you have a family line for which you have some basic information on your great-great-grandparents, for example, use one of their names rather than a name for which you know only a few scattered details. The more details you know about a person, the more successful your initial search is likely to be.

For example, if your grandmother told you that her father was a miner and immigrated from England to New South Wales to work in the coalfields, you have useful information that you can put to work when searching the internet for information about him. Being a coalminer, he probably lived in the industrial parts of northern England rather than in the middle of London. Likewise, after arriving in Australia, it's more likely he worked in the Hunter Valley region of New South Wales than in the middle of Sydney. For more information on how to extract genealogical information from your family to use in your research, see Chapter 1.

## Selecting a grandparent's name

Having trouble selecting a name? Why not try one of your grandparents' names? Using a grandparent's name has several benefits:

- If you find some information on an individual but aren't sure whether it's relevant to your family, you can check with relatives to see whether they have any additional information that can help you.

- This questioning may spur an interest in genealogy in other family members who can then assist you with some of your research burden or produce some family documents that you never knew existed.

With a name in hand, you're ready to see how much information is currently available on the internet about that individual. Because this is just one step in a long journey to discover your family history, you should keep in mind that you want to begin *slowly*. Don't try to examine every resource right from the start. You're more likely to become overloaded with information if you try to find too many resources too quickly. Your best approach is to begin searching a few sites until you get the hang of how to find information about your ancestors online. And keep in mind that you can always bookmark sites so that you can easily return to them later when you're ready for more in-depth researching.

To bookmark a site in Internet Explorer, the most popular web browser program, open the web page, select the 'Favorites' button on the toolbar, and then click on 'Add to Favorites' and 'Add'. You can give the website a new name if you wish. The website is now listed under the 'Favorites' button on the toolbar and you can return to the site at any time simply by clicking on it.

# Finding the Site That's Best for You

Your dream as an online genealogist is to find a site that contains all the information you ever wanted to know about *your* family. Unfortunately, these golden sites are few and far between (if they exist at all). In the meantime, you may discover a number of others that vary greatly in the amount and quality of genealogical information they offer. Knowing ahead of time what kinds of sites are available and what common types of information you may encounter is useful.

## Personal genealogical sites

A vast number of sites that you find on the internet are *personal genealogical sites*, established by individuals and families who have specific research interests. You're likely to find information on the site owner's immediate family or on particular branches of several different families, rather than on a surname as a whole. That doesn't mean that valuable information isn't present on these sites — just that they have a more personal focus.

You can find a wide variety of information on personal genealogical sites. Some list only a few surnames that the owner is researching; others contain extensive online genealogical databases and narratives. A site's content depends on the owner's research capabilities, time and computer skills. Some common items that you see on most sites include a list of surnames, an online genealogical database, pedigree and descendant charts (for information on these charts, see Chapter 9), family photographs and sometimes a list of the owner's favourite genealogical internet links.

Personal genealogical sites vary not only in content, but also in presentation. Some sites are neatly constructed and use soft backgrounds and aesthetically pleasing colours. Others require you to bring out your sunglasses to tone down the fluorescent colours, or use link colours that blend in with the background, making it very difficult to navigate through the site. Note that many personal sites use JavaScript, music players and animated icons that can significantly increase your download times.

A great example of a personal genealogical site is the Baker Family History site (www.vectisjon.com/familyhistory shown in Figure 3-2), which details the history of the family in the United Kingdom.

When you find a site that contains useful information, print out any pages of personal interest and write down the site owner's name and email address. If you have any questions or want to exchange information, contact the owner as soon as possible, because the next time you check you may find that the website has gone. Personal websites (along with their owners' email addresses) have a way of disappearing without a trace as individuals frequently switch internet service providers or stop maintaining sites.

**Figure 3-2:**
A typical personal site: The Baker Family History site.

# One-name study sites

If you're looking for a wide range of information on one particular surname, a *one-name study site* may be the place to look. These sites usually focus on one surname regardless of the geographic location where the surname appears. In other words, they welcome information about people with the surname worldwide. These sites are quite helpful because they contain all sorts of information about the surname, even if they don't have specific information about your branch of the family. Frequently, they have information on the variations in spelling, origins, history and heraldry of the surname. One-name study sites have some of the resources you find in personal genealogical sites, including online genealogy databases and narratives.

Although one-name study sites welcome all surname information regardless of geographic location, the information presented at these sites is often organised around geographic lines. For example, a site may categorise all the information about people with the surname by continent or country — such as Helms in the United States, England, Canada, Europe and Africa. Or the site may be even more specific and categorise information by state, province, county or parish. So, you're better off if you have a general idea of where your family originated from or migrated to. But if you don't know, browsing through the site may lead to some useful information.

The Drake Family website (www.xroyvision.com.au/drake/drakepage.htm), shown in Figure 3-3 overleaf, is a one-name study site crammed with information on the name Drake.

The owners of one-name study sites welcome any information you have on their surnames. These sites are often a good place to join research groups that can be instrumental in assisting your personal genealogical effort.

The Internet Directory in Appendix C at the end of this book identifies a couple more one-name study sites you may want to visit. It gives you just a sampling, though. To find one-name study sites pertaining to the surnames you're researching, you have to go elsewhere. Two sites that can help you determine whether any one-name study sites are devoted to surnames you're researching are

- ✔ Guild of One-Name Studies (www.one-name.org), shown in Figure 3-4

- ✔ Surname Web (www.surnameweb.org), which links to many of the worldwide ancestry databases

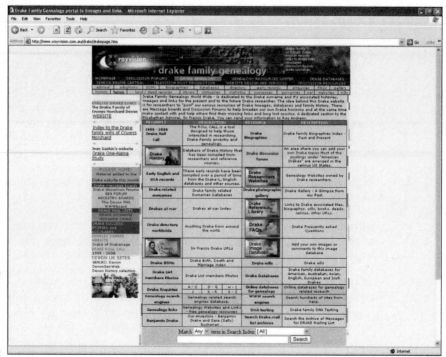

**Figure 3-3:**
The Drake
Family home
page.

Yep, as its name implies, Guild of One-Name Studies (commonly known as the GOONS) is an organisation of researchers devoted to collecting information on a specific surname of interest to them anywhere in the world. Follow these steps to find out whether any of the Guild's members focus on the surname of the person you're researching:

1. **Go to** www.one-name.org.

2. **Enter the surname in which you're interested in the Is Your Surname Registered with the Guild box and click on Search.**

   Alternatively, choose the Registered Names link on the top menu bar, and then either select the letter of the alphabet under which the surname is listed to browse, or type the surname in the search field and click on Search.

   The Results page appears with entries from the database that match your search. You can then email the Guild member, or if available, follow the link to the member's personal website.

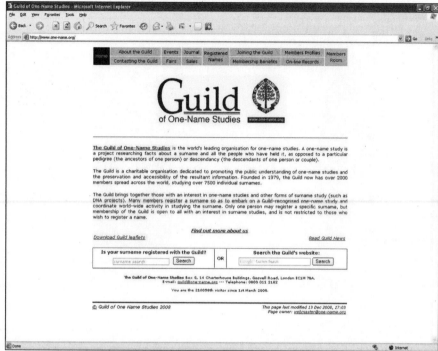

**Figure 3-4:**
The Guild of
One-Name
Studies
home page.

# Family associations and organisations

*Family association sites* are similar to one-name study sites in terms of
content, but they usually have an organisational structure (such as a formal
association, society or club) backing them. The association may focus on
the surname as a whole or just one branch of a family. The goals for the
family association site may differ from those for a one-name study. The
maintainers may be creating a family history in book form or a database of
all individuals descended from a particular person. Some sites may require
you to join the association before you can fully participate in their activities,
but the cost is usually minimal.

The Wingfield Family Society site (www.wingfield.org), shown in
Figure 3-5, has several items that are common to family association
sites. The site includes a family history, newsletter subscription details,
a membership form, reunion news, queries, mailing list information and
a directory of the society's members who are online. To access some of
the resources at the Wingfield Family Society site you're required to be a
member of the society.

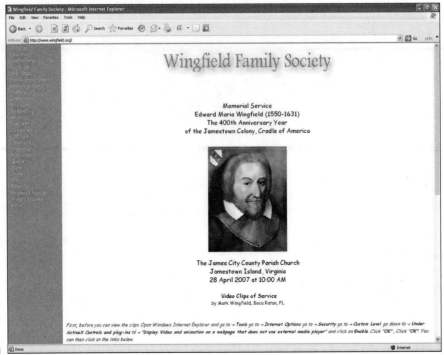

To find a family association website, your best bet is to use a search engine. The following section explains how to do that, and later in the chapter we give details on how to use online databases.

# Letting Your Computer Do the Walking: Using Search Engines

Imagine spending several hours clicking from link to link and not finding anything that relates to your research. Wouldn't it be nice to be able to just type in your ancestor's name and see whether any sites contain that name? Well, that's exactly what search engines allow you to do.

*Search engines* are programs that search huge indexes of information generated by robots. *Robots* are programs that travel throughout the internet collecting information on the sites and resources that they run across. You can access the information contained in search engines through an interface, usually through a form on a web page.

The real strength of search engines is that they allow you to search the full text of web pages instead of just the title or a brief abstract of the site. For example, say that you're looking for information on Charles Sleep who lived around the turn of the nineteenth century in Cornwall, England. You could consult a comprehensive genealogical directory (see 'Browsing Genealogy Gateways' later in this chapter), but unless someone has set up a specific website with the name of Charles Sleep in the title or abstract of the site, your chances of finding anything among the gateway's listings are rather slim. But, by conducting a search through a search engine that indexes the full text of websites, you can find websites that contain information about Charles Sleep. Search engines look right through the full data in websites and give you matches to investigate. In other words, they take away all the tedious online searching and go straight to sources that match the words in your queries.

You can conduct several different types of searches with most search engines. Looking at the search engine's Help link to see the most effective way to search is always a good idea. Also, search engines often have two search interfaces — a simple search and an advanced search. With the simple search, you normally just type your query and click on the Submit button. With advanced searches, you can usually use a variety of options to refine your search. The best way to become familiar with using a search engine is to experiment on a couple of searches and see what kinds of results you get.

Try using key phrases when looking for ancestors using a search engine's advanced search function. That's the easiest way to get sensible matches. For example, searching for Wilson using a search engine's main query form returns thousands of different types of matches for that word — business names, lighthouses, you name it! But if you use an advanced search for a key phrase, such as Humphrey Wilson, you narrow the search field and get listings for websites that contain the complete phrase — in this case, 'Humphrey Wilson'.

One search engine has become such a part of our everyday life that we now use its name in everyday conversation. Google (www.google.com.au) is the giant of search engines. To conduct a global search on Google for an ancestor's name, do the following:

1. **Go to** www.google.com.au.

   Using Google's home page is simple. It consists of a field to enter search terms and two buttons marked Google Search and I'm Feeling Lucky, along with additional links on the right-hand side for more advanced search functions.

2. **Click on the Advanced Search link on the right-hand side.**

   The Advanced Search screen appears.

3. **Type your ancestor's given name and surname into the Find Web Pages that have this Exact Wording or Phrase field and then click on the Advanced Search button.**

   The Results page appears with a list of website addresses and an abstract of the sites with the search term bolded (see Figure 3-6).

4. **Click on a search result that relates to your ancestor.**

   If you're looking for additional leads, Google allows you to view other pages that are similar to results that you receive from your original search.

Of course, Google isn't the only kid on the block. Other search engines to try include

- AltaVista (`au.altavista.com`)
- Yahoo! (`www.yahoo.com`)

In addition, some search engines let you meta-search — that is, search multiple search engines at once. These include

- Dogpile (`www.dogpile.com`)
- Metacrawler (`www.metacrawler.com`)

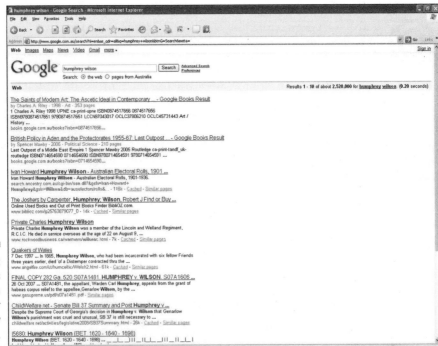

**Figure 3-6:**
Google's
search
results for
Humphrey
Wilson.

# Using Online Databases: Goldmines of Genealogy

Some of your ancestors may have immigrated to Australia during the gold rushes of the 1800s, lured by colourful stories that told of nuggets picked up in the streets of towns such as Ballarat and Bendigo in Victoria. They probably rushed to the diggings along with thousands of others, anxious to make their fortune — or at least a better life for themselves.

Some may have found that elusive nugget, but the vast majority spent several years sifting through piles of sediment without much success. Searching for family history on the internet can yield similar results. In fact, you may find yourself sympathising with the prospectors as you check out results from search engines only to find small nuggets of information here and there. However, don't lose hope. There may be some goldmines waiting for you if you can only stumble on the right site — and the right site may just be in the form of an online database.

*Online databases* are repositories of information that you can retrieve to assist you in compiling your family history. Most online databases are searchable and allow you to type in your ancestor's name and execute a search to determine whether any information stored in the database relates to that particular name. Databases can be large or small, they can focus on a small geographic area or have a broad scope that encompasses many different areas (even countries), and they can be fee-based or free. Each database may also have its own unique search method and present its information in its own format.

You can find online databases in many ways. You can find references to them through search engines (see the section 'Letting Your Computer Do the Walking: Using Search Engines' earlier in this chapter), gateway sites (see the section 'Browsing Genealogy Gateways' later in this chapter), and links that appear on personal and geographic-specific websites.

To give you a taste of the type of goldmines that are available, the following sections look at some of the larger online databases and some unique ones.

## FamilySearch

FamilySearch (www.familysearch.org) is the official research site for The Church of Jesus Christ of Latter-day Saints. This website allows you to search several databases (spanning many countries), including the Ancestral File, International Genealogical Index, Family History Library catalogue, census records, the Pedigree Resource File, Vital Records Index and a collection of abstracted websites, all for free.

Much of FamilySearch's large genealogical collection extracts information from original church records and census data collected through the church's extensive microfilming projects around the world. However, other records are submitted to the website by family history researchers, who may or may not have been careful in researching and documenting their family history. By all means extract data of value, but also verify (through original records) any information that you do find online.

To search FamilySearch, do the following:

1. **Go to** www.familysearch.org **and click on Search Records from the top menu bar.**

   The Search Records For Ancestors screen appears.

2. **Type in the first and last name of the ancestor you're researching in the fields marked First Name and Last Name, and then select the country where you want to search.**

   Don't be tempted to fill in the optional fields on the screen at this point. For your first search, just type in your ancestor's surname and given name. If your search returns too many hits you can always come back to the page and refine your search — for example, by selecting an Event (birth, marriage or death), a region from the Country drop-down box or typing in the names of your ancestor's parents in the Father and Mother fields.

   When using genealogy databases, always begin with a broad search. It's better to get too many results from an initial search than none at all, otherwise you're likely to decide that the site has nothing for you — and possibly miss important research leads.

3. **After you select the search options, click on the Search button.**

   The Results page contains links with descriptions to the resources that meet your search criteria. For example, a search for Charles Sleep in England receives matches in the British 1881 census and the International Genealogical Index for the British Isles (see Figure 3-7). Several of these entries originate from records in Cornwall in the UK, the place we're certain our Charles Sleep originates from. On the right-hand side of the screen you get a breakdown of how many entries are located in each of the databases searched.

4. **Click the link of any result to see more information.**

Try varying the search by turning off the 'exact spelling' option. You then receive matches for similar surnames (such as Sloop, Sleap and Slabe in the case of Sleep), as well as other entries that list more than one given name, such as Charles Robert Sloop, John Charles Sloop and so on. If the name you're searching is a popular one, then the number of records returned from this type of blanket search can be quite daunting; however, if you need to widen the net, turning off the 'exact spelling' option sometimes finds entries for a person hiding in a record under a different spelling of the name.

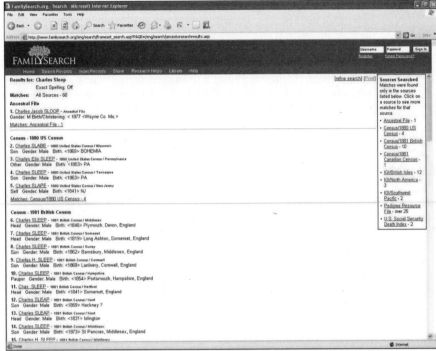

**Figure 3-7:**
Family-
Search
results for
Charles
Sleep.

*FamilySearch.org © by Intellectual Reserve, Inc. Used by permission.*

The FamilySearch website is especially useful because by default it allows family historians to search all resources at once — such as the International Genealogical Index (IGI) for the British Isles, the 1881 British census, US census records and other databases. This means you can use FamilySearch to look for records that show not only where a person was born, but also that list the same person as later living in other parts of the world at different dates. For example, a search for the name Sarah Hayhoe returns hundreds of results from English records, and one matches a Sarah Hayhoe listed in the 1880 US census as living in Kentucky. (In fact, by 1880, poor Sarah is 55 years old, widowed and a laundress living in the Kentucky Lunatic Asylum — so that's why no-one knows what happened to your great-grandmother's sister!)

## *Ancestry.com*

Ancestry.com (www.ancestry.com) is a commercial site that maintains millions of fully searchable records — including US and British census data and indexes to birth, marriage and death records — from more than 28,000 databases. Ancestry.com is the leading 'pay to view' site with sister sites for

British data (www.ancestry.co.uk) and Australian data (www.ancestry.com.au), as well as a growing network of European websites. Searching for people in Ancestry.com returns summaries of the databases that contain records that match the ancestor's name, and these indicate the number of individual records held in each database. Records that are available only to subscribers display a padlock icon next to the database summaries. Records without padlocks take you directly to listings or, in some cases, require you to register as a guest to view the records for free (presumably to tell you about special offers via your email address).

Ancestry.com's World Family Tree database is a free resource that requires you to register first, but it's worth the step because Ancestry's World Family Tree contains millions of names.

The range of records available for British and Australian research through Ancestry.com is discussed in Chapter 13.

## WorldVitalRecords.com

WorldVitalRecords.com (www.worldvitalrecords.com) is currently very US-focused in its content, but is beginning to cover more British records and has millions of Australian records on its site. Like Ancestry.com, WorldVitalRecords is a commercial site but you can undertake useful index searches to determine whether there are any 'hits' for the names you're researching before you pay any money.

## Find My Past

Find My Past (www.findmypast.com) was previously known as 1837online.com, chiefly because it began life as a commercial site offering access to the pre-1837 birth, death and marriage indexes for England and Wales. Find My Past has diversified in recent years, and is now an excellent site for checking out the English and Welsh census records as well as a large series of outgoing passenger records from various British ports and many other English records.

## The Origins Network

The Origins Network (www.origins.net) is a subscription-based website. Although you can search its specialised databases for occurrences of a surname for free, you have to pay to view the actual records.

The Origins Network is made up of three sister sites: British Origins (www.englishorigins.com), Scots Origins (www.scotsorigins.com) and Irish Origins (www.irishorigins.com). You can subscribe to sites individually rather than taking out a full subscription to the combined sites. Although the sites are 'pay to view', you don't have to outlay a large sum of money for an annual subscription: Current plans start at less than the price of a movie ticket, giving you access for 72 hours.

British Origins hooks into exclusive records held by England's Society of Genealogists. These records cover indexes of marriages, wills, witness depositions, passenger lists and apprenticeship records from archives not available online anywhere else on the Web. The site also offers many English and Welsh census records, including the full 1841,1861 and 1871 censuses.

Scots Origins lets you search Scottish marriage, birth and christening records from 1553 to 1875 from the International Genealogical Index for free, and allows you to search parish by parish (a trick that FamilySearch can't readily perform). Although you don't get the full record if a search is successful, you can follow the link through to the FamilySearch website (www.familysearch.org) and use the search function in conjunction with FamilySearch as a useful shortcut in Scottish research.

Irish Origins also maintains some notable online databases — including indexed records and digital images from the original documents compiled by Richard Griffith between 1847 and 1864 for Ireland's Valuation Office. The Griffith Valuation was the first systematic valuation of property holdings in Ireland and contains information on more than one million people — from the smallest farmer to the largest landlord. As the majority of Ireland's census records for the nineteenth century were destroyed by fire in 1922, when the Public Records Office in Dublin burned down, the Griffith Valuation represents the most comprehensive survey of households available for Ireland in that period. Irish Origins also contains some surviving census records, wills and many other useful databases.

# *Browsing Genealogy Gateways*

If you're unable to find information on your ancestors through a search engine or online database (or you want to find additional information), another resource to try is a genealogical gateway site. A *gateway site* is like a directory, containing categorised listings of links to online resources for family history research. Some are your ticket to worldwide resources, while others relate to a specific region or are designed for a specialised audience. Gateway sites can be organised in a variety of ways including by subject, alphabetically or by resource type. No matter how the links are organised, they usually appear hierarchically — meaning that you click from category to subcategory, and so forth, drilling down through the site until you find the link you're looking for.

Browsing has its rewards. Spending time looking through categories in gateway sites can often open up new avenues of research you haven't thought of before. For example, you can use a gateway site to locate websites that have information about shipping records in New South Wales, only to find that by looking at the different links you can actually search the records online. Gateways can also inspire you when you hit a brick wall in your research by prompting you with listings of sites you haven't previously explored and topics you hadn't thought to check.

Of course, one drawback to gateway sites is that they can be time-consuming to browse. You may sometimes need to make several clicks to get down to the area where you believe links that interest you are located. Then, after another several clicks, you find that no relevant links are in that area. This may be because the site's owner has not yet indexed a relevant site, or the site may be listed somewhere else in the index.

To avoid wasting time at genealogy gateways, you may want to check whether the site has a search facility. If it does, try a search before spending a lot of time clicking from one category to another in search of an elusive link.

In this section we highlight some potentially useful gateway sites, one with worldwide coverage, three that focus on Australia and one that focuses on the United Kingdom.

## Cyndi's List

Cyndi's List (www.cyndislist.com) is one of the most comprehensive and best known gateways to family history-related web pages on the internet. You may find the site a bit daunting when you first start out because of its size, but this really is the one to visit when you need to find a family history society in South Africa or background on the registration of births in Norway.

To give you an idea of how to find information in Cyndi's List, try the following example:

1. **Go to** www.cyndislist.com.

   This launches the home page for Cyndi's List.

2. **Under the portion of the main page labelled Main Category Index, click on the relevant letter of the alphabet and then on the category you wish to research.**

   For example, say you're looking for a page that contains information on your ancestors, the Rayment family. So you click on the letter 'S' for 'surnames' and then the category, Surnames, Family Associations & Family Newsletters.

3. **Click on the option you wish to access.**

   Under this category, you have a choice of looking at surname sites or projects or choosing a letter of the alphabet again to link through to sites relating to specific surnames. In this instance, since you're looking for sites about the Rayment family you select the letter 'R'.

4. **Click on a promising link.**

   Under Surname Specific Sites and Resources is one listing for Rayment (see Figure 3-8). You can then click on the link to determine whether it relates to your branch of the family.

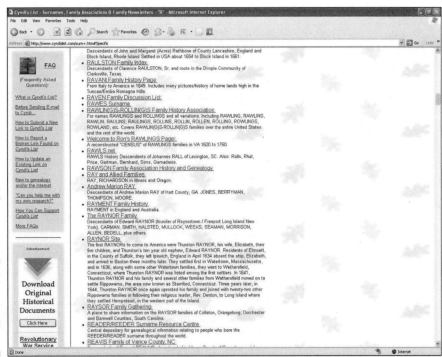

**Figure 3-8:** A surname subcategory page from Cyndi's List.

## Coraweb

If you specifically want a lead on Australian resources, a useful one to try is Coraweb (www.coraweb.com.au) — Cora Num's website for genealogists. This site is geared specifically for Australian research and lists the main categories in alphabetical order on the home page, which makes it less intimidating than Cyndi's List, especially if you're new to research.

To help you find your way around, work your way through the following example to find links to historical information about the gold rush in Victoria:

1. **Go to** www.coraweb.com.au.

   This takes you to the home page with a list of links running down the screen.

2. **Scroll down the list and select a category that's most relevant to your query.**

   For example, click the Local History link. This takes you to a page that provides subcategories of resources by each state in Australia.

3. **Scroll down to find the listings you require.**

   In this case, find the listings for Victoria.

4. **Click on a promising link.**

   Try the link for Ballarat, which was a known goldfield town. The link takes you to the website of the Ballarat & District Genealogical Society, which is dedicated to the local history of that area.

## Genealogy Search Australia

Genealogy Search Australia (www.searchwhateveraustralia.com.au) is another Australian gateway site, and one that is especially useful for finding family history websites: Currently, more than 4,000 are indexed on the site.

## Genealogylinks.net

The gateway site Genealogylinks.net (www.genealogylinks.net) may be particularly useful when you're trying to locate smaller websites that aren't listed by some of the larger gateways.

# GENUKI

GENUKI (www.genuki.org.uk) is one of the most popular regional genealogy gateways and is a fascinating site to browse. As its name implies, it relates to genealogy in the United Kingdom and Ireland, and is run by a cooperative of dedicated volunteers across the British Isles.

GENUKI is structured hierarchically and has identical topic headings at each different level (national, county and parish, town or village). So, you need to work out in advance whether the information you're seeking is of national, county or local interest. Online transcripts of a specific church in, say, Lancashire can be found by searching at the county level, while links to census records that were collected across the country can be found at the national level. Alternatively, you can use the GENUKI search engine to search the contents of all GENUKI resources if you're in a hurry. This works well if you know exactly what you're looking for.

Because GENUKI holds so much detailed information at different levels, we'd like to take you on a quick tour.

## National level

Follow these steps to browse GENUKI at the national level:

1. **Go to** www.genuki.org.uk.

   The home page appears with a green map of the United Kingdom and Ireland in its centre.

2. **Click on the green map to go to a page with a coloured and more detailed map of the region, and then click on the section of the map you're interested in.**

   For example, click on the England portion of the map, which takes you to a page with another coloured map of the country, with the counties listed either side of it and the main category headings listed below it.

3. **Click on the category link that interests you.**

   In this case, click on the Church Records link. The page lists sites that collect church records for the whole of the United Kingdom. Links include sites such as the Baptist Historical Society and the Methodist Archives and Research Centre.

### County level

To browse GENUKI's church records at the county level, you need to go to another level. Here's what to do:

1. **If you're not already there, go to** www.genuki.org.uk **and click on the green map of the United Kingdom and Ireland in the centre of the page.**

   If you were following the steps in the preceding sections, just click on your browser's Back button until you come to the page with the multi-coloured maps of England, Scotland, Ireland and Wales.

2. **Click on the section of the map that you're interested in.**

   For example, click on the red map of England.

3. **Click on the county link that you require.**

   For example, click the Cornwall link and the page displays a list of topics on Cornwall.

4. **Click on the topics link that you're interested in.**

   Say you're interested in the Church Records link. The page displays county-based resources for church records. One of these links to the Cornish OPC website. Click on this link and then enter **Sleep** in the Groom Surname box to see a list of Sleep marriages (see Figure 3-9).

### Parish, town or village level

You can also go directly to records at the parish, town or village level. Follow these steps:

1. **Follow Steps 1–3 of the preceding section.**

   The page shows the listing of resources for the county. For the sake of illustration, pretend you've followed the Cornwall example from the preceding section.

2. **Scroll to the top of the page and click on the Towns and Parishes link.**

3. **On the link page, click on the letter of the alphabet that represents the town, village or parish for which you want to find records.**

   So, on the Cornwall Towns and Parishes page, if you click on 'T' and then Tintagel, for example, you find a number of links to church records about halfway down the page — one of which leads to an online copy of transcripts for marriages that occurred in the parish between 1588 and 1812.

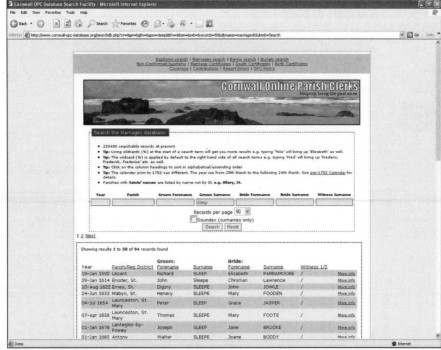

**Figure 3-9:**
Indexes of
marriages
from
Cornwall
parish
records in
GENUKI.

To have the most success with this site, you need to understand these different levels of searching. You won't find Tintagel marriage indexes if you search under Church Records for the whole of England. Similarly, you won't find out about the records of the Baptist Historical Society if you initially drill down to the parish level and then conduct your search. So first determine whether what you're looking for is likely to be of national, county-based or local interest, and then search accordingly.

# Query for One: Seeking Answers to Your Surname Questions

Even if you can't find any surname-specific sites on your particular family, you still have hope! This light at the end of the tunnel comes in the form of queries. *Queries* are research questions that you post to a particular website or mailing list so that other researchers can help you solve your research problems. Often, you may find that researchers have information they haven't yet made available about a family, or they may have seen some information on your family even though it isn't a branch that they're actively researching. And just like genealogists in the real world, online genealogists are usually very keen to share their research and knowledge with others.

# Web queries

One of the quickest ways of reaching a wide audience with your query is through a *forum* on the Web. One example of a forum is GenForum, a site hosted by Genealogy.com that has forums for surnames, geographic regions and related genealogy topics.

Follow these steps to search for a surname on GenForum:

1. **Go to** www.genforum.com.

2. **In the field under Forum Finder, type the surname you're looking for and click on the Find button.**

   Enter a surname that interests you. If you feel like browsing the forums, you can also select a letter beneath the word Surnames.

   Don't worry if your surname doesn't have a forum. The GenForum section is constantly growing and adding surnames. You may also want to take a look at the other surname forums by browsing in the Surnames section to see whether the name is included in a variant spelling.

3. **After you find a forum, click on its link.**

   As soon as your browser loads the forum's page, you should see a list of bulleted messages to choose from. For example, Figure 3-10 shows the Phillips Family Genealogy Forum. To read a message, click on the link. If you don't want to read all the messages, you have the option to see the latest messages, today's messages and any messages posted in the last seven days. These options are available as blue buttons at the top and bottom of the page.

   To post a new query on the site, proceed as follows:

4. **Find the Post New Message link in the row of blue buttons just above the list of messages.**

   Clicking this link generates another page that leads you to the registration section. If you haven't already done so, you must register with Genealogy.com in order to use the GenForum site. Registration is free and enables you to post and respond to all messages in any of the forums.

5. **Fill in the details on the Post New Message page and then click on the Preview Message button.**

   Fill in the Subject field and then write your message in the window. Notice that the page already includes the details about the surname forum you're writing a message to, your name and email address.

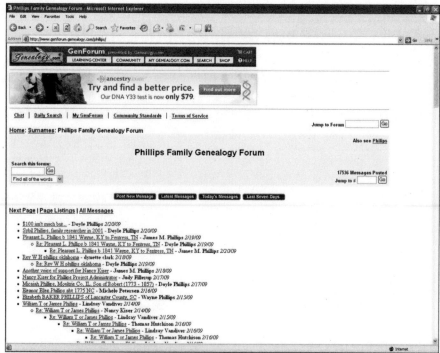

**Figure 3-10:**
The Phillips
Family
Genealogy
Forum
page at
GenForum.

Make sure that your message contains enough information to let other researchers determine whether they can assist you. Include full names, birth and death dates and places (if known), and geographic locations where your ancestors lived (if known). For more tips on how to create effective messages, see the sidebar 'Keys to an effective query' in this chapter.

Clicking on the Preview Message button is an important step because you can see how the message will look when it's posted. This option can prevent you from posting an embarrassing message.

6. **If you're satisfied with the way that the message looks, click the Post Message button.**

   After you've done that, your message is sent to everyone who's registered an interest in the same surname forum. Hopefully, at least one of these people has information that's going to help your research and will respond to your message.

## Keys to an effective query

Have you ever asked a question of thousands of strangers around the entire world? If you haven't, then you should be aware that this is exactly what you do when you post a query.

Many genealogical websites allow visitors to post questions (queries) about the people and places they're currently researching. Posting queries is a lot like calling the reference desk of your local library. Reference librarians can be a great help — if your questions contain enough detail for them to work with.

Keep these key things in mind when you post queries:

- ✔ Ensure that your query is appropriate for the site. Several sites have specific requirements for queries, especially those sites that focus on particular geographical areas.

- ✔ Format your query in a manner consistent with the site maintainer's instructions. Some sites don't have an automated posting process, so the maintainer probably posts all the queries by hand. It helps the maintainer to have all the queries in a standard format and it helps those reading each query to quickly determine whether they can help the person.

- ✔ Keep your query concise but add some concrete information. Dates of birth and death, specific locations where the person lived, and names of any spouses, parents or children are concise but concrete.

- ✔ Type the surnames in capital letters. HELM is much easier to see than Helm when reading through thousands of queries.

Your query should contain the basic elements that other researchers need to determine whether they can help you. A good guideline is that your query should, at a minimum, contain the answers to these questions:

- ✔ Who is the person you're looking for?

- ✔ What specific information do you want about the person?

- ✔ Where did the person live? Where was the person born? Where did the person die?

- ✔ When was the person born? When did the person die?

- ✔ How can someone contact you with a reply? Include your email address, but don't share your residential address or phone number in such a public forum. If you use a post office box for family history queries you can add those details, however.

Here's a good query example:

'CHAPMAN, John — I am looking for the parents of John CHAPMAN of Wellington NSW (1869–1923). His wife was Eliza HUNT and they had two sons Frederick and William. William enlisted in WWI and was killed in France. Frederick (1894–1964) is my grandfather. I can be contacted at cfosterXX1@yahoo.com'.

## Mailing list queries

When you think of mailing lists, you may have nightmares about the endless stream of junk mail that you receive every day as a result of some company selling your name to a mailing list. Well, fear no more. The type of mailing lists we refer to here deliver mail that you actually request. They also provide a means through which you can post queries and messages about your surnames and genealogical research in general.

*Mailing lists* are formed by groups of people who share common interests, whether those interests are in surnames, specific geographical areas, particular topics or ethnic groups. A list consists of the email addresses of every person who joins (subscribes to) the group. When you want to send a message to the entire group, you send it to a single email address that in turn forwards the message to everyone on the list. To join a mailing list, you send an email to a designated address with a subscription message. You should then receive a confirmation email letting you know that you're subscribed to the list and telling you where you need to send an email if you want to send a message to everyone on the list.

So how do you join a mailing list of interest to you? One way is to consult the comprehensive list of mailing lists found on the RootsWeb site (`lists.rootsweb.ancestry.com`). This section on RootsWeb breaks down more than 30,000 mailing lists by country, surname and genealogy topics.

Here's how you can find and join a mailing list for your surname at RootsWeb:

1. **Go to** `lists.rootsweb.ancestry.com`.

2. **Enter your surname in the Find a Mailing List keyword box and click on Find.**

   For example, if you're looking for a mailing list for the name Turner, you enter that name in the search field. When you click on Find, you see a number of Turner lists, some relating to the surname, some for places called Turner and others for DNA sampling done for the surname Turner.

3. **Scroll through the list and click on one of the surname links on the page (see Figure 3-11).**

   When you click on a name, the link takes you to a page that details the types of mailing list available.

4. **Follow the subscription instructions for your mailing list.**

   In our example, the page returns several entries for Turner — let's say you're interested in one specific to the United Kingdom.

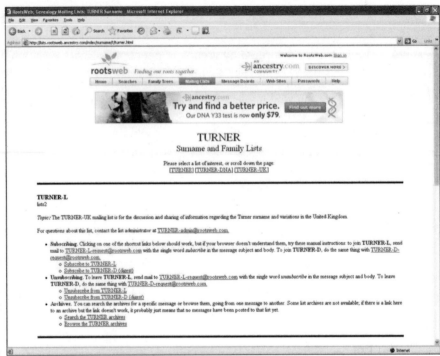

**Figure 3-11:**
A surname
mailing list
page from
RootsWeb.

You can subscribe to one of two delivery methods for receiving messages from the mailing list: Turner-UK-L (mail mode) or Turner-UK-D (digest mode). *Mail mode* simply forwards email messages to you every time someone posts to the mailing list. Although this practice is fine for small mailing lists, you probably don't want hundreds of messages coming in individually — unless you like to have lots of emails sitting in your inbox. To avoid this, try digest mode. *Digest mode* groups several messages together and then sends them out as one large message. Instead of receiving 30 messages a week, you may receive only two messages with the text of 15 messages in each.

The instructions for subscribing to either the Turner-UK-L or the Turner-UK-D mailing list tell you to send an email message with the word *subscribe* as the only text in the message body.

The reason for including only the word subscribe is to accommodate automatic processing by a computer. When you send a message to join a mailing list, chances are that the message is processed automatically without human intervention. That is, the computer automatically adds you to the mailing list when it reads the word subscribe in your message. If you add any other text, the computer doesn't know what to do with the message and it may not add you to the mailing list.

TIP

All mailing lists are free and you won't be asked to pay any money for subscribing in either digest or mail mode.

**5. Click on the required Subscribe to link.**

You've decided to subscribe to the digest mode of the Turner-UK mailing list, so click on the TURNER-UK-D link. Clicking the link automatically opens your email program and creates a new message addressed to the Turner-UK-D mailing list with only the word *subscribe* in the body (see Figure 3-12). Within a couple of minutes of sending the email, you receive a confirmation message welcoming you to the mailing list.

Within the text of the confirmation messages that most mailing lists send is some valuable information that you want to hold on to for as long as you subscribe to the list — such as how to unsubscribe from the list, how to post messages to the list for others to read, and what format you should use for posting queries.

After you've subscribed, you can read the messages without responding or posting your own messages for a while. Begin posting your own queries and responses to others' messages when you feel comfortable.

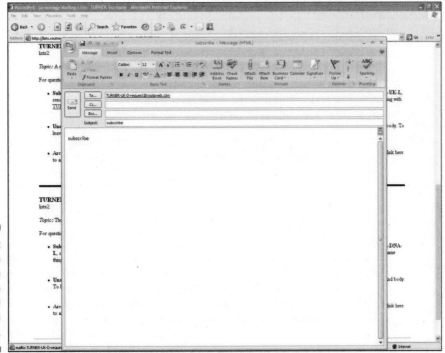

**Figure 3-12:** An email to subscribe to the Turner-UK-D surname mailing list.

Reading messages but not posting your own messages is called *lurking*. You may want to lurk on the mailing list to see what other messages look like and to become familiar with the general culture of the list. After you get a feel for the structure and attitude of the messages, jump in and begin sending your own queries and messages!

Most mailing lists have an archive section where you can read old messages. This section can be both informative and a useful indication of how active the site is and who's normally prepared to answer any queries posted by other subscribers.

Try exploring other kinds of mailing lists that are available. Many societies have their own lists where members post all sorts of queries, seeking help from others or asking for quick checks of records. For example, you can find the mailing list for the Society of Australian Genealogists (SAG) by selecting Mailing Lists from the RootsWeb home page (www.rootsweb.ancestry.com) and then entering **Society of Australian Genealogists** in the Find a Search List box on the Search page. The results list all possible matches: AUS-SAG is at the top of the list

# Using Email to Get Help

In addition to using email to research surnames — for example, using a mailing list — you can also use email to directly contact other researchers about a query. You just need to know where to find them.

Identifying potential email recipients by using online directories to find everyone with the surname you're researching, getting their email addresses and then mass emailing all of them with your questions is a bad idea. Although mass emailing everyone you can find with a particular surname generates return email for you, we can almost guarantee that the responses won't be helpful. Sticking with genealogical sites (like those we identify in the preceding sections) when looking for other researchers who are interested in the same surnames as you is the better way to go about it.

One of the oldest of the internet genealogy resources is the RootsWeb Surname List (RSL) (rsl.rootsweb.ancestry.com). The RSL is simply a list of surnames (and their associated dates and locations) accompanied by contact information for the person who placed the surname on the list. To contact other submitters about particular surnames, all you have to do is look at the contact information and send them email messages or letters in the mail detailing your interest in the surnames.

To search for a name using the Search the RootsWeb Surname List window on the RootsWeb website, follow these steps:

1. **Go to** `rsl.rootsweb.ancestry.com` **and click on Search the RSL Database.**

2. **Type the surname you're looking for into the Surname field and click on Submit.**

   If you want to narrow down your search, type the code for the relevant region in the Location field. If you don't know the code for the region you're querying, visit Abbreviations and Character Codes for RootsWeb Users (`helpdesk.rootsweb.com/codes`) — this page has the country and state codes for regions around the world, including Australia.

   Search results are displayed in table format (see Figure 3-13). Each line contains the surname, the earliest date for which the submitter has information on the surname, the most recent date the submitter has for the surname, locations through which the family passed showing migration patterns (using a list of standard abbreviations) and the submitter's name tag.

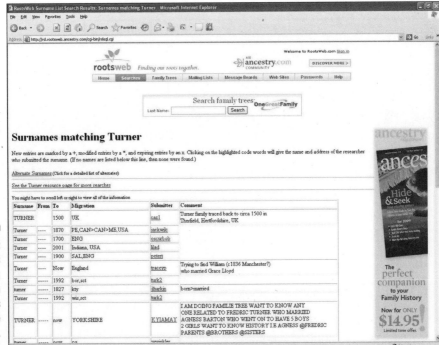

**Figure 3-13:** Surnames matching Turner in the Roots Surname List.

**3. Click on the name tag to contact a submitter.**

The link automatically takes you to a page that includes the submitter's email address and a mailing address if it has been provided. You can then email the submitter with your query.

# Chapter 4

# Locating Your Ancestors (Geographically Speaking)

*I*n your genealogical research, finding information about your family's surnames only isn't enough. To put together a truly comprehensive genealogy, you need to know where your ancestors lived and the times in which they lived. Although you can get some of this information from other relatives and from documents that belonged to your ancestors, much of what you're looking for is available only in or from the actual areas where your ancestors lived.

In this chapter, we examine some geographical resources that can help you develop the *where* and *when* in your genealogy.

## Are We There Yet? (Researching Where 'There' Was to Your Ancestors)

What did 'there' mean for your ancestors? You have to answer this question to know where to look for genealogical information. These days, coming from a family that has lived in the same general area for more than two or three generations is rather unique. If you're a member of such a family, you're a lucky person when it comes to genealogical research. However, if you're like most people, you come from families that have moved around at least every couple of generations, if not more often. Usually, finding out where all your ancestors lived — and when — presents a challenge. On the other hand, it's also a very rewarding challenge.

So, how do you find out where your ancestors lived and the approximate time frames they were there? A good starting point is to look for clues in the notes you made when interviewing your relatives and in the records you've collected so far, as these often give you a good idea of where your ancestors lived — and when.

## Using documents you already have in your possession

Go through any copies of records that you or others in the family have already collected, as well as your notes from interviews with family members and from other resources you've found on your ancestors. For example, you may have recorded a general statement such as 'Aunty Elsie recalled stories about her father building a slab hut on the banks of the Macquarie River near Dubbo when the family first settled there'. Of course, whether Aunty Elsie recalled the stories *first-hand* (those that she witnessed or lived through) or was recounting stories told to her by other family members does have a bearing on how much faith you can put in her recollection of time and place. Nonetheless, these stories give you a starting point.

In addition, most public records that you've already collected — such as vital records, land records and so on — provide at least two leads for you to follow. They tell you:

- ✔ The names of the people involved (and sometimes also the names of witnesses or parents)
- ✔ The date and place of the event, or at least when the event was recorded

Having this information points you in the right direction of where to begin looking for other records to substantiate what you believe to be true about your ancestors. Knowing a name to look for in a particular place and time gets you on your way to seeking other records.

Try to narrow down the time frame for a search *before* you set out to track down an ancestor's records. Knowing that you're looking for a shipping record in a three-month period is very different — and much simpler — than undertaking a search that spans a five-year time frame. If you know how old a great uncle was when he died, you can easily work out his approximate date of birth. This gives you the time frame in which to search for his birth record.

# *Looking at directories and newspapers*

If you have a general idea of where your family lived at a particular time, but no conclusive proof, post office directories and newspapers may help. (In some countries, census records are quite helpful too. We discuss census records in Chapter 5.) Directories and newspapers can help you confirm whether your ancestors indeed lived in a particular area and, in some cases, they can provide even more information than you expect. A newspaper obituary, for instance, may unearth some very graphic descriptions. Along with the name and age of the deceased and when he or she died, you may get additional information on the family's history or the circumstances of the death. In old regional newspapers especially, it's not unusual to find details of the family as well as the life of the deceased. A statement such as 'Maggie Carmichael was the eldest of seven daughters born to Fred and Annie Smithers, who came to New South Wales in 1855 on the *Ensign* and who had settled in this district more than 50 years ago', provides research gems for you to follow through. Such examples are not uncommon.

## *Directories*

Like today's telephone books, directories contained basic information about the people who lived in particular towns, cities, districts or counties. Typically, the directories identified at least the head of each household and the location of the house.

A large number of directories are now available online and more are being digitised all the time. Here are two websites to try for directories relating to Australia:

- ✔ **Ancestry.com.au** (www.ancestry.com.au): If you think the family you're researching was in New South Wales, you can find a run of the state's Sands Post Office directories for most years between 1861 and 1933 at this site. You can search the directories for free, but you have to subscribe in order to download the full image.

- ✔ **World Vital Records** (www.worldvitalrecords.com.au): This 'pay per view' site offers by far the most comprehensive coverage of Australian directories available. The range goes beyond post office, commercial and trade directories to many occupational lists, including medical, legal and religious bodies, which are useful if your family had an association with one of these occupations. You can search the indexes for free, but you need to subscribe to view the full image.

Many overseas sites also offer a wide range of directories online. For example:

- ✔ **United Kingdom:** The University of Leicester's digital library of historical directories (www.historicaldirectories.org/hd) provides free online access to local and trade directories for England and Wales from 1750 to 1919. You can search the collection by decade, by place or by keyword, you can search within the directory for a specific name or you can just browse through the entire book. If you search the online collection by keyword (such as surname, place or occupation), you view the results via a digital image of the original directory.

- ✔ **United States:** The City Directories site (www.uscitydirectories.com) offers a survey of many library and historical collections and allows you to check what directories are known to exist for a particular state. Some collections have links to online images, while others provide a call number for a book or microfilm in a specific library. A paid search service is also available, whereby you can order specific searches through a professional genealogical company.

### Newspapers

Newspapers are helpful only if your ancestors did something that was newsworthy — but you'd be surprised what was considered newsworthy in the past. Your ancestor didn't necessarily have to be a politician or a criminal to get his picture and story in the paper. Just like today, obituaries, birth and marriage announcements, advertisements and gossip sections were all relatively common in newspapers of the past. Your grandmother being listed as a finalist in the Kalgoorlie Agricultural Show's sponge cake making competition in 1912 may not seem a very newsworthy story to you, but it places her in a specific place at that time, which can be very important if she's proving hard to trace.

Today, numerous websites are devoted to digitised images of historical newspapers. Most sites are the result of large-scale digitisation projects aimed at large public libraries and academic institutions. Here are a few to whet your appetite:

- ✔ Australian Newspapers Online (www.nla.gov.au/npapers) has a range of local and national Australian papers and is hosted by the National Library of Australia.

- ✔ NewspaperARCHIVE.com (www.newspaperarchive.com) has nearly 3,000 US titles online and claims to be adding one new newspaper page per second to its site.

- ✔ Onlinenewspapers.com (www.onlinenewspapers.com) has links to various worldwide newspaper listings.

Australian libraries are cooperating through a project run by the National Library to digitise many early newspapers. The test website (`ndpbeta.nla.gov.au/ndp/del/home`) indicates the range of newspapers to be covered and the search capabilities of the site.

Similarly, Google is developing a News Archive website (`news.google.com/archivesearch`), which has the potential to be very helpful for family historians. You can search any time period from 1550 to 1995 by entering a search term (which can be a name, a place or an event) and clicking on the Show Timeline box. The resulting screen is just like a standard Google search, summarising the results, highlighting the term you searched and providing links to websites where you can get the full details.

In addition, many public libraries across Australia subscribe to Gale Digital Archive and so offer access to the Burney Collection of British newspapers from the seventeenth and eighteenth centuries, the British Library's collection of newspapers from the nineteenth century and The Times Digital Archive spanning 1785 to 1985.

- ✔ The Burney and British Library collections combined contain more than three million pages of historical newspapers published across the United Kingdom prior to 1900. You can search across numerous titles and download specific pages.

- ✔ The Times Digital Archive provides access to 200 years of the most important national newspaper in England. You can undertake focused searches and view full articles.

Individuals cannot subscribe to Gale Digital Archive, but check with your state library to see whether it offers access from home for its registered users.

Contemporary newspapers can also be useful, and online directories of these are widely available. The local newspaper for the area where your ancestors once lived may run a small enquiry on your behalf through one of its regular columns, or it may even be interested in you writing a short piece about your pioneer ancestors if the story is likely to have general appeal to its readers. This story, in turn, may generate new leads for you from locals.

Local and state libraries usually hold collections of current newspapers, and often list their holdings as part of their online catalogues. Of course, this doesn't mean you can get access to the newspapers' resources without physically visiting that library or hiring a professional researcher to do the job for you, but it does at least make you aware that the resource is there. Examples include

- ✔ The newspaper collections at the State Library of Victoria, Australia (www.slv.vic.gov.au/catalogues)

- ✔ The British Library's Newspaper Library (catalogue.bl.uk — click on Search the Integrated Catalogue and then use the Catalogue Subset Search feature and select newspapers)

An increasing number of online projects are cataloguing or transcribing information from newspapers, particularly birth, death and marriage records, resulting in some very useful online databases. One of the best of these is the Ryerson Index (www.ryersonindex.org), which currently name-indexes more than 2 million death, funeral, probate and obituary announcements from Australian newspapers, especially the *Sydney Morning Herald* (see Figure 4-1).

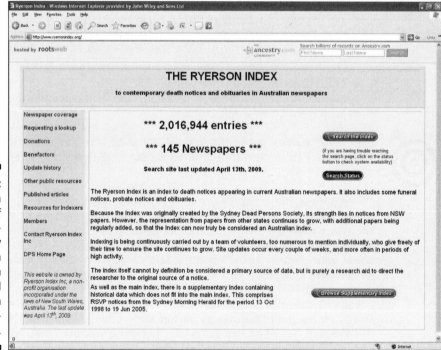

**Figure 4-1:**
The Ryerson Index of contemporary death notices from selected Australian newspapers.

You can find a free searchable database of some of the main Australian newspapers at www.newsstore.fairfax.com.au. The search results show you the date and name of the paper, giving you enough information to then visit your state library and trawl through the paper for that day, or for a small fee you can ask for a copy of the entry to be sent to you electronically.

You can also find specific newspapers using a geographical approach through a comprehensive genealogical gateway site. For example, if you're looking for a British paper you can use a site such as GENUKI (www.genuki.org.uk). Look under a specific county name and then the topic of Newspapers to see what's available for that county. For an Australian paper, try Coraweb (www.coraweb.com.au), following the link under the topic heading Online Publications: Newspapers and Newspaper Indexes. Alternatively, you can use a general internet search engine — especially if you know the location and time frame for the newspaper.

# *Where Is Gulgong, Anyway?*

At some point during your research, you're bound to run across something that says an ancestor lived in a particular town or county but contains no details of where that place was — no state or other identifier. How do you find out where that place was located?

A *gazetteer*, or geographical dictionary, provides information about places. By looking up the name of the town or county, you can narrow your search for your ancestor. The gazetteer identifies every known town or county by a particular name and provides varying information (depending on the gazetteer itself) about each. Typically, gazetteers provide at least the names of the state and country where the town or county is located. Many contemporary gazetteers also provide the latitude and longitude of the place.

Using an online gazetteer is easy. All online gazetteers are organised similarly and have query or search forms. Here's how to use Geoscience Australia's gazetteer:

1. **Go to Geoscience Australia's website at** www.ga.gov.au.

2. **From the Interactive Tools menu, click on Place Name Search.**

   When you click the Place Name Search link, the query form page appears (see Figure 4-2).

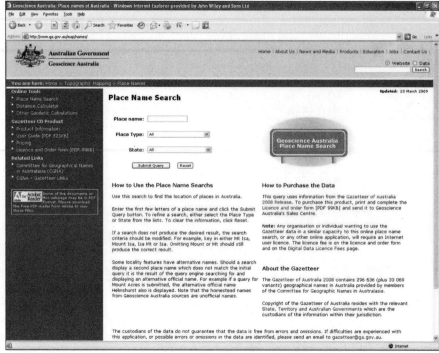

**Figure 4-2:**
The query
form for
Geoscience
Australia's
Place Name
Search.

Source: © Commonwealth of Australia, Geoscience Australia. All rights reserved. Reproduced by permission
of the Chief Executive Officer, Geoscience Australia, Canberra, ACT, www.ga.gov.au.

**3. Type your place of interest in the Place Name field and click the Submit Query button.**

For example, type **Barraba** in the Place Name field, leave the Place Type and State fields set to 'All', and then click the Submit Query button.

Geoscience Australia executes a search of its database and returns the results to you in list form. For example, a Place Name Search for Barraba returns numerous records for you to review (Figure 4-3 shows those appearing first in the list), including not only the town near Tamworth in northern New South Wales, but also a parish of that name in Queensland, as well as an airfield, a railway station, a school and a creek. Latitude and longitude information is provided for each entry, allowing you to plot this on a map.

By adding the information you get from the online gazetteer to the other pieces of your puzzle, you can reduce the list of common place names to just those that you think are plausible for your ancestors. By pinpointing where a place is, you can look for more records to prove whether your ancestors really lived there.

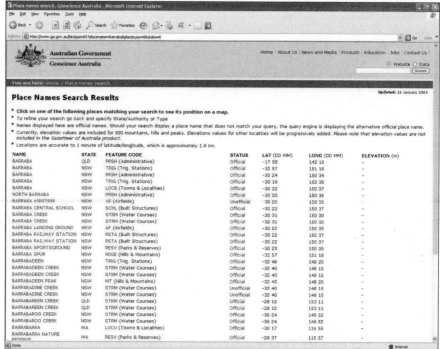

**Figure 4-3:**
The results
of a broad
Place Name
Search on
the name
Barraba.

For example, if your mother told you that your great-great-grandfather's uncle lived in a town called Barraba but didn't say where Barraba was, you can use the information you just collected in the Place Name Search database query to narrow your search for places called Barraba. To narrow your search to a specific type of place, select an item from the Place Type drop-down list; and to narrow your search to a specific region or locality, select an item from the State drop-down list.

From your initial Place Name Search query, you know that numerous places with the name Barraba exist in Australia. You can eliminate all the places that aren't actual towns or localities. (After all, your great-great-grandfather's uncle probably didn't live in an airfield or a school.) This process of elimination narrows your search down to two possible localities with different latitudes and longitudes — click on each entry to bring up a large-scale map showing the location of that place. Immediately, you can see that there is one town or locality called Barraba in New South Wales and a Barrabarra in Western Australia.

In addition to the Geoscience Australia database, many other online gazetteers identify places worldwide. Here are some for you to check out:

- Gazetteer for Scotland (www.geo.ed.ac.uk/scotgaz)
- Geographical Names of Canada (geonames.nrcan.gc.ca)
- Ordnance Survey UK (www.ordnancesurvey.co.uk/oswebsite/freefun/didyouknow)
- US Board on Geographic Names (geonames.usgs.gov)

The National Library of Australia provides a useful listing of its holdings of world gazetteers and has identified links to online international gazetteers for easy access at www.nla.gov.au/map/worldgazetteers.html#world.

GENUKI (www.genuki.org.uk) provides an online gazetteer that links to information on its website. Designed specifically for genealogists, this is a great way to locate a place in England, Wales, Scotland or Ireland and then find information relevant to it.

To use the GENUKI gazetteer, follow these steps:

1. **Go to** www.genuki.org.uk.

2. **Click on Contents & Search.**

   This takes you to the site map.

3. **Click on Search.**

   This takes you to a page with various search options. One of these options is the GENUKI Gazetteer.

4. **In the Gazetteer section, type the name of the place you're researching in the Place Name box, leaving the other search options defaulting to 'Any' and 'Plot Places on a Map'.**

   For this example, type the name Cullompton. The result is shown on a map: Cullompton, Devon (see Figure 4-4).

   Clicking on the link for Cullompton takes you to all the information contained in the GENUKI database for that town. So from not knowing exactly where the place was, you now have immediate access to genealogically relevant information for the town.

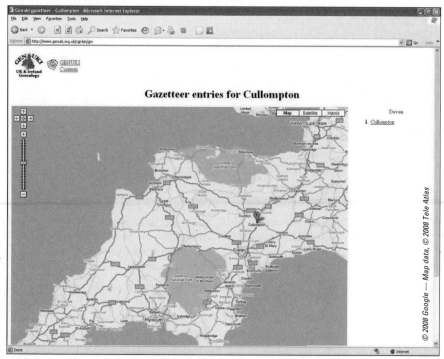

**Figure 4-4:**
Locating
the town of
Cullompton
using
GENUKI.

# Mapping Your Ancestors' Way

Maps can be an invaluable resource in your genealogical research. Not only do maps help you track your ancestors, but they also enhance your published genealogy by illustrating some of your findings.

Tracking the movements of your ancestors can be a lot of fun. Just reading about migrations in family histories, texts and records isn't the easiest way to understand where, why and how your ancestors moved. Charting movements on maps makes visualising the paths your ancestors took and the obstacles they may have encountered easier. Maps also make the genealogy you put together more interesting for others to read, because they enable the reader to see what you're talking about in your writing. Maps help tell your ancestors' stories, so to speak.

Different types of online sites have maps that may be useful in your genealogical research:

- **Images of maps:** Some websites contain scanned or digitised images of historic maps, which you can download or print out. For example, the Parish Map Preservation Project run by the New South Wales Department of Lands (parishmaps.lands.nsw.gov.au) provides online access to more than 35,000 parish maps in its historical collection. Another global collection is held by the Perry-Castañeda Library at the University of Texas (www.lib.utexas.edu/maps/historical/index.html), while Old Maps (www.old-maps.co.uk) and Genmaps (freepages.genealogy.rootsweb.ancestry.com/~genmaps) bring together historical maps of the United Kingdom listed in chronological order by county.

- **Interactive maps:** Most interactive map websites tend to offer current rather than historical information, so they're good if you're looking for the current location of a cemetery, church or house, but they're unlikely to help you find where a particular building was in the 1850s.

  A well-known Australian website is Whereis (www.whereis.com.au), which also provides step-by-step directions to reach a specific place from any destination. Two good international sites are MapQuest (www.mapquest.com), a US project that has interactive maps for too many countries to list here (including the United States, Australia, Canada, Germany, Italy, New Zealand and the United Kingdom); and Streetmap (www.streetmap.co.uk), which provides detailed maps for all of mainland Britain.

- **Specialised maps:** Some websites offer maps that come with tools and specialised functions. One example is ancestry.co.uk (www.ancestry.co.uk/learn/facts/default.aspx), which has a free mapping service for surname distribution in the 1891 British census available through its learning centre.

Found where your ancestors were living in the 1891 Scottish census? By typing the address or place name into Google Maps (maps.google.com) you can zoom in and out of an aerial map with that place name superimposed so that you can see what the locality looks like today. Google Maps is the best known of all mapping services and can add a whole new dimension to your family history. Using Google Maps you can quickly establish whether a place about which you know very little is a large town or a small rural area, and whether it is in a remote region or part of a busy metropolis. In addition, you can use Google Maps to find individual addresses, and sometimes its Street View function can help you to 'drive past' a house in another country where your ancestors once lived. It all adds to the information you're gathering about where your ancestors lived.

To launch the Street View feature, click on the yellow symbol representing a person on the map. Alternatively, when you search by place name using Google Maps, a white pop-up box appears in the middle of the screen. Click on Street View to launch the feature. Use the arrows to move along the image.

Suppose that you've just received the death certificate of a family member and found that she was born in a place called Longwood in Victoria. You aren't sure exactly where Longwood is in the state and whether in fact it still exists. Here's how you can use Google Maps to aid your research:

1. **Go to** `maps.google.com`.

2. **Type** Longwood, Victoria, **in the Search box and click on Search Maps.**

   An aerial view of this part of Victoria appears, showing you exactly where Longwood is. You can immediately see that it's a rural area, and you can zoom in and out to take a virtual aerial tour of the district.

---

# Crossing the line

Just as maps help you to track your ancestors' movements and where they once lived, so maps can help you to track when your ancestors *didn't* really move. Boundaries for towns, districts and even states change over time. Additionally, sometimes towns and counties change their names. Knowing whether your ancestors really moved or just appeared to move because of boundary or town name changes is important when you're trying to locate records for them.

To determine whether a town or county changed names at some point, check a gazetteer or historical text on the area. (Gazetteers are discussed in the earlier section, 'Where Is Gulgong, Anyway?') Finding boundary changes can be a little more challenging, but resources are available to help you. For example, historical atlases illustrate land and boundary changes. You can also use websites that have maps for the same areas over time. A few sites deal specifically with boundary changes in particular locations; for example, the Counties of England, Wales and Scotland Prior to the 1974 Boundary Changes link in the GENUKI website (`www.genuki.org.uk/big/Britain.html`). A program that tracks boundary changes across Europe and the Middle East is the Centennia Historical Atlas (`www.clockwk.com/download.html`). A free downloadable version covers the years 1789 to 1819 and you can purchase an upgrade, which makes the mapping feature fully functional for the period 1000 AD to the present day.

# There's No Place Like Home: Using Local Resources

A time will come (possibly early in your research) when you need information that's maintained on a local level — say, a copy of a record stored in a state archive, confirmation that an ancestor is buried in a particular cemetery or even just a photo of the old homestead. So how can you find and get what you need?

Finding this information is easy if you live in or near the place where the information is maintained — you decide what you need and where it's stored, and then go and get a copy. Getting locally held information isn't quite as easy if you live in another state or country because, while you can determine what information you need and where it may be stored, finding out whether the information is truly kept where you think it is and then getting a copy is another thing. Of course, if this situation weren't such a common occurrence for genealogists, you could just make a holiday out of it — travel to the location to finish researching there and get the copy you need while sightseeing along the way. But unfortunately, needing records from distant places is a common occurrence, and you probably can't afford to pack your bags and hit the road every time you need a record or an item from a faraway place — which is why it's nice to know that resources are available to help you.

From geographic-specific websites to local genealogical and historical societies to libraries with research services and even individuals who are willing to do research in public records, a lot of resources are available to help you locate local documents and obtain copies. Some resources are totally free, others may charge you a fee for their time and still others want money only for copying or other direct costs.

## Geographic-specific websites

*Geographic-specific websites* are those pages that contain specific information about a particular town, county, state, country or other locality. They typically provide information about local resources, such as genealogical and historical societies, government agencies, cemeteries and civic organisations. Some sites include local histories and biographies of prominent residents online. Often, they list and have links to other web pages that have resources for the area. And sometimes, they even have a place where you can post queries about the area or families from there with the hope that someone who reads your query will have some answers for you.

How can you find geographic-specific websites, you ask? Doing so is easy. Try these options for finding a place in the United Kingdom:

- ✔ Use a search engine, such as Google (www.google.com.au). Type the place name of interest and click on Google Search. You get links to local parish sites, tourist sites, local government sites and links to the area's genealogical records via the GENUKI gateway site.
- ✔ Visit UKvillages.co.uk (ukvillages.co.uk), type the place name of interest in the Search box and click on Find.

In addition, gateway sites such as Coraweb (www.coraweb.com.au) and GENUKI (www.genuki.org.uk) lead you to geographic-specific sites.

## Genealogical and historical societies

Most genealogical and historical societies exist on a local level and attempt to preserve documents and history for the area in which they're located. Genealogical societies also have another purpose — to help their members to research their ancestors whether they lived in the local area or elsewhere. Although historical societies don't primarily exist to provide genealogical information, many are able to assist family historians and frequently compile databases or retain information that may be of value to others researching the region.

Often, if you don't live in the area where you need a record or some other information, you can contact a local genealogical or historical society to get help. This assistance can vary from the society undertaking a search or retrieval of documents service in its own collection to carrying out more extensive research. Such groups are always not-for-profit and are run by volunteers, so expect to make a donation towards their work in return for anything they do for you if they don't advertise a specific fee.

Before you contact a local genealogical or historical society for help, be sure you know what services it offers. Some groups are large and active, and have teams of volunteers waiting to answer enquiries, while others are small and struggle to maintain any kind of research advice. Many genealogical and historical societies have their own websites where they post details about the services they offer for both members and non-members. Read this information before you send an email enquiry: That way, you're not wasting your time waiting for help that can't be provided.

Try these websites to find a society in the region you're researching:

- Australasian Federation of Family History Organisations (www.affho.org)

- Cora Num's Web Sites For Genealogists (www.coraweb.com.au)

- Genealogy and Family Heritage at CyberPursuits (www.cyberpursuits.com/gen/default.asp)

- Irish Ancestors at Irish Times.com (www.irishtimes.com/ancestor/browse/addresses/family.htm)

- Royal Australian Historical Society (www.rahs.org.au)

- Scottish Association of Family History Societies (www.safhs.org.uk)

- The USGenWeb Project (www.usgenweb.org)

- UK Federation of Family History Societies (www.ffhs.org.uk)

## Libraries and archives

Often, the holdings in local libraries and archives can be of great value to you — even if you can't physically visit the library or archive to do your research. Check the organisation's website to see whether it has an online catalogue you can consult, to determine whether it has the book or document that you need. An increasing number of libraries in Australia are now part of the Libraries Australia project (outlined later in this section), which means you can search for a specific title across all participating repositories. Many allow you to borrow the book you require through interlibrary loan for a nominal charge. Alternatively, the library may offer a copying service you can utilise to copy the document that you require.

Use these links to locate libraries and archives in a particular place:

- **Australian Libraries Gateway** (www.nla.gov.au/libraries): This site is the Australian National Library's one-stop-shop for finding a library anywhere in Australia.

- **Directory of Archives in Australia** (www.archivists.org.au/directory-of-archives): This online directory lists hundreds of archives, including those held by government departments, schools, religious groups, businesses and not-for-profit groups.

- **Libraries Australia** (librariesaustralia.nla.gov.au/apps/kss): Check the holdings of most public, state, academic and specialist libraries across the country: More than 42 million items are listed.

- **UNESCO Libraries Portal** (www.unesco.org/webworld/portal_bib) **and UNESCO Archive Portal** (www.unesco.org/webworld/portal_archives): Search for libraries and archive institutions worldwide.

# Professional researchers

*Professional researchers* are people who research your genealogy — or particular family lines — for a fee. Some people engage a professional genealogist to research their family tree for them because they don't have the time to do it themselves, or because the professional genealogist has specialised knowledge in researching certain types of records. Others live too far away from the records they need, so engage a professional researcher on a one-off basis or short-term assignment to locate and copy specific records for them.

Shop around to ensure that you find the best person for the job you want done: Professional genealogists are no different than other professionals — their services, rates, experience and reputations vary. Here's a list of questions you may want to ask before engaging a professional researcher:

- ✔ Is the researcher certified or accredited and, if so, by what organisation?

- ✔ How many years research experience does this person have?

- ✔ What is the researcher's educational background?

- ✔ What languages does the researcher speak fluently?

- ✔ Does the researcher have any professional affiliations? In other words, does he or she belong to any professional genealogical organisations and, if so, which ones?

- ✔ What records and resources does the researcher have access to?

- ✔ What is the researcher's experience in the area where you need help? For example, if you need help interviewing distant relatives in a foreign country, has the researcher conducted interviews in the past? Or if you need records pertaining to a particular ethnic or religious group, does he or she have experience researching those types of records?

- ✔ How does the researcher charge for services — by the record, by the hour or by the project? What methods of payment does the researcher accept? What is the researcher's policy on refunds if you're dissatisfied with the service?

- ✔ How many other projects is the researcher working on presently and what kinds of projects? How much time will he or she devote to your research project? When will he or she report the results?

- ✔ How does the researcher report on the results?

- ✔ Does the researcher have references that you can contact?

One way to find a researcher is to contact a professional association of genealogists. Members of these associations must be accredited and sign an agreement to abide by a code of ethics. The associations also provide help if issues or complaints arise about their members. If you're looking for a researcher, try the following organisations:

- Association of Genealogists and Researchers in Archives (UK) (www.agra.org.uk)

- Association of Professional Genealogists (www.apgen.org) (**Note:** The organisation differs from other organisations listed here in that anyone who supports its objectives and abides by its code of ethics can join. No accreditation is required.)

- Association of Professional Genealogists in Ireland (www.apgi.ie)

- Association of Scottish Genealogists and Researchers in Archives (www.asgra.co.uk)

- Association of Ulster Genealogists and Record Agents (www.augra.com)

- Australasian Association of Genealogists and Record Agents (www.aagra.asn.au)

The Society of Australian Genealogists publishes a list of researchers who've successfully undertaken its Diploma in Family Historical Studies and who are available for private commissions (see www.sag.org.au/downloads/diplomates.pdf).

# Part II
# Finding the Elusive Records

*'Researching government records was great fun until I discovered dad's family was in a witness protection program.'*

# In this part ...

This part covers how to locate sites with hard-to-find information about groups of people and particular types of records — and figuring out how to use those sites effectively in your genealogical research. Here you find information about the following:

- Finding Australian government records
- Finding other miscellaneous records and information on various groups
- Tracking down ancestors in overseas records

# Chapter 5

# Australian Government Records

· · · · · · · · · · · · · · · · · · · · · · · · · · · · · ·

· · · · · · · · · · · · · · · · · · · · · · · · · · · · · ·

**G**overnments are bureaucratic institutions no matter where you live. Fortunately, you can tap into some of the information that the Australian government has collected over the years, going right back to colonial times — when the authorities kept close tabs on all the early residents, both convict and free. Records at all levels of government are immensely valuable to genealogists, and getting access to some of these records can make tracing your family history much easier.

Many government departments have begun to digitise some of their older records, and these are available online to save you a lot of travel time.

This isn't to say that you're going to find every government record online — for example, it's unlikely you'll ever be able to access your grandparents' tax returns. Increasingly, records are becoming more restricted to ensure the protection of people's privacy, but most government websites at least provide pointers to specific information, which may cut down your search time.

In this chapter, we show you what kinds of records are currently available and some of the major projects you can use as keys for unlocking the government treasure chests of genealogical information.

# Chasing Births, Deaths, Marriages and Divorces

Sometimes, it seems that with every major event in people's lives comes a government record. One is generated every time someone is born, gets married, has a child and passes away. *Vital records* (also called civil registrations) are the collective name for records of these events. Originally, only churches in Australia kept such records (see Chapter 6). Then each state set up its own registry and introduced civil registration. Today, no national system of registration exists for these types of records, which means you have to look for specific birth, death, marriage or divorce records in the state or territory in which the event occurred.

## Births, deaths and marriages

Civil registration indexes serve much the same purpose as other indexes: They point to the locations of original records. You can use indexes to confirm that an ancestor's vital records are available prior to purchasing a copy of the records. And knowing the exact location of a record can often make retrieval of the record a lot easier.

The easiest way to find civil registration indexes on the internet is to search along geographical lines — that is, look to resources in the state or territory where your ancestors lived. You can use some of the tips we give in Chapter 4 to locate your ancestors geographically, and this can help you narrow your search.

Check out the following for information about civil registration resources in Australia:

- **Australian Capital Territory:** The Registry of Births, Deaths and Marriages (www.ors.act.gov.au/bdm/WebPages/bdm_deaths.html) provides an online historical death index for the years 1930 (when records commenced) to 1973. All records prior to 1930 can be found in the New South Wales indexes.

- **New South Wales:** The NSW Registry of Births, Deaths & Marriages (www.bdm.nsw.gov.au) provides historical online indexes for baptisms/births from 1788 to 1908, marriages from 1788 to 1958 and deaths from 1788 to 1978. You can search the indexes for free and order certificates online. Birth indexes to 1918 are available on CD-ROM through many libraries and family history societies.

- ✔ **Northern Territory:** Records commenced in 1870 and are held by the Northern Territory Department of Justice (www.nt.gov.au/justice/bdm). It has no online indexes, but you can consult microfiche records of births from 1870 to 1918, marriages from 1870 to 1913 and deaths from 1870 to 1913.

- ✔ **Queensland:** Records are kept by the Queensland Department of Justice and Attorney-General (www.justice.qld.gov.au/bdm), which has online indexes of births from 1829 to 1914, marriages from 1829 to 1929 and deaths from 1829 to 1929. Some additional years are available on CD-ROM and microfiche. Pre-1856 records can be found in the New South Wales indexes.

- ✔ **South Australia:** The Office of Consumer and Business Affairs (www.ocba.sa.gov.au/bdm) currently doesn't have any online indexes. However, you can consult records for births from 1842 to 1928, marriages from 1842 to 1937 and deaths from 1842 to 1972 on CD-ROM and microfiche.

- ✔ **Tasmania:** The Department of Justice (www.justice.tas.gov.au/bdm) has online indexes of baptisms/births, marriages and burials/deaths from 1803 to 1899. Further years are indexed on CD-ROM and microfiche.

- ✔ **Victoria:** The Department of Justice (www.justice.vic.gov.au) has online indexes for baptisms/births from 1836 to 1908, marriages from 1836 to 1942 and burials/deaths from 1836 to 1985. You have to pay a fee to view the indexes online, and if you order a certificate online it's supplied to you electronically via the department's website. Births to 1920 are also available on CD-ROM. Some pre-1851 entries can be found in the New South Wales indexes.

- ✔ **Western Australia:** The Department of the Attorney-General (www.bdm.dotag.wa.gov.au) offers online indexes of births from 1841 to 1932, marriages from 1841 to 1927 and deaths from 1841 to 1953).

The date ranges of searchable online indexes are often restricted by privacy laws, so check with your local library or family history society to see whether it has indexes that go beyond those dates available online. The Society of Australian Genealogists (www.sag.org.au) has a complete set of all available Australian birth, death and marriage indexes in its library, and for some states these extend beyond the dates of the records available online.

Online indexes of birth, death and marriage records take much of the hard yakka out of tracking down your ancestor's vital records. The following steps show you how to search online indexes at the NSW Registry of Births, Deaths & Marriages website to cut your research time to shreds:

1. **Go to** www.bdm.nsw.gov.au **and click on Family History.**

2. **Click on Search Historical Indexes.**

   You're assuming for this exercise that you're an experienced user of the index and so click on Search Now.

3. **Choose whether you wish to search Birth and Death Records or Marriage Records and click on the relevant link.**

   For example, click on the Births and Deaths Records link.

4. **Click on the radio button to indicate the type of record you're searching for, enter a surname in the Last Name field and at least a starting date for the search, then click on Search Now.**

   For example, select the Births radio button, type in the surname **Dalton** and then type in **1890** and **1900** in the Years From and To fields, respectively. Don't worry about entering information in the other fields at this stage.

5. **Scroll through the search results available on-screen.**

   The results screen shows all the records that match the search criteria. In the different columns you can see each entry's registration number, last name, given name, father's name and mother's name and the district in which the birth was registered, as shown in Figure 5-1. You can click on a column heading to reorganise the list.

   If your search generates a large list (as in Figure 5-1), clicking on the Father's Given Name(s) column heading, for example, reorganises the list alphabetically by father. You don't need to do this if your search results return only a few matches.

   If you get too many search results, you can go back to the Search screen and refine your search. For example, you can confine your search by asking only for people called Henry Dalton born between 1890 and 1900, or only for people called Dalton born between 1890 and 1900 who had a mother named Mary.

The registration number in the left-hand column of the search results table (see Figure 5-1) is a combination of the year in which the event was recorded and the unique number applying to that event. Be careful not to make assumptions about the year shown in the registration number — this doesn't indicate the individual's birth or death year, for example, but the year when the event was registered. So, if your grandmother was born in

1891 but the nearest entry you can find specifies 1892, then the record may well belong to her, especially if she was born late in December and the family didn't get around to advising the authorities about her birth until early the following year.

After you find the entry you're looking for you can order a copy of the certificate online by following the Buy Now link. The full certificate gives you a lot more information than that provided in the online index — especially if the event occurred after 1856 when official civil registration was first introduced. For example, a birth certificate from the 1890s is likely to tell you the age of the parents, where they were born, when they married, the father's occupation, other children already born to the couple, who registered the birth and who was the witness to the event (often the mother or sister of the woman giving birth).

Tracking down death certificates is certainly worthwhile, but keep in mind that some of the information they contain — such as the deceased's age — may not always be 100 per cent accurate. See Chapter 3 for more details.

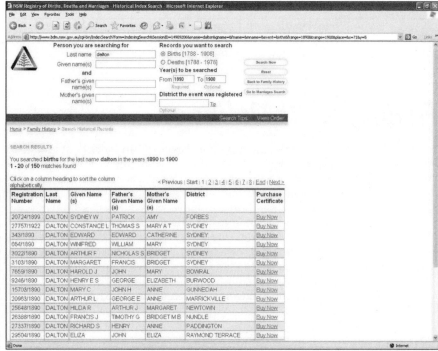

**Figure 5-1:**
A search results page from the NSW Registry of Births, Deaths & Marriages website.

*Source: This material is reproduced with the permission of the NSW Registry of Births, Deaths & Marriages on behalf of the Crown in the right of the State of New South Wales. It is subject to Crown Copyright.*

## Divorces

Divorces used to fall into that 'black sheep' category that no-one talked about much, but these days the prevalence of divorce has changed people's views and most people aren't too concerned if they find out that an ancestor's marriage ended in the divorce court. Records are beginning to be opened up, and you can find records for the following states available online:

- ✔ **New South Wales:** The State Records Authority of New South Wales (srwww.records.nsw.gov.au/indexes/searchform.aspx?id=16) has divorce records from 1873 to 1923 searchable by petitioner and respondent. The index is currently being extended to 1930.

- ✔ **Queensland:** The Queensland State Archives (www.archives.qld.gov.au/research/index/divorces.asp) has a browsable PDF of divorce cases from 1861 to 1894.

- ✔ **Tasmania:** The Archives Office of Tasmania (portal.archives.tas.gov.au/menu.aspx?search=3) has divorce records from 1861 to 1920 searchable by surname.

- ✔ **Victoria:** Macbeth Genealogical Services (www.macbeth.com.au/cgi-bin/divsearch.pl) offers a record retrieval service covering divorces in Victoria between 1861 and 1900.

# Finding Wills Online

A *will* is one of the most personal records an individual creates because it sets out what the person wants to have happen to his or her property and possessions after he or she dies. This is where clues about family favourites and long-running feuds may surface. For example, why did grandma leave £50 to all the grandchildren but give the youngest £200? Or, how come your great-grandfather divided his estate equally between eight of his children, but specifically declared that the eldest son should receive nothing? Did they have a falling out, or had that son been adequately provided for already with gifts during his father's lifetime? And what happened to the six family portraits detailed in your great-grandmother's will that she left to her youngest daughter living somewhere in England?

Several states provide online indexes to wills. To find out what you can access, see the following:

✔ **New South Wales:** The State Records Authority of New South Wales (srwww.records.nsw.gov.au/archives/early-probate_11821.asp) has an online index to a small series of supplementary probate records for the period 1790–1875.

More importantly, the organisation holds probate packets (the working documents for the settling of estates in New South Wales between 1880 and the 1960s) and these are gradually being entered into Archives Investigator, its main site catalogue (investigator.records.nsw.gov.au). Check for probate packets by using the Simple Search feature, entering the surname of the person you're seeking and the word **death** (for example, **Simpson death**). If you find the probate packet you're looking for but are unable to visit the Western Sydney Search Room at Kingswood, you can use the record retrieval service to obtain a copy.

In addition, the State Records Authority has an index to intestate estates from 1823 to 1888 (where people died without leaving a legal will) available through its Indexes Online section (www.records.nsw.gov.au). This can be very useful, as many people didn't make provision for their families by having a legally written will and so the authorities had to step in and administer their estates.

✔ **Queensland:** The Queensland State Archives Wills Index (www.archives.qld.gov.au/research/index/wills.asp) allows you to search for files from all districts in Queensland between 1857 and 1900 and from the southern district (Brisbane area) from 1900 to 1915.

✔ **Tasmania:** The Archives Office of Tasmania, Index of Wills (portal.archives.tas.gov.au/menu.aspx?search=9) allows you to search for wills and probate records in the state from 1824 to 1989.

✔ **Victoria:** Public Record Office Victoria (www.prov.vic.gov.au) holds probates from 1841 onwards and records are being progressively digitised to be available online for viewing. At www.prov.vic.gov.au/access/probate.asp you can search an online index for probates approved between 1841 and 1925 and download a PDF of an original probate file for free.

✔ **Western Australia:** To find an ancestor's will in Western Australia, download an information sheet from the State Records Office website (www.sro.wa.gov.au/pdfs/infosheet-probate.pdf).

You can track down microfiche copies of will and probate indexes at many local family history societies. Likewise, the Society of Australian Genealogists (www.sag.org.au) holds copies of all available indexes to wills published in Australia.

# Counting on the Census

Census records are one of the most valuable tools available to genealogists, but their importance varies according to the country you're searching. For example, in Australia old census records have mostly been destroyed and family historians tend to rely on vital records to help fill the gaps. Conversely, in the United Kingdom and the United States, census data are crucial to genealogical research, while vital records don't always provide as much identifying information as they do in Australia.

Although Australia conducts a national census every five years, because records have been systematically destroyed for more than 150 years, today only fragments of historical information remain.

How did this come about? Well, some say it has a lot to do with Australia's convict origins. Although today having a convict in your family tree is fashionable, in the past people went to great lengths to hide the fact that grandad got a free passage to one of the colonies after being caught stealing a sheep. People thought that if census records were available for public scrutiny, they could give away too many clues about a family's background. So, for privacy reasons, Australian authorities began to destroy the census records, and today Australia remains one of the few countries in the Western world to still do so.

However, in the 2001 census Australians were given the option to have their census forms retained for 100 years and then released publicly, and 53 per cent of the population agreed to do so. As a result, the same option was offered for the 2006 census (with 56 per cent agreeing to do so). So, in 2102 genealogists will be able to find out something about at least some of their forebears — although that doesn't help those people tracing family histories today.

Of course, some earlier Australian census records have survived. As a family historian, these are of value because they allow you to determine where someone was living on a particular date. Just as importantly, they sometimes tell you who else that person was with (other members of the household), as well as his or her occupation, age and birthplace. Likewise, the person's year of arrival in Australia and ship name was often listed. Being able to find an ancestor in a census record may give you enough information to add one more generation to your family tree, and often leads back to other records.

Here's the type of census information you can find in Australia:

- ✔ **Census records:** Information collected by *enumerators*, who went from house to house to compile information about residents.

- ✔ **Muster records:** These usually relate to the convict period and refer to government instructions for certain groups of individuals to gather or muster together at a specific time and place to have their details taken. They may contain details of convicts, ex-convicts and free settlers.

- ✔ **Victualling lists:** Lists drawn up by the authorities detailing everyone who was eligible for government rations.

## Finding your ancestors in Australian census records

The first — and best known — census of the colony of New South Wales was taken in November 1828. It contains information about both free people and convicts in the colony, and gives good identifying information about individuals. Two copies of the census were taken; one was retained in the colony and the other returned to England. The Australian version has been published in book form and on CD-ROM, while the English version is available through Ancestry.com.au's website (www.ancestry.com.au).

Ancestry.com.au also has a database called 'Australia Convict Musters 1806–1849', which contains indexes and digitised images of musters for New South Wales in the period 1806 to 1837 and Tasmania in the period 1808 to 1849. Although the database is accessed via the Convict Musters link, a number of the indexes also include free persons.

The State Records Authority of New South Wales (www.records.nsw.gov.au) has several online indexes to surviving New South Wales census records. However, the index to the 1841 census provides only basic identifying information, such as name, residence (district) and the reference number from the original return, which can be consulted on microfilm. In addition, only details of the head of the household are included and for some districts no name-identified records survive. For both the 1891 and 1901 censuses an online index to the Collectors' Books is provided, but these have details of the districts covered only and don't name individuals.

Try this sample search to discover how to find individuals in the 1841 census:

1. **Go to** `www.records.nsw.gov.au` **and click on Indexes Online on the home page.**

2. **Click on Census and then under 1841 Census click on Search.**

   This brings up a query page where you can search by surname, first name and residence.

3. **Type the name you're researching into the Surname field, then click on the Submit button.**

   For example, if you're interested in finding relatives with the surname Cormack, but don't know where exactly they lived in New South Wales in 1841, just type **Cormack** into the Surname field.

   *Note:* You can use the '%' sign to do a wildcard search, so that the search picks up alternative spellings of a name. For example, typing **%Cormack%** results in all entries that have Cormack in the name, such as McOrmack.

4. **Review the results page.**

   The results page shows the surnames of any matching entries, along with their given names or initials, and their place of residence as given in the 1841 census.

   Using Cormack results in two entries, or three if the wildcard is used (shown in Figure 5-2).

   The results page also lists the relevant reference number for the microfilm copy of the original census. To purchase a copy of an entry from the 1841 census online, click on the relevant Order button and then click on Submit Order. Alternatively, you can visit one of the State Records centres and view the entry yourself (see `www.records.nsw.gov.au/state-archives/use-the-archives/getting-started/visit-us/visit-us` for more details).

Because government authorities compiled muster records and census returns, the best place to look for surviving records is in each state or territory's archive website. These addresses are listed in Chapter 1.

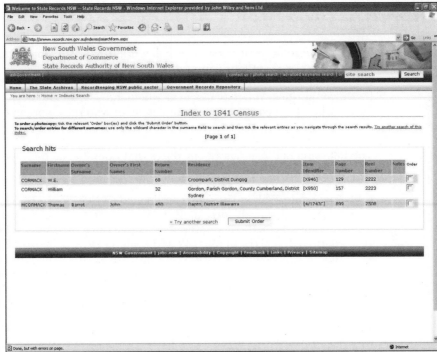

**Figure 5-2:**
A search
results page
from the
1841 census
online
index.

# Making use of muster and victualling lists

The earliest records in Australia are muster and victualling lists and these date back to the arrival of the First Fleet in 1788. Regular musters of convicts and free persons in the colonies continued to be collated throughout the late eighteenth and early nineteenth centuries. Unfortunately, not all these records have survived.

See the Research Guide, *Basics on Australian Musters and Censuses*, found on the Society of Australian Genealogists website (www.sag.org.au) for more information. The guide lists all known New South Wales census and muster records and details their current location. The society also publishes many of the early muster and census records for New South Wales through its Australian Biographical and Genealogical Record (the ABGR). These records aren't yet available online, but you can find information about the collection under 'Research Guides' on the society's website.

# Piecing Together Convict Records

Having convicts in your family tree can work to your advantage, since you're likely to find out a lot more about them than your law-abiding ancestors! Because convicts were prisoners, their daily lives were well documented by the authorities. You may discover when and where they were tried, their crime, when they got their freedom, details of who they worked for and any punishments they received for misdemeanours.

The following outlines Australian states that operated as penal settlements and where you can find convict records:

- **New South Wales:** The penal settlement of New South Wales was established with the arrival of the First Fleet on 26 January 1788. Although the settlement stopped taking convicts in 1840, a few ships continued to arrive until 1842 and again between 1849 and 1850. The State Records Authority of New South Wales (www.records.nsw. gov.au) provides online indexes for the following (under 'Convicts'):

  - Certificates of Freedom (1823 to 1869)

  - Convict Bank Accounts (1837 to 1870)

  - Convict Exiles (1846 to 1850)

  - Tickets of Leave, Certificates of Emancipation and Pardons (1810 to 1819)

  The Society of Australian Genealogists (www.sag.org.au) has an online index to Tickets of Leave issued between 1810 and 1875 (found under 'Databases' on the main menu).

- **Queensland:** The colony of Moreton Bay was established in 1825 as a place of secondary transportation (in other words, it didn't receive convicts from overseas, but only those who were already in another colony who reoffended). Convict records are maintained by the Queensland State Archives (www.archives.qld.gov.au), although no records are online at present. Up until 1859, Moreton Bay was administered by New South Wales.

- **Tasmania:** Van Diemen's Land (Tasmania) took in convicts from 1804, although direct transportation didn't commence until 1818. The state was also used as a place of secondary transportation, but ceased taking convicts in 1853. The Archives Office of Tasmania (www.archives.tas.gov.au) provides an online Index to Convicts (1802 to 1853), which includes those tried within the local system: 76,000 names are listed, with the last record dated c.1893. Convict Applications to Marry (1829 to 1857) are also available on this site.

- **Victoria:** Public Record Office Victoria (www.prov.vic.gov.au) has available a Register of Convicts (1838 to 1852) as a digitised online index, and this includes convicts who were assigned in Port Phillip (Victoria) or who obtained their Ticket of Leave there.

- **Western Australia:** Male convicts were sent to Western Australia from 1850 until 1868. The State Records Office of Western Australia provides online information about how to access the records it holds (see www.sro.wa.gov.au/collection/convict.asp). The Perth Dead Persons' Society also has some interesting items on its site (www.convictcentral.com).

In addition, you can try these sources:

- Ancestry.com.au is adding digitised images of many original records still held in archives in the United Kingdom and relating to the Australian convict period to its website (www.ancestry.com.au). These include Australian Convict Transportation Registers for the years 1788 to 1868, Convict Savings Bank Books (New South Wales) for the period 1824 to 1886, and many muster and census records.

- The National Archives of Ireland (www.nationalarchives.ie/search/index.php?category=18) has available online the Ireland–Australia Transportation Index, 1791–1868, which contains the records of thousands of convicts sent from Ireland to Australia.

- The Proceedings of the Old Bailey Central Criminal Court, London, from 1674 to 1913 are available online and are fully searchable (www.oldbaileyonline.org). Many convicts sent to Australia were sentenced through this court.

- The State Library of Queensland has an online index of 123,000 convicts sent to the Australian colonies between 1787 and 1867 (www.slq.qld.gov.au/info/fh/convicts).

No convicts were sent to South Australia. It was founded in 1836 as a free settlement. Likewise, convicts were not sent to Victoria, although a few went there with their masters as part of the Port Phillip settlement of 1804. Victoria was officially established by free settlement in 1834.

# Ship Ahoy! Tapping Into Your Ancestors' Arrival Records

Finding out how, when and even why your ancestors immigrated to Australia can be one of the most rewarding aspects of genealogy. In Chapter 1, we outline the different ways your ancestors could have arrived, but to find out when — and maybe even why — state government archive websites can help, especially if you know into which colony your ancestors first arrived.

Australia has no national index of early shipping records. Each state archive maintains its own records. However, after 1923, immigration became a federal responsibility, and from that date on records are with the National Archives of Australia — for more information, see the project 'Making Australia Home' at the National Archives website (www.naa.gov.au).

## Locating shipping records

Because shipping records are so important to family historians, much effort has gone into preparing indexes, transcriptions and associated information about arrival details from government archives, and many of these have resulted from extensive volunteer projects. Digitised images are also becoming available online. In this section, we step you through some examples to show you how to look for your ancestors in shipping records.

### New South Wales

The State Records Authority of New South Wales provides online indexes on assisted or bounty immigrants (those who were sponsored or who had their passages paid for them) for the period 1844 to 1896. These are divided into three separate online indexes, which all work in the same way: 1844 to 1859, 1860 to 1879 and 1880 to 1896. You can find them at the State Records Authority website (www.records.nsw.gov.au) by clicking on Indexes Online and then Immigration & Shipping.

In the same section of the website you can also access an index to Miscellaneous Passengers 1828–1843 and an index to Unassisted Passengers (those who paid their own fare) 1842–1855.

In association with the State Records Authority, a private volunteer-run project is indexing all unassisted shipping arrivals into New South Wales (mariners.records.nsw.gov.au), and currently this index has good coverage for the period 1854 to 1880, with work progressing well on subsequent years. Images of many shipping lists are linked to the index.

In addition, Ancestry.com.au has recently indexed the shipping records of NSW Assisted Immigrants (1828–1896) and NSW Unassisted Immigrants (1826–1922) (www.ancestry.com.au). Images of the actual shipping records are expected to be made available online as part of this project.

Here's how to search the 1844 to 1859 index at the State Records Authority website:

1. **Go to** www.records.nsw.gov.au **and click on Indexes Online.**

2. **From the list click on Immigration & Shipping and then the Search button under Sydney and Newcastle 1844–59.**

   The resulting search page allows you to search by surname, first name, vessel name or year (or all years — 1844 to 1859). Note also that this site provides a wildcard search facility to allow you to broaden your search — that is, it allows you to look for names with alternative spellings and so on.

3. **Type the name you're looking for into the Surname box then click on the Submit Query button.**

   For example, type in the surname **Rivett**, but don't use the wildcard facility. The results screen returns two pages of indexes on the name Rivett, all of whom arrived on different vessels.

   To hone in on a particular individual, you can refine the search to surname and vessel name.

4. **To refine your search, click on your browser's Back button to get back to the search query page.**

   The main search page appears, showing the surname you typed in the previous query.

5. **Type a ship's name in the Vessel Name box or select one from the drop-down list, then click on the Submit Query button.**

   For example, if you type in the name **Sultana**, the results screen shows seven matches, all from the same family — William and Susan Rivett and their five children (see Figure 5-3).

   Note that the index lists microfilm reference numbers in the Reel column, which you can use to consult the actual records on microfilm at one of the State Records centres or your local library or family history society to get more details about the person you're searching for.

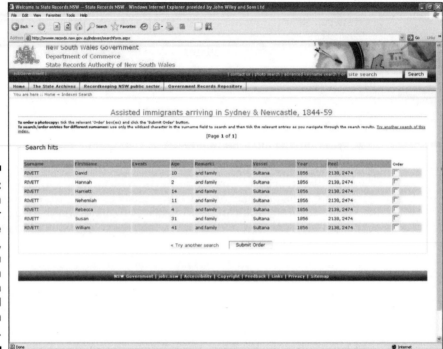

Figure 5-3:
Search
results for
the surname
Rivett,
arriving in
New South
Wales on
the vessel
*Sultana* in
1856.

The search engine at the State Records website also allows you to find everyone who arrived on one particular voyage. For example, to list everyone who arrived on the *Sultana* in 1856, start a new search query and type % in the surname field, then type **Sultana** in the Vessel Name field and **1856** in both the From and To date fields. Now click on the Submit button and the first page of the full passenger list for that voyage appears on your screen.

What if one of your ancestors arrived in New South Wales but didn't stay? Unfortunately, few surviving records detail people who actually left the colony prior to 1896. However, an index of ships musters, covering passengers and crews departing the colony between 1816 and 1825 is available online at the Society of Australian Genealogists website (www.sag.org.au) under Databases.

Need an overview of early shipping records and how to look for them online? See the State Records Authority's online guides on Shipping and Arrival Records (www.records.nsw.gov.au).

## Victoria

The colony of Victoria — or Port Phillip as it was first known — was originally administered by New South Wales, so early shipping records are held by the State Records Authority in Sydney. You can find a searchable index covering the period 1839–1851 at the State Records Authority website (www.records.nsw.gov.au) by clicking on Indexes Online and then Immigration & Shipping.

Public Record Office Victoria (www.prov.vic.gov.au) provides an online index to Unassisted Inward Passenger Lists to Victoria 1852–1923 and an index to Assisted British Immigration 1839–1871. In addition, work is progressing on uploading an index of Outward Passengers to Interstate, UK and Foreign Ports 1852–1876. Follow the links under Immigration Records and Family History on the website.

Say you want to search for family members who arrived in Victoria in the late 1800s using the index to Unassisted Inward Passenger Lists to Victoria 1852–1923. To do so, follow these steps:

1. **Go to** www.prov.vic.gov.au **and click on Immigration Records and Family History.**

   This brings up the locating and copying ships' passenger lists page.

2. **Scroll down to find Index to Unassisted Inward Passenger Lists to Victoria 1852–1923 and click on it.**

   The search query page appears on your screen. You can search by family name, first name, ship, month and year. Note that you can also sort results by family name and ship. This groups together family members with the same surname in the search results.

3. **Type a name into the Surname field and select Family Name from the Primary Sort drop-down list and Ship from the Secondary Sort drop-down list, then click on the Search button.**

   For example, type **Smith** in the Surname field. The search result displays all results sorted by surname and ship, as well as the arrivals' given names, ages, month and year of arrival, whether they boarded at a British or foreign port and reference details. From these details you can then visit the Public Record Office in Melbourne or another repository to view the complete shipping record.

## Queensland

Like Victoria, the colony of Queensland (or as it was first known, Moreton Bay) was originally administered by New South Wales, which still holds its early records. For an online index on assisted immigration to Queensland for the period 1848 to 1859, go to the State Records Authority website (www.records.nsw.gov.au) and click on Indexes Online and then Immigration & Shipping.

Queensland State Archives has indexes to assisted immigration arrivals into the colony for the period 1848 to 1912. The indexes are a series of PDFs sorted by individual letters of the alphabet containing details from the immigration register. They can be accessed at www.archives.qld.gov.au by clicking on Indexes under Research Services and then following the links.

### South Australia

Some South Australian passenger lists for the period 1803 to 1850 are available online at www.familyhistorysa.info. If you have German ancestors, you may find The Ships List site helpful (www.theshipslist.com/ships/australia/SAgermanindex.htm).

### Western Australia

Western Australia was a very important point of entry into Australia, especially from the late 1800s. The National Archives of Australia (www.naa.gov.au) has begun indexing arrival records for Fremantle for the years 1921 to 1950. To access these records, click on RecordSearch and Search Now, then click on Passenger Index. Don't discount this port as a place of arrival into the country — many passengers arrived in Western Australia before moving on to other Australian ports.

## Tracking down overseas shipping records

Branches of families can be spread around the world. For example, it's not unusual to find that one branch of an Irish family came to Australia, while another settled in the United States. If you can track down other branches of your own family, not only can you have fun making contact with them, but they may also have an interest in family history and have information they can share with you.

Try the following online resources to help you track down shipping records to other countries:

- Ancestry.co.uk (www.ancestry.co.uk) has a database of shipping arrivals into the United Kingdom from foreign ports outside of Europe and the Mediterranean between 1878 and 1888, and 1890 and 1960. The database is an index to the Board of Trade's passenger lists of ships, and can be found by following the links under Immigration & Emigration.

- Ellis Island Foundation (www.ellisisland.org) has an online index of arrivals entering New York between 1892 and 1924.

✔ Find My Past (www.findmypast.com) lists details of shipping departures from the United Kingdom during the period 1890 to 1960 and covers more than 24 million people. This can be a useful way of tracking down some of your better-off ancestors, who may have 'gone home for a visit' to the old country during their lifetime.

## Coping when you're cut adrift

Now, we know that as family historians you hate to give up, but sometimes you just have to accept that you aren't going to be able to find an ancestor's name on any shipping lists. Why? As we explain in Chapter 1, some vessels' captains never bothered to note down the names of passengers they were carrying.

If the ancestors you're looking for were relatively well-to-do, arrived in the colony as free settlers paying their own way and had their own cabin during the voyage, chances are they're on arrival records somewhere. Same goes with convicts — the authorities wanted to keep a tight rein on them. But if the ancestors you're looking for were among the hundreds of hopefuls who paid the cheapest possible passage to reach Australia (for example, during the height of the gold rush in the mid-1800s), the authorities may never have taken down their details — and if they did, the entry may have been no more than 'Mr Bridge' or 'Mrs Johnson'.

So, this is one area of research where it's worth looking for the record, but at the same time keep in mind that you may reach a point where you need to recognise that you can go no further and should move on to other research areas.

If you're stuck, but want to know whether you can go further, seek advice from family history societies, archives and other researchers you meet on the internet. These can help you to establish whether the search you're undertaking for your ancestor's arrival is a futile one.

# Investigating Naturalisation Records

Yes, Australia was once a British colony, but if your ancestors came from other lands — such as Italy, Germany, China or the United States — they may have become naturalised so they could buy land or vote.

*Naturalisation records* are documents showing that a person became a citizen of a particular country without being born in that country. Sometimes these documents can prove difficult to track down on the internet, especially if you don't know where to begin looking. Also, not all people of non-British background applied to be naturalised, so your family's ancestors may not appear in any records.

Naturalisation became a Commonwealth responsibility in 1904. All records from that date onwards are held by the National Archives of Australia, which provides online fact sheets on naturalisation and citizenship at its website explaining what you can access and how to tap into records. (To access these fact sheets, go to www.naa.gov.au, select Fact Sheets under Quick Links and then click on Migration, Citizenship and Travel.)

Prior to 1904, each Australian colony was responsible for its own naturalisation records. The National Archives of Australia maintains two of these collections — records for the colony of Victoria and the province of South Australia. For naturalisations that took place before 1904 in New South Wales, South Australia and Tasmania, check out the following:

- ✔ **New South Wales:** The State Records Authority has a searchable naturalisation index for the years 1834 to 1903 (go to www.records.nsw.gov.au and click on Indexes Online and then Naturalization). This is a complete index to all naturalisations during this period and contains more than 5,500 entries.

  Additionally, a database of Chinese naturalisations for the period 1857 to 1887 can be found on the Chinese Heritage of Australian Federation website at www.chaf.lib.latrobe.edu.au/naturalisation.htm under the Resources link.

- ✔ **South Australia:** Family History South Australia lists naturalisations in the state between 1839 and 1891 (www.adelaideco-op.familyhistorysa.info/naturalizations.html).

- ✔ **Tasmania:** Archives Office of Tasmania has a searchable online index to applications for naturalisation in the state for the period 1835 to 1905 (portal.archives.tas.gov.au/menu.aspx?search=6).

There are no online searchable indexes currently available for naturalisations that took place in either Queensland or Western Australia. The records should be held with the relevant state archives. For more information, visit

- ✔ **Queensland:** www.archives.qld.gov.au/downloads/BriefGuides/BG15Naturalisations.pdf

- ✔ **Western Australia:** www.sro.wa.gov.au/collection/passenger.asp#naturalisation

Some naturalisation records for the period after 1904 can be found on the National Archives website (www.naa.gov.au). Many of these entries include digitised images of the actual documentation. To check whether a naturalisation record has been catalogued for a member of the family you're tracing, follow these steps:

1. **Go to** www.naa.gov.au **and click on RecordSearch and then Search Now.**

   This opens the general search page.

2. **Click on Name Search.**

   This opens the general search page.

3. **Type in the name of the family you're researching in the Family Name box, and select Immigration and Naturalisation Records from the Category drop-down menu. Then click on Search.**

   For example, try typing in **Kurtz**. You're best bet is to turn off the Use Exact Spelling option, since the family may have been known as Kurz or even Kerz when they arrived from Germany.

4. **Click on Display and review the results page.**

   This search returns 36 entries for the surname Kurtz, including several for people who arrived in Australia by aircraft after the 1950s as well as a number of naturalisation records. If the Digital Copy symbol appears next to an entry, you can instantly download a copy of the original document to view, free of charge.

# Looking for Land and Property Records

Historical land records don't always contain detailed demographic information, but they do place your ancestors in a time and location — and sometimes in an historical context as well. Land records include applications for land grants, requests for surveys and surveyor's reports, as well as other matters in relation to the management of Crown Land — including disputed claims and leaseholds. Each state in Australia is responsible for land records in its region, and most provide online resources that also point to archives.

Understanding the history of land records before you conduct a lot of research is a good idea, as these can be a complicated set of records to tackle. Most of the repositories that hold records of interest have useful online guides, so spend some time tracking these down and reading them.

Online searching is possible at the following sites:

- ✔ **New South Wales:** The Department of Lands (www.lands.nsw.gov.au) provides basic information on land records, but the State Records Authority has a number of excellent online indexes relating to land records (go to www.records.nsw.gov.au and click on Indexes Online and then Land).

- ✔ **Queensland:** Queensland State Archives has an online index to land selections prior to 1884 as well as an index to mineral leases for the period 1871 to 1940 (available under Indexes at www.archives.qld.gov.au).

- ✔ **South Australia:** Land Services Group (www.landservices.sa.gov.au) has a section on searching land records for family historians.

- ✔ **Victoria:** Public Record Office Victoria has digitised its index to the Treasurer's correspondence relating to pastoral runs for the years 1838 to 1855 (www.prov.vic.gov.au; click on Access the Collection and then PROV's Digitised Records and Online Indexes).

The Western Australian Land Information Authority provides information on modern maps and title searches and offers an online ordering service (www.landgate.wa.gov.au). The Tasmanian Archives Office gives brief details of holdings of land records in its guide, 'Records Useful for Genealogical Research' (see www.archives.tas.gov.au/guides/genealogy).

# Reviewing Military Tales: In the Service of their Country

You've probably heard family stories about how your grandfather fought in World War I or World War II. Or maybe you have letters he wrote to family members while in service? Either way, you can find more information about the part that he played in Australia's military history fairly easily.

# Searching service records online

Online military resources come in several different forms, depending on where and when the individual served. To track down your ancestor's records, try the following:

- **Australian War Memorial** (www.awm.gov.au): This site provides online databases you can search to find out more about family members who served in overseas wars or other military conflicts in which Australian troops served. These databases begin with the Sudan Contingent in 1885 and go right through to the 1990–1991 Gulf War. The information available for each conflict varies, but less identifying information is publicly available for the more recent campaigns. To search a database, click on Biographical Databases and Nominal Rolls and then follow the links to the relevant conflict:

  • Sudan Contingent, 1885

  • Boer War, 1899–1902

  • Boxer Uprising, China, 1900–1901

  • World War I, 1914–1918

  • Korean War, 1950–1956

  • Vietnam War, 1962–1975

  • Gulf War, 1990–1991

  For World War II, 1939–1945, use the database developed by the Department of Veterans' Affairs. You can reach this database via the links provided on the War Memorial's website, or you can access it directly at www.ww2roll.gov.au. This is an extremely valuable database of more than one million Australian men and women who served in the various forces, as it's searchable not only by name but also by place of enlistment or birth.

- **Commonwealth War Graves Commission** (www.cwgc.org): Search the online Debt of Honour Register to find an ancestor's final resting place, and burial and next of kin details.

- **National Archives of Australia** (www.naa.gov.au): The National Archives is the custodian of all World War I and World War II service records. Digitisation of service records for all World War I personnel is now complete and you can download a copy of a file free of charge. Files can be located by clicking on RecordsSearch and then Search Now and doing a NameSearch.

Understanding more about the conflicts in which your ancestors served gives you a better understanding of their experiences and may even lead you to more information about your ancestors. Try the following websites:

- ✔ **Australian War Memorial Online Encyclopedia (**www.awm.gov.au/encyclopedia**):** This resource provides extensive information about military history and the role Australians have played during times of war. Browsing its database also lets you tap into online databases of war records and links to many other resources.

- ✔ **Australians at War Film Archive (**www.australiansatwarfilm archive.gov.au**):** The recollections of more than 2,000 personnel involved in all military conflicts since World War I have been recorded and transcripts of their interviews are available. This is a marvellous resource, not only if you have a family member mentioned, but also as background information on what it's like to serve your country.

## Digging into early military records

Many of Australia's early settlers arrived as marines or as members of one of the early British military regiments. These records date from 1778 through to 1870, when the last British regiments departed. Most of these records have been microfilmed by the Australian Joint Copying Project and are available for viewing at major libraries. However, some online resources describe military records or allow you to search online indexes. Here are a few examples:

- ✔ **Australia's Red Coat Settlers (**freepages.history.rootsweb.ancestry.com/~garter1**):** This privately run website aims to include the names of all British soldiers who served in Australia and currently contains more than 36,000 names.

- ✔ **Coraweb's Service Personnel (**www.coraweb.com.au/service.htm**):** This site links to many Australian military records and websites devoted to military service.

- ✔ **Graham Jaunay's British Regiments in the Colonies (**www.jaunay.com/garrisons.html**):** This website provides an overview of early British regiment detachments.

- ✔ **Society of Australian Genealogists (**www.sag.org.au**):** The society has an online index to soldiers and marines who served in Australia from 1788 to 1830. To find the index, follow the link to Soldiers & Marines from Databases.

# Exploring Institutions, Hospitals and Agencies for Institutionalised Ancestors

If a member of your family spent time in a government institution — such as a hospital, an asylum or a gaol — you may be able to source some valuable information about that person. In earlier times, not only did many institutions use admission registers to record details about people — such as each person's name, age, place of birth and ship of arrival — but they also put on record personal information that can tell you a lot about their background.

Records collected by most colonial government-run institutions are now in the hands of each state or territory's archive authority (see the Internet Directory in Appendix C at the end of this book for their web addresses).

Examples of the type of online indexes or transcriptions of institution records you may find include

✔ Gaol and police records such as:

- Braidwood Gaol, New South Wales, Entrance Book for 1856 to 1899 (www.pcug.org.au/~ppmay/braidwood.htm)

- Criminal and other case files found in Victoria Police correspondence files (members.ozemail.com.au/~hdharris/criminals.htm)

- Gaol Photographic Description Books (www.records.nsw.gov.au) listing more than 20,000 records of those who went into New South Wales gaols between 1870 and 1930 (this database can be searched by following the link from the home page to Indexes Online and then Court, Police and Prison)

- Queensland Police Watchhouse Records (www.judywebster.gil.com.au/police.html)

✔ Hospital and agency records such as:

- Consumptive patients in Queensland (www.archives.qld.gov.au/research/indexes.asp)

- Deaths in the Melbourne Hospital, 1867–1880 (www.tfoenander.com/meldeath.html) taken from reports in the *Argus* newspaper

- Mittagong Farm Home for Boys, Register of Committals, 1907–1921 (www.records.nsw.gov.au/indexes/searchform.aspx?id=27)

- Randwick Asylum for Destitute Children, 1852–1915 (www.record.nsw.gov.au/indexes/searchform.aspx?id=26)

# Chapter 6

# Records Off the Beaten Track

*M*any people who are familiar with genealogy know to use vital records, census records and other historical resources to find information on their ancestors. These records tend to provide an historical 'snapshot' of an individual's life at a particular point in time. But as a genealogist, you want to know more than the bare details of your ancestors' movements — you want to know something about them as people.

In this chapter, we look at some examples of hard-to-find or specialised records that can be quite useful in family history research. These include records held by Aboriginal groups, religious organisations and cemeteries; along with photographs, and adoption and child migration records.

## Tracking Down Aboriginal Records

If your ancestry includes Indigenous Australians and you're trying to find out where you came from or are looking to locate family members, online resources may be able to help you track records. In some cases, you may find people of Aboriginal background detailed in some of the records we discuss in earlier chapters — such as birth, death and marriage records (covered in Chapters 1 and 5). You may also be able to find specific records relating to Aboriginal communities.

Start your search with the following helpful websites:

- ✔ **The Aboriginal Family History Unit of the Australian Institute of Aboriginal and Torres Strait Islander Studies (**`www.aiatsis.gov.au/library/family_history_tracing`**):** The unit provides extensive guidance on how to trace Aboriginal and Torres Strait Islander heritage in the section, Family History Information Kit (see Figure 6-1). You can download the numerous PDF guides that the unit has compiled and then link to the information sheet on further leads for your state or territory.

- ✔ **National Archives of Australia — Indigenous Records (**`naa12.naa.gov.au/NameSearch/Interface/LinkATSI.html`**):** The majority of these records relate to people from Victoria and the Northern Territory.

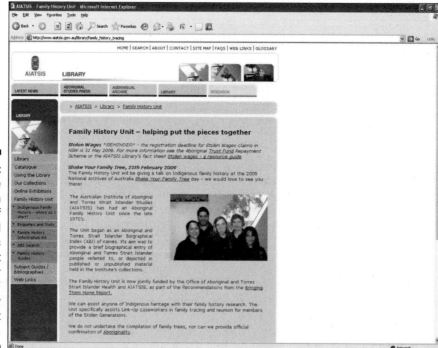

**Figure 6-1:**
The
Australian
Institute of
Aboriginal
and Torres
Strait
Islander
Studies'
Family
History Unit
website.

State government archive websites also provide information about how to access the records they collected on Indigenous Australians before Federation. For example:

- ✔ Public Record Office Victoria (www.prov.vic.gov.au) has a Koorie Records Unit

- ✔ The State Records Authority of New South Wales (www.records.nsw.gov.au) has an Aboriginal Liaison Officer on staff who can assist researchers wanting to trace Indigenous ancestors in the records it holds. For more information follow the links under Resources for Indigenous People on the website.

If you're trying to locate Aboriginal family members, you can also contact Link Up, an organisation dedicated to helping reunite Aboriginal people who've been separated from their families. The NSW branch has links to other useful sites (at www.linkupnsw.org.au, follow the Links button on the left-hand tool bar).

# Sourcing Church Archives

In Chapters 1 and 5, we discuss the importance of birth, death and marriage records in family history. Mostly these are official government records. However, churches have always maintained similar records associated with these events — in fact, long before governments started recording births, deaths and marriages.

Records kept by churches can back up vital records and provide you with more leads about your ancestors. For example, even if you don't remember your grandmother ever going to church, she was probably baptised and married in one. Likewise, if you track down an online death record that may belong to an ancestor, you can turn to parish church records for more information — for example, the record of the funeral service conducted in the local church or at the graveside by the local minister.

Church records can include baptismal records, parish registers, marriage records, death or burial records, meeting minutes and service registers.

Although few Australian church records are available online, you can use the internet to help you establish whether archives exist for the records you seek, and if so, where and how you can access them.

Start by typing the word **church** into the online search facility of a general archival directory such as that of the Australian Society of Archivists (www.archivists.org.au). This gives you a list of all known religious archives in Australia. Most of the major churches have their own archives, but bear in mind that many of these archive facilities are small and can't accommodate family historians or conduct genealogical research on behalf of enquirers. In some instances archives have allowed copies of their records to be microfilmed, so that they can be accessed elsewhere.

Here are a few examples of archives relating to specific church groups:

- ✔ Anglican Archives (www.anglican.org.au — click on Archive Page)
- ✔ Catholic Archives (www.sydney.catholic.org.au/about/archives.shtml)
- ✔ Lutheran Archives (www.lca.org.au/resources/archives.html)
- ✔ The Uniting Church of Australia — NSW Synod Archives (nsw.uca.org.au/church/archives.htm)

Try the following if you're after websites that provide information about Jewish genealogy:

- ✔ Australian Jewish Genealogical Society (www.ajgs.org.au), which also has an online forum that you can join
- ✔ Australian Jewish Historical Society (www.ajhs.info), which outlines a history of the Jewish faith in Australia, and provides links to the Australian Jewish Genealogical Society and the Great Synagogue Archives

Of course, at some point you may want to access church records overseas. As in Australia, finding church records in other countries online can be quite challenging, but sites such as GENUKI (www.genuki.co.uk) can help you track down what's available in the United Kingdom and Ireland. For details about how to search for church records using GENUKI, see Chapter 3.

# Digging into Cemetery Records

If you're like other family historians, you're going to love tracking down cemetery records. Not only do they take you to an ancestor's final resting place, but also in many cases the cemetery may hold vital clues about the person's life to help you understand more about your family.

Of course, we know what you hope for: Finding one of those fabulous monuments that tells you when and where an ancestor was born and died, as well as his or her occupation and next of kin. Additional information may outline the cause of death — such as 'Died as a result of an accident', which can lead you to newspapers and coroner's records for more details. Or, you may discover new information about your ancestor's life that gives you a whole new angle of research — for example, an inscription that reads 'Former Mayor of this town'.

Not all graves have headstones: What you eventually track down may simply be an unmarked grass plot.

## Searching close to home

Looking for cemeteries on Australian soil? Try these websites to start your search:

- ✔ Australian Cemeteries (www.ozgenonline.com/aust_cemeteries), where you can search or browse an index for every state and territory to find a specific cemetery. Entries indicate whether online data (including photographs) are available, whether searches can be done, whether transcripts are known to have been compiled and whether the cemetery has its own home page.

- ✔ Interment.net, Australian Cemeteries (www.interment.net/aus), again where you can search or browse by state or territory.

Because the genealogical community values cemetery records so highly, many groups and individuals have worked to collect information on burials in their local cemeteries and have published their findings in book form or on the internet. An increasing number of cemeteries and crematoriums also have websites and provide online details about the people buried or cremated there. The following are some examples of the types of cemetery records available online:

- ✔ Australian Cemeteries Index (cemindex.arkangles.com), with data for nearly 300 cemeteries across Australia (mostly in western New South Wales) including transcriptions of headstones and photographs of graves

- ✔ Catholic Cemeteries (www.catholiccemeteries.org.au), where you can undertake a combined search of the Catholic sections of Rookwood, Field of Mars, Liverpool, North Rocks and Kemps Creek cemeteries, all located in the Sydney suburban area

- ✔ Eastern Suburbs Memorial Park (www.esmp.net.au), where you can search the databases of the cemetery and crematorium, both of which are located in the south-eastern suburbs of Sydney

- ✔ Hawkesbury Cemetery and Grave Register (www.hawkesbury.net.au/cemetery), a great resource for searching many of the smaller country cemeteries in this historic part of New South Wales

- ✔ Metropolitan Cemeteries Board (Western Australia) (www.mcb.wa.gov. au), which allows searches of Karrakatta, Fremantle, Pinnaroo Valley, Midland, Guildford and the new Rockingham Regional cemeteries and memorial parks in Western Australia (this site is also one of the first to offer webcasting of funerals)

- ✔ Necropolis Deceased Search (www.deceasedsearch.com), which covers Melbourne General, Springvale Botanical and St Kilda cemeteries, the latter two of which have searchable databases

 Many genealogy societies catalogue the cemetery records they hold on their websites, even though the records themselves may not yet be available online. For example, the Society of Australian Genealogists (www.sag.org. au) has extensive cemetery holdings, covering all regions of Australia. To browse the online catalogue, click on the Library Catalogue link. You can search by typing the place of interest, such as Cooma, into the catalogue and doing a keyword search. If you get a large number of hits, you can narrow your search by adding the word 'cemetery' as an additional keyword in your search.

## Searching overseas

If you're looking for cemeteries in different parts of the world, try the Interment.net Cemetery Transcription Library (www.interment.net) — a cooperative website that enables family historians to share their cemetery information with others online. The site lets you tap into the records of thousands of cemeteries around the world. Note that Interment.net relies mainly on volunteers to provide information about cemeteries and add burial records to its database, so listings aren't complete.

# Appreciating that a Photo Is Worth a Thousand Words

Sure, it'd be great to dig up a photo of your great-grandmother on her wedding day or find a picture of your great-great-grandfather to add to your family history records. But a lot of people don't have photographs of their family beyond two or three generations, and in some cases they may have almost no pictorial record at all.

Now we're not suggesting that somewhere out there on the World Wide Web you may be able to find that elusive photo of great-grandmother in her wedding dress. But in Chapters 3 and 4 we show you how to use the internet to contact other family historians researching the same family line. These other branches of the family may have photos of gatherings or special events, and if they've made electronic copies they're likely to be more than happy to share them with you.

You may also be interested in pictures of places where your ancestors lived. Being able to describe how a certain town, estate or farm looked at the time your ancestors lived there adds colour to your family history. For example, if your ancestors lived in Gulgong, New South Wales, do you know what the town looked like at the time they lived there? If one of your ancestors ran the local butcher shop, for example, you may be able to find a photograph of the town's main street that shows the butcher shop somewhere in the image.

You can find various types of photographic websites on the internet that can assist you with your research. Some of these sites explain the photographic process and the many types of photographs that have been used throughout history (see also 'Dusting Off the Old Photo Albums' in Chapter 1), some sites contain collections of photographs from a certain geographical area or time period in history, some sites contain historical photographs for sale, and other sites contain photographs of the ancestors of a particular family. The following list gives some examples of various photography websites:

- **General information:** City Gallery (www.city-gallery.com) has a brief explanation of the types of photography used during the nineteenth century. Although this is a US-based site, much of the information it contains is of general interest — but bear in mind that some techniques took several years to reach the colonies.

- **Personal photographs:** Colin Hinson's Blunham website (blunham. com) is an example of a personal website with a photo gallery of sites of interest to family historians in Blunham — a small village in Bedfordshire in the United Kingdom.

- **Photographic collections:** The National Archives of Australia's online photographic collection (www.naa.gov.au, using the PhotoSearch link) and Picture Australia (www.pictureaustralia.org) are the two most prominent archives of Australian historical photographs and images.

Picture Australia (www.pictureaustralia.org) is hosted by the National Library of Australia and brings together pictorial collections from many libraries, museums, galleries, archives and cultural institutions throughout the country. To search for images at Picture Australia, follow these steps:

1. **Go to** www.pictureaustralia.org.

2. **Type the name of the town you're researching in the Find Pictures Of query box, then click on the Search button.**

   For example, typing **Geraldton** returns several hundred hits, and displays thumbnails of images along with captions.

**3. Click on an image of interest.**

When you click on an image, the image is displayed in full-page view and includes catalogue details such as probable date, photographer, location and identifying information on the subject of the photo. Depending on the policy of the holding institution, you can either save the photo to your hard drive or order a print of the photo online

*Note:* Photos at Picture Australia are high quality, but most can be used for research purposes only: You cannot publish or use them commercially unless you obtain permission.

You can also use Picture Australia to search for photos of people. Try typing in your family name — you never know who you may find.

Picture Australia searches sites such as Flickr, so sometimes the results you get show modern-day photographs rather than historical ones.

Most historical societies have photographic collections pertaining to the area in which they are located. You can find links to historical societies at the Royal Australian Historical Society website (www.rahs.org.au) or by visiting Coraweb's Family History and Historical Societies page (www.coraweb.com.au/society.htm).

# Getting Your Hands on Adoption Records

Adoption records are of interest to a lot of family historians, including those who were adopted themselves, those who gave up children for adoption and those who have ancestors who were adopted.

If you were adopted or gave up a child for adoption, some online resources may help you. In the main, these are support services and government agencies that have set up online resources to help adoptees to find their families, and to assist people who gave up babies for adoption to re-establish contact with them.

Online resources include registries, reference materials, advice and discussion groups, and information on legislation pertaining to adoption. Registries enable you to post information about yourself and your adoption with the hope that a member of your birth family may see the posting and contact you. (Likewise, if you're the birth parent of an adoptee, you can post a message with the hope that the adoptee sees it and responds.)

Unfortunately, you won't find online sites that contain actual adoption records — privacy laws protect the rights of all individuals involved in such highly emotional and sensitive cases. Also, in earlier times the needs of future generations were rarely considered in adoption cases. Children were often removed from their birth mothers and placed with another family, completely overriding the needs of the biological family. In fact, records were usually destroyed or altered to make the paper trail difficult to follow.

If you do have a successful reunion with your birth parent(s) by registering with an online site, hopefully you can obtain information about their parents, grandparents and so on — so that you know where to begin your genealogical pursuit of that family line.

Check out the following websites to find adoption registries, reference materials, advice and discussion forums and/or legislative information:

- ✔ **New South Wales and the Australian Capital Territory:** Post Adoption Resource Centre at www.bensoc.org.au/parc and New South Wales Department of Community Services Adoption Information Unit at www.community.nsw.gov.au/parents_carers_and_families/ fostering_and_adoption/adoption.html

- ✔ **Northern Territory:** Department of Health and Families at www. health.nt.gov.au/Children_Youth_and_Families/Adoption/ index.aspx

- ✔ **Queensland:** Jigsaw Queensland Post Adoption Centre at jigsawqld. server101.com

- ✔ **South Australia:** Adoption and Family Information Service at www.dfc. sa.gov.au/pub/tabid/257/itemid/881/default.aspx

- ✔ **Tasmania:** See Children and Families under Your Health and Wellbeing at www.dhhs.tas.gov.au

- ✔ **Victoria:** Adoptive Families Association of Victoria at home.vicnet. net.au/%7Eafav

- ✔ **Western Australia:** Department for Child Protection at www. community.wa.gov.au/DCP/Resources/Adoption

If you're interested in adoption records because you have ancestors who were adopted, you may have a more difficult time finding information. Bear in mind that official adoption is a relatively new procedure: In earlier times adoption and foster care were often private arrangements made between families or institutions, occasionally with the help of a solicitor. You may have to rely on the regular genealogical resources — particularly query pages and discussion groups — and the kindness and knowledge of other researchers to find information about your adopted ancestors.

Adoption as a legal process began in England and Wales on 1 January 1927. Anyone adopted before that date was considered fostered. Unfortunately, tracing the birth parents of a fostered child, especially if there was a change of surname, is a very difficult and specialist exercise.

If you're searching for Australian historical records about children separated from their families, the online version of the New South Wales Department of Community Services' *Connecting Kin* guide to child welfare records may be of help. This 384-page guide is downloadable in PDF format and covers substitute care in New South Wales after 1900. To access the guide, go to www.community.nsw.gov.au and follow the link to Publications through the Parents, Carers and Families tab.

# Uncovering Child Migration Records

During and after World War II, the UK government sent up to 130,000 British children and youths to Australia, New Zealand, Canada and South Africa as orphans. However, for many of these children, one or both of their parents were still alive but they were never given the opportunity to see them again.

Government enquiries have brought public attention to the plight of these people in recent years. If you're one of them and you're trying to trace any remaining family members, several websites can offer advice, point you towards records, and provide reference materials and information on legislation.

Try the following resources:

- **National Archives Australia:** *Good British Stock: Child and Youth Migration to Australia*, at www.naa.gov.au (go to the Shop link under Services, click on Browsing the Online Shop and then Research Guides, and then select Immigration and the title *Good British Stock*; a link at the bottom of the page allows you to read the publication online for free)
- **Parliamentary Library:** *Child Migrants From the UK* at www.aph.gov.au/library/intguide/sp/childmigrantuk.htm

# Using Civil and Court Records

Now, don't jump to conclusions. We're not suggesting your ancestors had to be criminals for civil and court records to be useful in your genealogical research. Many of your model-citizen ancestors may have had their day in court as witnesses or to serve on juries, or they may have been to court to take action against someone else who owed them money.

Of course, they may also have been on the wrong side of the law. If so, you may be able to find out a great deal about them.

The availability of court records varies according to the place and type of judicial records created. For example, in local areas many people appeared before the Court of Petty Sessions, sometimes for minor misdemeanours such as being drunk and disorderly or for failing to pay council rates on time. These types of records may not necessarily have survived. However, if an ancestor was involved in a major crime, such as a murder or bank robbery (either as the accused or as a victim) then the records are more likely to still be available. State government archives hold most of these records, although privacy laws place access restrictions on records less than 80 years old. Also, keep in mind that some records, especially those covering minor cases, may not have survived.

You can find the web addresses of the state and territory archives in Appendix C or on Cora Num's gateway site (www.coraweb.com.au).

# Chapter 7

# Zeroing In on Your Origins

*F*inding information about ancestors in foreign records can be challenging. Even though every country has records that are unique to it, the further back you go the less reliable or helpful resources may be. Or, members of your family may have been very mobile — making it difficult for you to track down records that do exist. In some cases, you may find no records at all, because they were lost during periods of war.

Despite the difficulty in finding some of these records, larger population bases overseas mean that many resources are available online to help you zero in on your family's origins. These resources can give you a clearer picture of your ancestors' part in history and provide unique sources of information that can add colour to your family's story.

In this chapter, we examine some of the online resources available to help you track down your origins overseas.

## Finding Ancestors in England and Wales

Because England and Wales are administratively and historically similar, most genealogy websites group resources from these two countries together. And just as state-based boundaries divide Australian online resources, the county or parish system carves up resources pertaining to genealogy in England and Wales.

Here's how it works: Historically, the further back you go, the smaller the administrative area. So, if you're looking for a birth record from the 1920s it's probably waiting for you in records held at the national level (with both England and Wales in the one resource). But if the information you seek dates back to the 1720s, it's more likely to be in a record created by the local parish, which is now held at county level. This means that determining your ancestors' exact place of origin depends entirely on your ability to focus your research on a small geographical area.

Need an excuse for a holiday in England? Here's one: As we state at the beginning of this book, you can't expect to trace your entire family tree using the internet alone. At some point you have to contact libraries, county record offices and family history societies to get hold of your English or Welsh ancestors' records. That's because although some English and Welsh genealogy resources provide online information about the records they hold, not all let you conduct searches or view records online.

However, this situation is changing rapidly. In particular, you find fierce competition between the large 'pay to view' commercial providers to make records available to their subscribers. And while that means you have to pay to access some of this information, when you weigh it all up this option is far cheaper than going to England yourself to conduct the research, and much quicker — even if it isn't quite so much fun.

## Sourcing English and Welsh birth, death and marriage records

The General Register Office (www.gro.gov.uk) maintains official records on births, deaths and marriages for England and Wales. These records go back as far as 1837, although nineteenth-century civil registrations contain little identifying information — usually just the name of the person being registered, the place of registration, a reference number and a few specific details relating to that person. Certainly, these records are nowhere near as comprehensive as those found in Australia. The department's website explains how you can obtain copies of individual certificates and order certificates online.

You can search the post-1837 birth, death and marriage indexes for England and Wales online. These indexes are available at various websites, including the following:

> ✔ **Ancestry.co.uk** (www.ancestry.co.uk): This site offers free access to the birth, death and marriage indexes prepared by the FreeBMD transcribers (see below). It also offers access to images of the microfiche indexes from which these records were compiled for the years 1837 to 1983 and has transcribed the indexes for deaths and

marriages for the years 1984 to 2005 and for births for the years 1916 to 2005.

✔ **Find My Past (**www.findmypast.com**):** This 'pay to view' site offers online access to the birth and death indexes for 1837 to 2006 and to the marriage index for 1837 to 2005 (see Figure 7-1). When you do a search, you download an image from the microfiche index, which you can then read through.

✔ **FreeBMD (**www.freebmd.org.uk**):** FreeBMD is a cooperative project run by volunteers who're busy transcribing the birth, death and marriage indexes for England and Wales from 1837 onwards. You can search for names over a range of dates, but because information is copied from microfiche indexes (not original certificates), the site warns that errors due to illegibility can occur. And since this site is a work in progress, gaps in the indexes exist. An online graph shows what years have been covered to date and it's worthwhile checking this first. To access the graph, click on Information and then follow the links to Statistics and Coverage Charts. At the time of writing, volunteers had keyed nearly all the index information from 1837 to 1915, but after 1915 coverage is a little patchy.

**Figure 7-1:** At Find My Past you can search online indexes of English and Welsh birth, death and marriage records from 1837 to 2006.

Basically, the quickest and cheapest way to check the birth, death and marriage indexes is to use the FreeBMD site if it covers the time period you need. Otherwise, for searches post-1915 you need to use one of the 'pay to view' sites.

Civil registrations were recorded in district registries, so it can be worthwhile checking to see whether the local registry for the area of interest to you has placed any records online. For example, the county of Cheshire has these records available online at www.cheshirebmd.org.uk. The records held at district registries have a different reference number to the centralised system held at the General Register Office, so if you find a record you want at a district registry, you need to obtain a copy of the record from the registry, not the General Register Office.

Looking for records associated with births, deaths and marriages prior to 1837? Then you need to check websites that contain parish registers. For more details see 'Looking for parish records in England and Wales' later in this chapter.

## Following the census trail

Censuses have been conducted in England and Wales every ten years since 1801 (except for 1941 during World War II). However, most of the returns from 1801 to 1831 were purely statistical and didn't contain names. Beginning in 1841, the administration of the census became the responsibility of the Registrar General and the Superintendent of Registrars, who were responsible for recording civil registrations. This changed the focus of the census from simply counting the size of the population to recording details on individuals and families. Today, historical census records are maintained by the National Archives (www.nationalarchives.gov.uk), which provides public access to census information only after 100 years, although with legislative approval earlier access has been granted to the 1911 census.

Census records for the period 1841 to 1911 are available online through a number of commercial sites. For example, each of the following websites provides access to at least some of the census records for England and Wales:

- www.ancestry.co.uk
- www.findmypast.com
- www.origins.net
- www.worldvitalrecords.com

In addition, FamilySearch (www.familysearch.org), the genealogy research service of The Church of Jesus Christ of Latter-day Saints (see also

Chapter 3), now provides free indexes to many national census records. The site has an affiliate partnership with Find My Past, so you can follow the link from the index to that site and subscribe to view an original census document online if you wish to do so.

Each commercial company that provides census data online uses its own team of transcribers and indexers to create its database, so you may like to check more than one company's site, especially if you don't find what you're looking for or have some doubts as to the accuracy of the transcription. Where the image of the original census page is available to download, you should always do so in order to verify the details for yourself.

Don't forget to check beyond the well-known websites to see whether other databases are available to you. For example, a number of private transcriptions and projects completed by individual family history societies have made copies of the census for individual counties available online for free. Use a gateway site like GENUKI (www.genuki.org.uk) and work through to the county of interest to you, then select Census and follow the links. Or check out a website like FreeCEN (freecen.rootsweb.com/statistics.html) to determine whether a volunteer project has covered the year and area you're researching.

## Looking for parish records in England and Wales

The further back you go in your English and Welsh ancestry research, the more important parish records become. Principally established by the Church of England or the Church of Wales, parishes were once responsible for just about everything that went on in the locality — from keeping records of baptisms, marriages and burials, to looking after the poor and maintaining the local roads.

Most parish records are now held by County Record Offices throughout England and Wales. Many of these offices have their own websites and in some cases provide online access to catalogues and records. The easiest way to find a County Record Office is to use GENUKI. Here's what to do:

1. **Go to** www.genuki.org.uk.

   The home page appears with a green map of the United Kingdom and Ireland in its centre.

2. **Click on the green map to go to a page with a coloured and more detailed map of the region, and then click on the section of the map you're interested in.**

   For example, click on the United Kingdom portion of the map, which takes you to a page with another coloured map of the country, with the counties listed either side of it and the main category headings listed below it.

3. **Click on the county you're interested in.**

   For example, click on Devon. The page lists categories of links relevant to the county.

4. **Click on the Archives and Libraries link.**

   The results show the Devon County Record Offices and other useful archives in that county.

---

# Where there's a will ...

Wills and probate records are useful to family historians not only because they can provide details about an individual's possessions, but also because they include information such as the deceased's date and place of death, occupation and in some cases other personal details. Probate records are actually court records that deal with the settling of an estate after a death.

In 1858, England and Wales nationalised probate records, and microfiche indexes of records from 1858 to 1942 are available for searching at some family history societies, such as the Society of Australian Genealogists (www.sag.org.au). Alternatively, Her Majesty's Courts Service website (www.hmcourts-service.gov.uk) provides information about accessing post-1858 probate records and finding probate registries (follow the links under Wills and Probate).

Prior to 1858 a number of different courts conducted probate administration, principally the Prerogative Court of Canterbury (PCC) and the Prerogative Court of York (PCY). PCC wills are indexed at DocumentsOnline (available via www.nationalarchives.gov.uk: Click on Search the Archives and follow the links to DocumentsOnline). You can search more than 800,000 wills from the period 1384 to 1858 by family name, occupation and place.

Searching the index is free, although there is a charge to download a digital image of a document. Many PCY wills are available through the subscription-based site British Origins (www.englishorigins.com). You may also like to check the holdings of the relevant local County Record Office, as some local wills may be lodged there. You can do this through GENUKI (www.genuki.org.uk) or by using the Advanced Search feature of the Access to Archives site (www.nationalarchives.gov.uk/a2a).

In addition, an index to an associated set of records — death duty registers — for the period 1796 to 1903 is available online at Find My Past (www.findmypast.com). Death duty register records may show how an estate was administered and include the last address and occupation of the deceased and the date of his or her will, as well as the addresses, occupations and sometimes relationships of others named, such as beneficiaries. Most helpfully, these records were sometimes annotated long after the deceased had died to show information such as the death of a spouse. Not every estate required death duties to be collected on it, but the death duty register index does serve as a useful aid for finding more details of deaths in the period 1796 to 1903.

Don't forget to also visit the GENUKI page for the town, village or parish in which you're interested. Many individuals have provided online indexes to, or transcriptions of, the baptism, marriage or burial records for specific parishes, and these can be a great find if they cover the period you need. Sometimes these are freely available (such as the transcripts to St Mary's Taunton (Somerset) marriages, 1728–1812, provided by Roy Parkhouse at `www.genuki.org.uk/big/eng/SOM/Taunton/Tmar.html`), other times a fee is involved (such as Paul Joiner's listing of marriages for the north of England, Hertfordshire and Norfolk pre-1837, which contains more than 1.25 million entries: See `www.joinermarriageindex.com`). Before paying a site owner to obtain the full record, you can usually do a free search to see how many hits the site finds for the details you enter.

Some websites provide resources that are unique or specific to researching English or Welsh ancestry at the county or parish level. Try these examples:

- **Access to Archives** (`www.nationalarchives.gov.uk/a2a`): Also known as A2A, this site contains about 30 per cent of all archive catalogues across England and Wales, containing more than 10.3 million items. You can search across the country by region or by repository.

- **FamilyRecords.gov.uk** (`www.familyrecords.gov.uk`): This site links to government departments and agencies that hold historical records.

- **The National Library of Wales** (`www.llgc.org.uk`): Along with pages devoted to tracing family history, this site offers online catalogues of the library's extensive collections, including newspapers.

- **The (UK) Society of Genealogists** (`www.sog.org.uk`): This site offers an online catalogue of its holdings and many useful guides to its records.

# Searching for Everything Irish

Many Australians can trace their family history back to Ireland. In fact, at various times it's been suggested that one in every three Australians has an Irish ancestor somewhere in their background. The Irish came to Australia in huge numbers during the mid-nineteenth century when famine forced them to seek a new life in a different land. Many were also shipped out as convicts, or packed up and left home when gold was discovered in Australia.

## Working with Irish online resources

One of the first things you may notice when researching your Irish ancestry on the Web is that resources are county-based, which means you need to know the county your Irish ancestors came from if you want to find information about them online.

Information gathered about the Irish-born population in Australia during the colonial period usually referred to them only as originating from Ireland, but in 1922, what was historically known as Ireland was divided into Northern Ireland (Ulster) and the Republic of Ireland, and today separate government agencies maintain the official records of these two regions.

This makes it even more important for you to find out as much as you can about your Irish ancestors in Australia first, *before* you turn to overseas resources to track them down. If you can establish the name of the village, town or county they came from, you know which government holds relevant records and where to look online to find out more about them. Unfortunately, if all you know is that your ancestors came from 'Ireland', this is going to make your search very difficult.

Supposing you already know where your Irish ancestors came from and want to consult a range of general Irish genealogy resources? Okay, try these:

- **Irish Genealogy (**www.irishgenealogy.ie**):** This gateway site offers free index searching that links through to an Irish heritage centre or a similar organisation that then provides more details for a prescribed fee. The index, which includes almost 400,000 gravestone inscriptions from ten Irish counties, provides quite useful search results.

- **Irish Origins (**www.irishorigins.com**):** This site has a range of databases available on a subscription basis.

- **Ulster Ancestry (**www.ulsterancestry.com**):** This is one example of the many commercial sites offering help with researching your Irish ancestry. It provides an extensive range of free databases that you can search before deciding whether you'd like to approach the company to undertake work on your behalf.

## Searching for Irish birth, death and marriage records

As we explain in the preceding section, Northern Ireland — the six counties of Ulster (Antrim, Armagh, Down, Fermanagh, Londonderry and Tyrone) — became separate from the Republic of Ireland in 1922. However, civil registrations began in Ireland in 1845, although it wasn't until 1864 that Catholic marriages were also registered and all births and deaths were recorded.

All records for the years 1845 to 1922 are maintained by the Republic of Ireland's General Register Office in Dublin (www.groireland.ie) — along with all civil registrations recorded in the Republic of Ireland through to this day. Civil registrations recorded in Northern Ireland after 1922 are held by the General Register Office in Belfast (www.groni.gov.uk). At both websites you can order civil registration certificates online, although neither site provides online access to records.

Parish registers contain local church records, such as baptisms, marriages and funerals. You can find information about where these types of records are held at the National Library of Ireland (www.nli.ie) or use genealogy databases or online gateways (see Chapter 3) to find transcribed records online.

## Using Ireland's archives and libraries

The National Archives of Ireland (www.nationalarchives.ie) provides comprehensive online information sheets for family historians that you can access by following the Genealogy link on the home page. You can also search its online databases, including the Ireland–Australia Transportation index for the years 1780 to 1868.

Likewise, the Public Record Office of Northern Ireland (www.proni.gov.uk) holds many archives from government departments, courts, non-departmental public bodies and local authorities in Northern Ireland — including records on emigration to Australia, wills, estates, churches, cemeteries and much more. If you'd like an introduction to using the Public Record Office's records for family history, you can download several information sheets (available under the Family History link). Its searchable online indexes include

- Pre-1840 freeholders' records of those men entitled to vote, including links to the digitised images of the Returns and Poll Books. These records can be used as a useful census substitute.

- The Ulster Covenant, containing the signatures of nearly 500,000 people who signed the Covenant in 1912 to express their opposition to the proposal from Westminster to grant limited Home Rule. The index is linked to the original signatures and also provides addresses.

- Will calendar entries for the District Probate Registries of Armagh, Belfast and Londonderry from 1858 to c.1900.

## Tracking down Irish census records

Although Ireland began taking censuses of its population every ten years from 1821, only fragments of early records survive. Two census records that are available for free online are

✔ The 1901 census for Clare, which is available through Clare County Library at www.clarelibrary.ie (follow the links under Genealogy)

✔ The 1911 census for Dublin, Antrim, Down and Kerry, which is available at the National Archives of Ireland (www.nationalarchives.ie) and provides excellent background information on the social conditions in those areas at that time

# Going Back to Scotland

The Scottish government makes it easy for genealogists to trace their Scottish ancestry — it has centralised all the main family history resources in the one place at ScotlandsPeople (www.scotlandspeople.gov.uk).

At the ScotlandsPeople website (see Figure 7-2) you can search the following online indexes for Scotland:

✔ Banns and marriages for the years 1538 to 1933

✔ Baptisms for the years 1538 to 1854

✔ Births from 1855 to 2006

✔ Burials for the years 1538 to 1854

✔ Coats of Arms granted between 1672 and 1907 (this database is free)

✔ Complete census returns for the years 1841 to 1901

✔ Deaths from 1855 to 2006

✔ Wills from 1513 to 1901 (this database is free)

To search the indexes and download the associated images, you must be a registered user and pay a fee. This fee is currently £6: This provides 30 credits, which you have 90 consecutive days to use. Any unused credits remain in your account, but after 90 days have expired you need to pay a further £6 to reactivate the account.

Take the time to learn to use the ScotlandsPeople website properly, and you'll find that your fees are money well spent. Downloading a certificate or census page costs five credits, so with careful planning you can actually progress your research a long way for little outlay. You also get immediate access to your search results, making this truly a site where within a few hours you can progress your Scottish research back several generations.

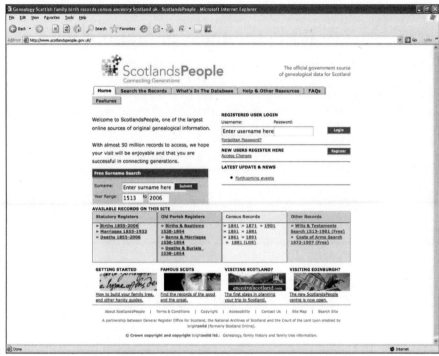

**Figure 7-2:**
The
Scotlands-
People
website.

In addition, the site has a great bonus feature: It stores all your previous searches and you can download again for free any record for which you've already paid the retrieval fee of five credits. Say you're in the middle of a census search and need to check when your great-great-grandfather was married: If you've already obtained his marriage certificate through the site, you can look at it again for free before returning to your census search.

After you identify your ancestors in the ScotlandsPeople database, you can find more information about them in other online resources. Try these websites:

✔ The National Archives of Scotland's Family History section (www.nas.gov.uk) has many online guides detailing resources for genealogists.

✔ Scotlands Family (www.scotlandsfamily.com) is a gateway site that helps researchers to find free information on the Web. It has links to many private online databases covering subjects such as censuses, births, deaths, marriages and poorhouse records.

✔ Scottish Archive Network (www.scan.org.uk) allows you to search the catalogues of 52 Scottish archives and record offices simultaneously, as well as providing research guides to help you.

✔ The Scottish Genealogy Society (www.scotsgenealogy.com) provides a number of useful guides on subjects related to Scottish family history.

## Making the most of mailing lists

In Chapter 3 we show you how to use family history mailing lists to search for individual surnames. However, many mailing lists are geographically based — they can help you make contact with other family historians researching the same region as you, and point you in the direction of other resources you didn't know existed. You may even find someone researching the same family tree!

RootsWeb (lists.rootsweb.ancestry.com) is home to many English, Irish and Scottish mailing lists that you can join to interact with other researchers who may already be knowledgeable about resources in specific regions. For example, its English index contains mailing lists that are county based or cover specific places, such as Bodmin Moor in Cornwall or English pubs and inns. Likewise, a number of RootsWeb's mailing lists for Scotland are clan-based, which can lead to useful contacts to help you trace your family's history. You can also find similar resources on Ireland.

# Looking Beyond the United Kingdom

While traditionally most Australians can trace their heritage back to the United Kingdom, over the past 220 years people from many different ethnic backgrounds have settled in Australia. The following section gives you some starting points if your ancestors didn't come from England, Wales, Scotland or Ireland.

## Tracking down European resources

If one or more of your ancestors came from Europe, your level of genealogical success depends greatly on the areas in which they lived. Ancestors from places that weathered several wars and border changes may have fewer surviving records than those who lived in a more stable environment. The following are just two examples of the resources available for specific regions:

  ✔ The Federation of East European Family History Societies (www.feefhs.org) works to promote genealogy in eastern and central Europe and contains useful information on its website. The society covers Albania, Armenia, Austria, Belarus, Bosnia, Bulgaria, Croatia, Czech Republic, Denmark, Estonia, Finland, Georgia, Germany, Greece, Hungary, Kosovo, Latvia, Lithuania, Macedonia, Moldova, Montenegro, Norway, Poland, Romania, Russia, Serbia, Slovakia, Slovenia, Sweden, Switzerland and the Ukraine.

✔ FamilySearch covers many European countries through its collection of microfilmed resources and has useful online guides that you can download to learn more about each country's historical background and how to conduct research there. From the home page (www. familysearch.org) click on the Research Helps link and either search for a specific country or browse the list.

One of the best ways to find out what's available for the country of interest to you is to use the gateway site Cyndi's List. Here's what to do:

1. **Go to** www.cyndislist.com.

2. **Scroll down the home page to the Main Category Index and select the letter from the alphabet that represents the country you're researching.**

   For example, select G for Germany: You can see that more than 1,000 links are available for Germany.

3. **Click on the name of the country you're interested in and browse the Category Index.**

   The Category Index for Germany lists broad topics such as Societies, Maps, General Resource Sites, Mailing Lists, Newspapers and so on.

   *Note:* If you're just starting out, click on the How To link in the Category Index. Not all of Cyndi's List's country pages have this category, but where provided it points to websites that can best help you to get started tracing your family history in that region.

Because the geographical boundaries of many European countries (such as Germany) have changed over time, the place of birth recorded on an ancestor's death certificate in 1873 may no longer be in the same country. To pinpoint a place name, consult online gazetteers and maps. Some online maps even show boundary changes over time. A good range of historical maps is available at the website of The Federation of East European Family History Societies (www.feefhs.org).

Many European countries have online family history societies and associated organisations, but once you start dealing with countries where English is not the native language you may encounter communication difficulties. Even if a website is available in English, making contact by email or letter is likely to be frustrating if you can't converse in the site's first language. Look for websites that provide translation details about basic genealogical terminology or that supply online form letters you can use.

Mailing lists can also help you to get around language barriers. For example, RootsWeb's international directory of mailing lists (lists.rootsweb. ancestry.com) covers most European countries, and although many lists conduct discussions in a foreign language, you can usually find one where people speak English. However, make sure you determine the geographic location of your family first, before you start posting requests for help on these mailing lists.

## Chasing New Zealand resources

A great deal of movement took place between the Australian colonies and New Zealand from the 1840s onwards. Some families moved between the two countries on a regular basis; others embarked on a new life in one before moving across the Tasman to settle in the other. This means that New Zealand may be worth putting on your research list if you've lost an ancestor or you can't establish Australian arrival details.

Check out the following websites:

- **Archives New Zealand** (www.archives.govt.nz): This site includes online access to Archway, the Archives' catalogue of holdings, which allows you to search some of the records by surname. Holdings include probate records (wills), immigration records, coroners' reports, notices of intention to marry and military service records prior to 1913. The site also contains many excellent research guides for the family historian.

- **Auckland City Libraries** (www.aucklandcitylibraries.com): This network of libraries has online databases of a number of different records, including: Auckland area passenger arrivals (1838 to 1886); original Crown land grants for inner Auckland; the 1842 to 1846 Auckland police census; various cemetery records; and the 1881 electoral roll.

- **Dictionary of New Zealand Biography** (www.dnzb.govt.nz/dnzb): At this site you can tap into some 3,000 online biographies of deceased New Zealanders.

- **National Library of New Zealand** (www.natlib.govt.nz): This site offers a number of useful online databases, including

  - Pictures Past, which has more than one million digitised images from 45 New Zealand newspapers covering the period 1839 to 1920

  - Timeframes, an online database of heritage images from the Alexander Turnbull Library

- **New Zealand Society of Genealogists** (www.genealogy.org.nz): Along with other resources, this site has a useful guide to New Zealand research (follow the links under the Research tab on the home page).

# Pacific and Asian resources

If your ancestors came from Asia or the Pacific Rim, your success at finding records depends greatly on the history of your ancestors' ethnic group and its record-keeping procedures. Here's a sample of some websites that deal with Asian and Pacific Rim regions:

- **China:** Geocities' Chinese Surname Index at www.geocities.com/Tokyo/3919/atoz.html, an alphabetical listing of Chinese surnames with links to known family websites

- **India:** Families in British India Society at www.fibis.org, which offers free access to many databases compiled by its volunteers. These databases focus on tracing British, European and Anglo-Indian family history in countries such as India, Burma, China, Pakistan, Malaysia and Bangladesh between 1600 and 1949. The site is of particular interest to those who had ancestors serving in the East India Company.

- **Japan:** Japan GenWeb at www.rootsweb.ancestry.com/~jpnwgw

- **Philippines:** Philippines Genealogy Web Project at www.geocities.com/Heartland/Ranch/9121

- **South Korea:** South Korea GenWeb Project at www.rootsweb.ancestry.com/~korwgw-s

Repositories of Primary Resources for Asia and the Pacific (www.uidaho.edu/special-collections/asia.html) is a gateway to government archives and libraries in Asia and the Pacific.

If you need to translate a website, try using Google Translate (translate.google.com/translate_t#). The service enables you to translate a word, a piece of text or even a website into English.

# Finding resources in the United States

Many of the major online resources we refer to throughout this book are based in the United States. This means these websites put just as much effort — if not more — into compiling information and records on American genealogy as they do for other countries.

The following websites (also covered in more detail in Chapters 13 and 14) make researching family history in the United States easy:

- ✔ **Ancestry.com** (`www.ancestry.com`): Being a US-based company, `Ancestry.com` has developed a huge range of databases to help Americans to trace their family trees.

- ✔ **Cyndi's List** (`www.cyndislist.com`): This gateway site links to thousands of US genealogy resources.

- ✔ **FamilySearch** (`www.familysearch.org`): The Church of Jesus Christ of Latter-day Saints' internet genealogy service focuses on gathering genealogical records from all over the world, and is one of the easiest to use for accessing US data.

- ✔ **Genealogy.com** (`www.genealogy.com`): This site's stronghold is genealogy software and providing online resources for family historians.

If you're looking for a good reference book that covers tracing family history in the United States in more depth, we recommend *Genealogy Online For Dummies*, 5th Edition, by Matthew and April Helm (Wiley Publishing Inc.).

# Part III
# Keeping Your Ancestors in Line: Organising and Presenting Your Findings

'I'm your great second cousin Rex, but you
may know me better by the family ID
JohnsonR/SA/24-J0001.'

# In this part ...

**D**o you know how to organise what you find in your research and preserve it for the future? The chapters in this part cover some traditional methods of organisation in the genealogical field, how to safely preserve documents and photos, and how to use your computer and genealogical software to store information. We also explore various computer components and peripherals that you may find handy.

# Chapter 8

# Finetuning Your Organisational and Preservation Skills

*A*fter you collect all this great genealogical data, your findings won't do you much good if you can't locate a particular item when you need it. You don't want to run all over the house trying to pull together all those scraps of paper — notes from your research at the library in your desk, letters from relatives in your mail-to-be-sorted basket, photocopies of some pedigree charts mixed in with your magazines. You may forget where you put a specific item and miss something important because your documents aren't organised and kept in a centralised location.

In this chapter, we examine ways of organising and preserving genealogical information and documents using traditional storage methods and preservation techniques.

## Getting a Firm Foundation in Traditional Methods of Genealogical Organisation

No finer tradition exists in genealogy than that of collecting tonnes of paper and photographs. Until now, you've probably used whatever means possible to take notes while talking with relatives about your ancestors or looking up information at the local library — from notebook paper, to receipts you have in your pocket or purse, to stick-on notes. You may have used your camera to take pictures of headstones in the cemetery where some of your ancestors are buried or the old family homestead that's now abandoned and barely standing.

And you've probably collected some original source documents — like the certified copy of your mother's birth certificate that your grandmother gave you, the family Bible from Aunty Rose and the old photograph of your great-great-grandfather as a child that you found while digging through boxes in the shed. Now what are you supposed to do with all these things? Organise, organise, organise!

Even if you decide to use genealogical software to track your research progress, you always have paper records and photographs you want to keep. The following sections offer some tips to help you become well organised (genealogically, anyway).

## Establishing effective organisational skills

You've probably already discovered that taking notes on little scraps of paper works adequately at first, but the more notes you take, the harder time you have sorting through them and making sense of the information on each. To avoid this situation, establish some effective note-taking and organisational skills early by being consistent in how you take notes.

Write the date and place that you research and the names of the family members that you interview at the top of your notes. This information can help you later on when you return to your notes to look for a particular fact or when you try to make sense out of conflicting information.

Be as detailed as possible when taking notes on particular events, persons, books and so forth — include the who, what, where, when, why and how. And most importantly, always cite the source of your information, keeping the following guidelines in mind:

- **Book or magazine:** Include all bibliographic information, such as the title of the publication, the author, the date of issue, the page number of the article or chapter and the repository where you found the publication.

- **Microfilm or microfiche:** Include all bibliographic information and note the document format (microfilm, microfiche), document number and repository name.

- **Person:** As well as the information, include the person's full name, relationship to you (if any), contact data (address, phone number and email address), and the date and time that you and this person communicated.

✔ **Record:** Include the name or type of record, record number, book number (if applicable), the name and location of the record-keeping agency, and any other pertinent information.

✔ **Website or other internet resource:** Include the name of the copyright holder for the site (or the name of the site's creator and maintainer if no copyright notice appears on it), the name of the site, the address or uniform resource locator (URL) of the site, the date the information was posted or copyrighted, and any notes with traditional contact information for the site's copyright holder or creator.

Print a copy of the web page or other internet resource that contains information about your research interest to keep in your paper files. Some websites have a tendency to disappear over time, so your best bet is to get documentation of the site while it exists.

# Understanding genealogical charts and forms

Many charts and forms can help you to organise your research and make your findings easier to understand for those you share them with. Some examples include pedigree charts that show the relationships between family members, descendant charts that list every person who descends from a particular ancestor and census forms that contain the data for particular years. Some of these charts and forms are available from places such as the Society of Australian Genealogists (www.sag.org.au) and Gould Genealogy (www.gould.com.au). The sooner you become familiar with the most common types of charts and how to read them, the sooner you can interpret a lot of the information you receive from other genealogists. We discuss some forms you can generate using your computer in Chapter 9.

# Assigning unique numbers to family members

If you have ancestors who share the same name, or if you've collected a lot of information on several generations of ancestors, you may have trouble distinguishing one person from another. To avoid confusion and the problems that can arise from it, you may want to use a commonly accepted numbering system to identify each individual.

Some people find it easier to keep track of their ancestors using one of these established numbering systems. Conversely, many family historians find the numbering systems a bit off-putting and prefer to let their database sort individual people for them so they don't have to show complicated-looking numbers beside each name.

Keep in mind that time spent grappling with a numbering system you don't understand is wasted research time. Also, other family members may be a little bit intimidated if you send them a very official-looking chart or report that contains a lot of numbers they don't understand. If you need their help in providing family history information, the last thing you want to do is to frighten them off.

Systems you may encounter include

- The *ahnentafel system* (or Sosa-Stradonitz system): This well-known numbering system is a method of numbering that shows a mathematical relationship between parents and children (see Figure 8-1). Ahnentafel means 'ancestor' (*ahnen*) and 'table' (*tafel*) in German. You may also hear the ahnentafel system referred to as the Sosa-Stradonitz system, because it was first used by a Spanish genealogist named Jerome de Sosa in 1676 and was popularised in 1896 by Stephan Kekule von Stradonitz.

- The *Henry system* or code: This well-known numbering system assigns a particular number to the progenitor, or the ancestor farthest back in a particular family line (that you know about). Then each of the progenitor's children is assigned a number in sequence that starts with his number and adds the numbers one, two, three and so forth through to nine. (If the progenitor had more than nine children, the 10th child is assigned an X, the 11th an A, the 12th a B and so on.) Then the children's children are assigned the parent's number plus a number in sequence (again one through to nine, then X, A, B and so on).

- The *tiny tafel system*: Some people confuse ahnentafel with tiny tafel, which is a compact way to show the relationships within a family database. Tiny tafel provides only the Soundex code for a surname, and the dates and locations where that surname may be found according to the database. (For an explanation of Soundex codes, check out the glossary in Appendix A.) Computer programs sometimes use tiny tafels to match the same individual in two different genealogy databases.

By no means are these systems the only genealogical numbering systems in existence. Ahnentafel and Henry are just two of the easier systems to learn. Several others have been designed to display genealogies in book form. If you're curious about some of these systems, take a look at the article 'Numbering Systems in Genealogy' by Richard Pence (www.saintclair.org/numbers), where you can find descriptions of each major numbering system.

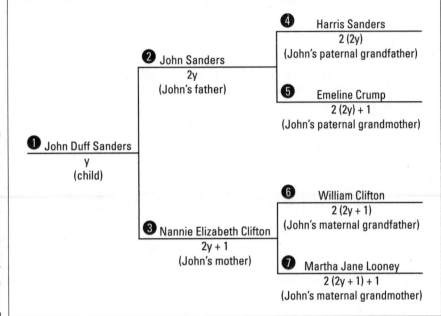

**Figure 8-1:** An illustration of the ahnentafel numbering system as applied to an ancestor (pedigree) chart.

Some computer software packages have an in-built numbering system that can be displayed on reports or when you set up a book. Check your software program to see what it offers. If it has an in-built numbering system but you're unsure whether this feature may be useful to you, try applying the numbering system to one branch of your family tree. Do you find it easier to work out relationships using the numbering system? If so, you may want to engage this feature on your software.

If you decide to use a numbering system, place the corresponding unique number for each individual on the file that you set up for that person in your paper record-keeping system, as well as in your genealogical software.

## Making copies of source documents

You don't want to carry original records with you when you're out and about researching. The chances of misplacing or forgetting a document are too great. You have several options:

- ✔ Copy the data from your desktop computer to an online storage system such as Google Docs or a flash drive to take with you.

- ✔ Enter the information into a database on your laptop, notebook computer or hand-held device to take with you.

- ✔ Make photocopies of data that you must take with you when researching.

- ✔ Print out your data and take the hard copies with you.

- ✔ Scan the documents and store them on your laptop or notebook computer to take with you. (We talk more about using computers for your notes in Chapter 9.)

Place the original documents in the safest place you can think of that is available to you — fireproof filing cabinets, safes and safe-deposit boxes are all good options.

## Deciding on a storage method

How are you going to store all the information you collect? You have to admit that your current system isn't working if you just spent all night searching the house for research material you know you put in a safe place, somewhere. A filing system is in order! You can set up a good filing system in many ways, and no one system is right or wrong. Just use one that's comfortable for you.

If you're at a loss as to how to start a system, try thinking about the various family lines you're tracing and divide your research notes and documents accordingly. Many people like to store documents and notes in sturdy two-ring folders. Don't punch holes in your research documents; instead use pre-punched plastic A4 sleeves and slip your papers into these. Make sure that the sleeves you buy are 'copysafe' — you can see this word imprinted down the white margin where the holes are punched. This means that the surface of photocopies and certificates you place in them won't transfer onto the plastic and damage your original material, which can happen with some of the cheaper sleeves. Likewise, you're less likely to harm your documents because the plastic sleeves protect them from fingerprints. Perhaps start with four folders: One for each of your grandparents' surnames. As you progress backwards you can set up extra folders. You can even number each folder, and later use these numbers as cross-references in the notes field of your genealogical database.

Some family historians like to set up similar systems using manila folders placed in a metal filing cabinet. While a metal filing cabinet provides very good protection against fire, loose papers stored in manila folders can easily become dislodged or get out of order — especially if you drop a folder!

Scan your documents onto your computer, and then make back-up copies using a Zip or flash drive or writable CD-ROM/DVD. Store these back-ups in a location away from where the originals are stored.

# *Preserving Your Treasured Family Documents*

Time is going to take its toll on every document in your possession. The longer you want your records and pictures to last, the better care you need to take of them now. The following sections discuss some tips for preserving your family treasures so that you can pass them down to future generations in the best possible shape.

## *Storing vital records under the right conditions*

Place precious original documents like birth and marriage certificates between acid-free paper in albums. Keep these albums in a dark, dry and temperature-controlled place. Ideally, you should store these documents in a place that is about 18 degrees Celsius year-round, with a relative humidity of less than 50 per cent. You may consider placing these albums in a steel filing cabinet.

Avoid using ink, staples, paper clips, glue and tape around your documents (unless you use archival products designed for document repair).

Of course, one of the best methods of preservation is to make electronic copies of your documents using a scanner. Then keep disk back-ups at a fire-safe, off-site location. A safe-deposit box is a good choice, or you can copy and distribute your documents among family members — or even deposit a set with your local family history society. Organisations like the Society of Australian Genealogists (www.sag.org.au) have large repositories of original research papers and documents that they preserve for the benefit of family historians. If your research focuses on a particular region, contact the local society there and ask whether it can take a copy of your material for its collection. Then, if anything untoward happens to your originals, you can reconstruct the information from the copies.

Some websites give more information about preserving family documents. The Department of Veterans' Affairs provides an online copy of its book *Caring for Your Wartime Memorabilia: A Guide to Preserving Your Family's Heritage* (www.dva.gov.au/media/publicat/2001/memorabilia), which offers useful tips for looking after everything from war medals to photos and diaries (see Figure 8-2).

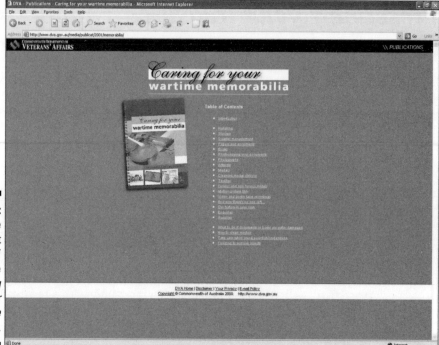

**Figure 8-2:**
The Department of Veterans' Affairs online book, *Caring for Your Wartime Memorabilia.*

## *Protecting your photographs*

Fight the urge to put all your photos of every ancestor on display, because light can damage them over time. Keep your most-prized pictures in a dark, dry and temperature-controlled place. If you use a photo album for storage, make sure that it has acid-free paper or chemically safe plastic pockets, and that you affix the pictures to the pages using a safe adhesive. Other storage options include acid-free storage boxes and steel filing cabinets. Store the photographs in a place about 18 degrees Celsius year-round, with a relative humidity of less than 50 per cent. Avoid prolonged exposure of photographs to direct sunlight and fluorescent lights. You can also preserve your photographs by scanning them into your computer and then storing a copy of the images on a CD-ROM, DVD or external hard drive.

Here are a few websites that provide more detailed tips on preserving your family photographic treasures:

- *Document and Photo Preservation FAQ* by Linda Beyea at
  `www.loricase.com/faq.html`

- *Guidelines For Preserving Your Photographic Heritage* by Ralph McKnight at `www.geocities.com/Heartland/6662/photopre.htm`

- *Protecting and Handling Photographs* by the National Archives of Australia at `www.naa.gov.au/services/family-historians/looking-after/photographs.aspx`

Additionally, a number of suppliers such as Albox Records Management (`www.albox.com.au`; see Figure 8-3) stock chemically safe storage products (albums, paper, boxes and so forth) for your photos and records. Albox also has a useful series of EBooklets on its website that you can download as PDFs. These booklets advise the best way to store various records and items such as photographs and CDs.

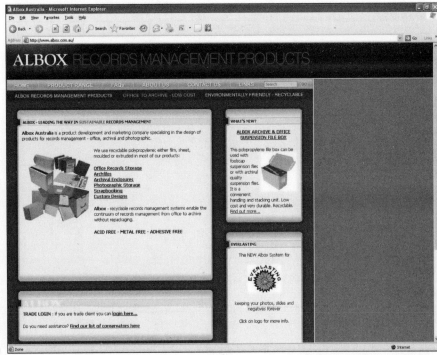

**Figure 8-3:** Albox Records Management's online store sells a variety of storage products.

Even though you want to preserve everything to the best of your ability, don't be afraid to pull out your albums to show visiting relatives and friends if you want to do so. On the other hand, don't be embarrassed to ask these guests to use caution when looking through your albums. Depending on the age and rarity of some of your documents, you may even want to ask guests to wear latex gloves when handling the albums, so that the oil from their hands doesn't get all over your treasures. Upon realising how important these treasures are to you, most guests won't mind using caution.

If you're taking original material with you on a visit to family or friends, be very careful. Months or even years of research could be lost forever if you absent-mindedly jump off the bus or train and leave the bag containing all your research carefully tucked under the seat. Similarly, taking those original photos to a family reunion may seem like a good idea, but can you keep track of each item as it's passed around between everyone gathered for the occasion — and that may number in the hundreds? Be sensible with your original material. Remember, once lost it's gone forever. You're better off taking copies with you.

# Chapter 9

# Using Your Computer to Store and Organise Information

After organising your paper records and photographs, put your computer to work storing and manipulating your family history.

Although some people still like using manual systems, a computer really is your best friend when it comes to storing, organising and publishing your genealogical information. Specially developed genealogical software guides you through the recording process and makes sharing your information with other researchers much easier and quicker in the long run.

With your computer, you can use genealogical software to

✔ Access CD-ROMs containing valuable genealogical records

✔ Scan images to preserve your family heritage

✔ Share information with researchers throughout the world via the internet

✔ Store information on thousands of individuals

In this chapter, we examine genealogical database software and what it can do for you. We also look at computer hardware and other gadgets that you can use to enhance your genealogical files.

# Purchasing Genealogical Software

Many different kinds of software programs are available that enable you to keep track of your ancestors. You can store facts and stories about them, attach files containing scanned photographs of them with their biographical information and generate numerous reports at the click of your mouse. Many programs allow you to store audio and video recordings too. (This capability is especially wonderful if you want to put together a multimedia presentation on your genealogy to share at a family reunion or conference.)

## Working out your system requirements

Minimum system requirements for software programs are usually similar, but you should always check first to ensure that your computer is capable of running the software you purchase and that it can utilise all the features the program offers. Genealogical software can literally store thousands of names — some now boast of being able to store millions — so the more powerful your system, the better the software will operate, especially if you plan to create a large database of information on it.

In general, the following list is what we recommend as the minimum requirements for your computer system to adequately run most genealogical software. However, keep in mind that if you want additional accessories for your computer to assist your genealogical effort (such as scanners, other software and so forth), or if you want to store electronic images, you may need to have a higher-end system — that is, a faster processor, more random access memory (RAM) and more free hard drive space.

For a PC, you need at least the following:

- A 1 GHz Pentium III or equivalent
- Windows Vista or XP
- A DVD drive
- A minimum of 40 gigabytes of free hard drive space
- 512 megabytes of RAM
- A 1024 × 768 resolution monitor

For a Macintosh computer, you need at least the following:

- An Intel, PowerPC G5 or PowerPC G4 (867 MHz or faster) processor
- A DVD drive

✔ A minimum of 9 gigabytes of free hard drive space

✔ 512 megabytes of RAM

Some features require a compatible broadband internet service provider; fees may apply

## Finding a research mate (of the software variety)

You probably think that you already have the perfect research mate — that special person you drag to every library, cemetery and archive centre to do your research, right? Wrong! The research mate we're referring to comes in a little box, with CD-ROMs or DVDs, and you load it onto your computer and then let it perform all sorts of amazing tasks for you.

Software programs can store and manipulate your genealogical information. They all have some standard features in common; for instance, most serve as databases for family facts and stories, have reporting functions to generate already-completed charts and forms, and have export capabilities so that you can share your data with others. Each software program has a few unique features that make it stand out from the others, such as the capability to take information out of the software and generate online reports at the click of your mouse.

Here's a list of the features you want to look for when evaluating different software packages:

✔ **Can your current computer system support this software?** If the requirements of the software cause your computer to crash every time you use the program, you won't get very far in your genealogical research.

✔ **Does the software generate the reports that you need?** For instance, if you're partial to Family Group Sheets, does this software support them?

✔ **Does the software allow you to export and/or import a GEDCOM file?** GEDCOM is a file format that's widely used for genealogical research. For more info about GEDCOM, see the sidebar 'GEDCOM: The genealogist's standard' later in this chapter.

✔ **Does this software provide fields for citing your sources and keeping notes?** Including information about the sources you use to gather your data — with the actual facts, if possible — is sound genealogical practice. For more information about the importance of citing sources and how to do so, take a look at Chapter 11.

✔ **Does the software allow you to include photographs, video and audio material?** If you think you may make use of multimedia, make sure that the program allows you to include scanned images of documents and family photographs and is capable of running audio and video clips. You may not think this an important feature now, but as you get more involved in recording the history of your family, you may regret not having this feature available.

✔ **How easy is the software to use?** Is it graphics-friendly so that you can see how and where to enter particular facts about an ancestor?

✔ **How many names can this software hold?** Make sure that the software can hold an adequate number of names (and the accompanying data) to accommodate all the ancestors about whom you have information. Keep in mind that your genealogy continues to grow over time. While most registered software has the capacity to store more ancestors than you'll ever be able to trace, some programs that you can download for free from the internet actually limit the number of names you can enter.

To see a comparison of some of the main software programs on the market, check out the section 'Family History Software Programs' on Cora Num's website at www.coraweb.com.au/software.htm, which has links to a number of reviews of software programs. Spend some time looking at the comparisons, as well as visiting the websites of the companies that sell the packages to get an idea of what features each program offers.

For further help, try the following:

✔ Ask around your genealogical friends and colleagues to find out what software they use and whether they recommend it.

✔ Contact your local family history society, as many societies offer demonstrations of specific software and seminars on genealogical computing. For example, the Society of Australian Genealogists (www.sag.org.au) holds regular sessions about Family Tree Maker, The Master Genealogist and Reunion for Macintosh, to name a few.

The prices of software have come down enormously in recent years, so the outlay you make on a particular product may no longer be quite as significant as it once was. However, there's a learning curve involved in adapting to every new program, plus you spend time entering your genealogical data into it. So, the time you spend researching the best software for you, rather than just jumping in and buying the first package you see, will be time well spent.

The CD that accompanies this book includes some sample software programs for you to try out. Some of these are trial versions that don't offer the full features of the main package; others only allow you to input a limited amount of data before the program is blocked. To continue using such a program, you need to purchase the full version or pay the necessary registration fee.

# Entering Information into a Family History Software Package

To help you get a better idea of how software can help you to organise your records and research, this section outlines the basics of using a software program.

Before you start entering data in your program, spend time looking at any tutorials or 'getting started' tips that the program provides. These guidelines show you how to use the different features of the software.

Family history software programs usually prompt you to enter information about yourself first, then your spouse and children, and work backwards through your parents, grandparents, great-grandparents and so forth. After you complete your direct lines back as far as you can, you may add details about siblings, nieces and nephews, cousins and other relatives.

---

## GEDCOM: The genealogist's standard

As you've probably already discovered, genealogy is full of acronyms. One such acronym that you hear and see over and over again is *GEDCOM* (*GEnealogical Data COMmunication*). GEDCOM is the standard for individuals and software manufacturers for exporting and importing information from or into genealogical databases. Simply put, GEDCOM is a file format intended to make data transferable between different software programs so that people can share their family information easily.

The Church of Jesus Christ of Latter-day Saints first developed and introduced GEDCOM in 1987. The first two versions of GEDCOM were released for public discussion only and weren't meant to serve as the standard. With the introduction of subsequent versions, however, GEDCOM was accepted as the standard.

Having a standard for formatting files is beneficial to you as a researcher because it enables you to share the information that you collect with others who're interested in some or all of your ancestors. It also enables you to import GEDCOM files from other researchers who have information about family lines and ancestors in whom you're interested. And you don't even have to use the same software as the other researchers! You can use Reunion on a Macintosh system and someone with whom you want to share information can use Family Tree Maker on a PC; having GEDCOM as the standard in both software programs enables you both to create and exchange GEDCOM files.

To convert the data in your genealogical database to a GEDCOM file, follow the instructions provided in your software's manual or Help menu. Most software programs automatically generate a GEDCOM file of your data for you to export.

Spend your time wisely keying in the data. Follow these general guidelines for entering information:

- ✔ Avoid the temptation to add in as many people as you possibly can to your family tree. There isn't much point having 14,000 people in your database if you can identify directly with only about 700 of them and never look at the others. Concentrate on entering detailed information on your direct family lines first.

- ✔ Spend the time entering the correct data from the start: This can save you a lot of time re-entering information later on. Don't simply key in a person's name and date of birth and marriage before moving on to the next family member. Learn how to also record the source of the information you have; for example, how you know someone was born on 14 January 1873 or died on 30 June 1930. You can go back later and add further details you find out about the person, but you'll be glad you spent the time entering the details properly from the start. To find out how to record source information, check your program's Help menu or manual.

Bear in mind that the majority of software programs are developed for the American market, where the date format differs from that used in Australia. These programs are likely to default to showing, say, 5 April 1925 as 04-05-1925. Australians read that as being 4 May 1925, but Americans read it as 5 April 1925. Because different countries use different date formats, if you rely on numerals other genealogists and family members around the world may interpret your dates incorrectly. Stick to entering your dates in full and never change the settings to allow the system to display abbreviated numerals. By all means change the default format to display day, month and full four-digit year (that is, 5 April 1925) if you wish, but never change the default setting to record the month as a numeral.

## Sharing Your Genealogical Success with Others

After you organise all your paper documents and enter as much information as possible into your genealogical software, you can share what you've gathered with others, or you can generate notes to take with you on research trips. (If you haven't organised your information yet, Chapter 8 can help you.)

Your genealogical software can help you by generating printed reports reflecting the information that you collected and entered. Most genealogical software packages have several standard reports or charts in common, including a pedigree chart, descendant chart, family outline, family group sheet and kinship report.

In this section, we examine the different types of reports and show what they look like using one of the most popular genealogical software programs around, Family Tree Maker (www.familytreemaker.com).

# Pedigree charts

A *pedigree chart* flows horizontally across a page and identifies a primary person by that person's name, date and place of birth, date and place of marriage, and date and place of death. The chart uses lines to show the relationship to the person's father and mother, then their parents and so on until the chart runs off the page. Figure 9-1 shows an example of a three-generation pedigree chart generated using Family Tree Maker.

# Descendant charts

A *descendant chart*, as shown in Figure 9-2, contains information about an ancestor and spouse (or spouses if more than one exists), their children and their spouses, grandchildren and spouses, and so on down the family line. A descendant chart usually flows vertically on a page, rather than running horizontally across the page like a pedigree chart.

# Family outlines

A *family outline* is a list of the descendants of a particular ancestor. (Family Tree Maker calls it an *outline descendant report*.) As shown in Figure 9-3, the first numbered line contains the name (and sometimes the years for birth and death) of the primary ancestor. The next line shows a spouse, followed by the next numbered line, which contains the name of the ancestor and spouse's first child. If that child is married and has children, the child's spouse follows, as do the names and information on each of the child's and spouse's children.

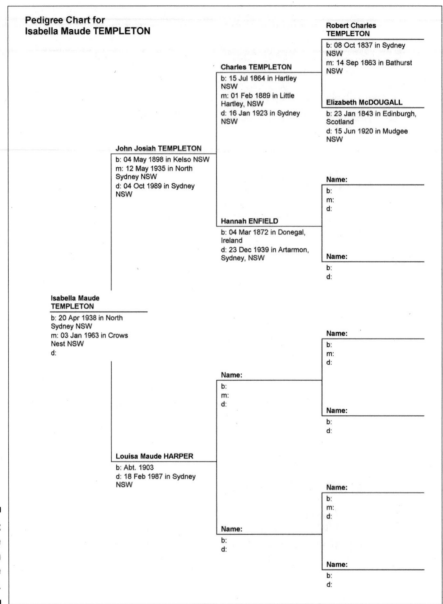

**Pedigree Chart for
Isabella Maude TEMPLETON**

**Robert Charles TEMPLETON**
b: 08 Oct 1837 in Sydney NSW
m: 14 Sep 1863 in Bathurst NSW

**Charles TEMPLETON**
b: 15 Jul 1864 in Hartley NSW
m: 01 Feb 1889 in Little Hartley, NSW
d: 16 Jan 1923 in Sydney NSW

**Elizabeth McDOUGALL**
b: 23 Jan 1843 in Edinburgh, Scotland
d: 15 Jun 1920 in Mudgee NSW

**John Josiah TEMPLETON**
b: 04 May 1898 in Kelso NSW
m: 12 May 1935 in North Sydney NSW
d: 04 Oct 1989 in Sydney NSW

**Name:**
b:
m:
d:

**Hannah ENFIELD**
b: 04 Mar 1872 in Donegal, Ireland
d: 23 Dec 1939 in Artarmon, Sydney, NSW

**Name:**
b:
d:

**Isabella Maude TEMPLETON**
b: 20 Apr 1938 in North Sydney NSW
m: 03 Jan 1963 in Crows Nest NSW
d:

**Name:**
b:
m:
d:

**Name:**
b:
m:
d:

**Name:**
b:
d:

**Louisa Maude HARPER**
b: Abt. 1903
d: 18 Feb 1987 in Sydney NSW

**Name:**
b:
m:
d:

**Name:**
b:
d:

**Name:**
b:
d:

**Name:**
b:
d:

**Figure 9-1:**
A pedigree chart in Family Tree Maker.

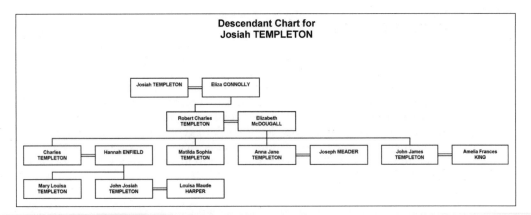

**Figure 9-2:** An example of a descendant chart in Family Tree Maker.

## Outline Descendant Report for Josiah TEMPLETON

..... 1  Josiah TEMPLETON (1800 - 1853) b: 13 Mar 1800 in London, England, d: 12 Oct 1853 in Hartley NSW

.....  + Eliza CONNOLLY (1809 - 1873) b: 03 Apr 1809 in Stepney London, m: 10 Dec 1836 in St James Church, Sydney NSW, d: 04 Dec 1873 in Kelso NSW

.......... 2  Robert Charles TEMPLETON (1837 - 1900) b: 08 Oct 1837 in Sydney NSW, d: 08 Sep 1900 in Dubbo NSW

..........  + Elizabeth McDOUGALL (1843 - 1920) b: 23 Jan 1843 in Edinburgh, Scotland, m: 14 Sep 1863 in Bathurst NSW, d: 15 Jun 1920 in Mudgee NSW

................ 3  Charles TEMPLETON (1864 - 1923) b: 15 Jul 1864 in Hartley NSW, d: 16 Jan 1923 in Sydney NSW

................  + Hannah ENFIELD (1872 - 1939) b: 04 Mar 1872 in Donegal, Ireland, m: 01 Feb 1889 in Little Hartley, NSW, d: 23 Dec 1939 in Artarmon, Sydney, NSW

...................... 4  Mary Louisa TEMPLETON (1893 - 1972) b: 23 Jun 1893 in Bathurst NSW, d: 04 Aug 1972 in Sydney NSW

...................... 4  John Josiah TEMPLETON (1898 - 1989) b: 04 May 1898 in Kelso NSW, d: 04 Oct 1989 in Sydney NSW

......................  + Louisa Maude HARPER (1903 - 1987) b: Abt. 1903, m: 12 May 1935 in North Sydney NSW, d: 18 Feb 1987 in Sydney NSW

............................ 5  Isabella Maude TEMPLETON (1938 - ) b: 20 Apr 1938 in North Sydney NSW

................ 3  Matilda Sophia TEMPLETON (1868 - 1870) b: 04 Sep 1868 in Hartley NSW, d: 09 Nov 1870

................ 3  Anna Jane TEMPLETON (1872 - 1933) b: 06 Apr 1872 in Hartley NSW, d: 02 Feb 1933 in Sydney NSW

................  + Joseph MEADER m: 15 Jun 1893 in Bathurst NSW

................ 3  John James TEMPLETON (1875 - 1923) b: 04 Nov 1875 in Bathurst NSW, d: 04 Mar 1923 in Melbourne Vic

................  + Amelia Frances KING (1870 - 1933) b: 04 Feb 1870 in Bathurst NSW, m: 12 Dec 1885 in Melbourne Vic, d: 18 Sep 1933 in Melbourne Vic

**Figure 9-3:** A family outline in Family Tree Maker.

## Family group sheets

A *family group sheet*, as shown in Figure 9-4, is a summary of information about a particular family unit. At the top of the page, it shows the husband, followed by the wife, and then any children of the couple, as well as biographical information (such as dates and places of birth, marriage and death). However, information on the children's spouses and children isn't included on this family group sheet; you can generate a separate family group sheet for each child's family (if applicable). Family group sheets generated by Family Tree Maker allow you to include a photograph of each individual.

## Kinship reports

A *kinship report* is a list of family members and how they relate directly to one particular person. The report includes the name of each family member and the person's relationship to the primary ancestor. The civil and canon codes reflecting the degree of relationship between the two people can also be generated for this report. Figure 9-5 shows an example of a kinship report generated by Family Tree Maker.

*Civil* and *canon codes* explain a bloodline relationship in legal terms — in other words, they identify how many degrees of separation (or steps) are between two people who are related by blood. *Civil law* counts each step between two relatives as a degree, so two people who are first cousins have a degree of separation equal to four, which is the total of two steps between one cousin and the common grandparent and two steps between the other cousin and the common grandparent. *Canon law* counts only the number of steps from the nearest common ancestor of both relatives, so the degree of separation between two first cousins is two: Two steps separate the grandparent from each of the cousins.

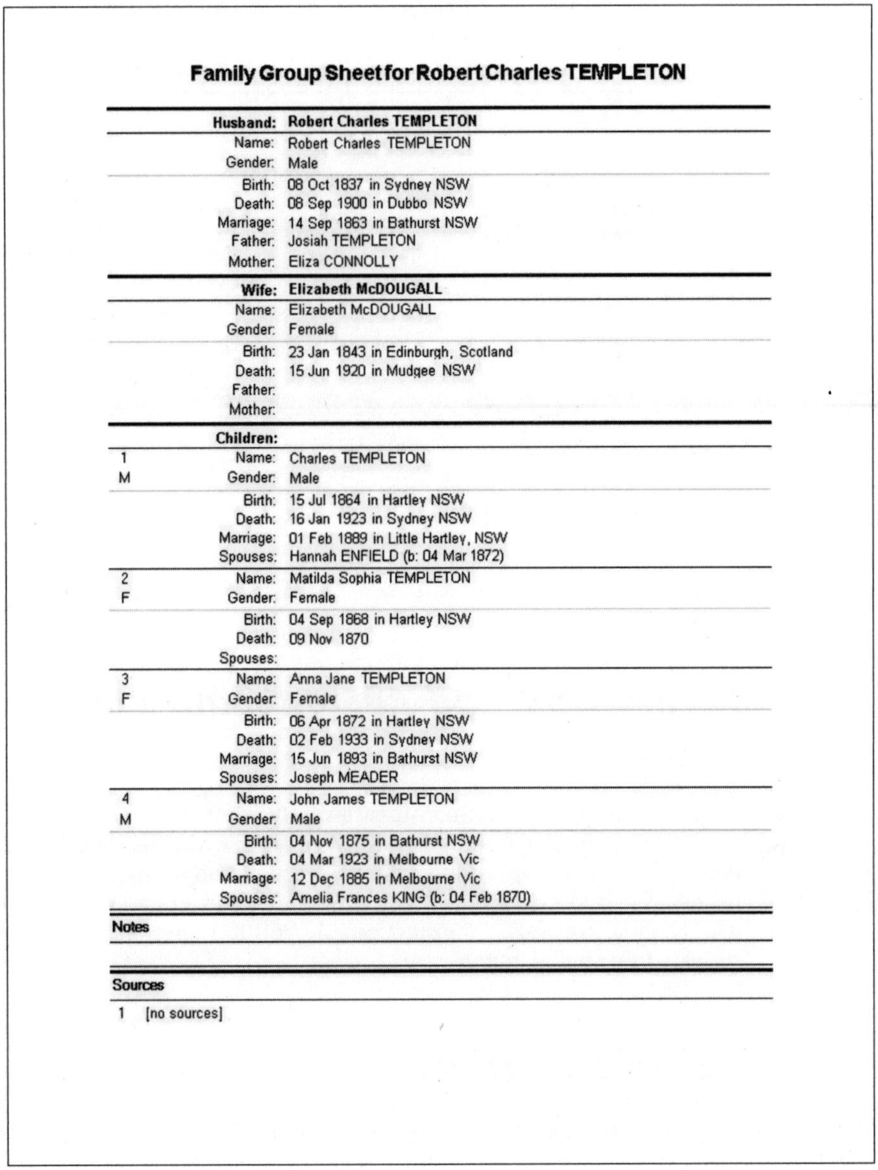

**Family Group Sheet for Robert Charles TEMPLETON**

| | | |
|---|---|---|
| **Husband:** | **Robert Charles TEMPLETON** | |
| | Name: | Robert Charles TEMPLETON |
| | Gender: | Male |
| | Birth: | 08 Oct 1837 in Sydney NSW |
| | Death: | 08 Sep 1900 in Dubbo NSW |
| | Marriage: | 14 Sep 1863 in Bathurst NSW |
| | Father: | Josiah TEMPLETON |
| | Mother: | Eliza CONNOLLY |
| | **Wife:** | **Elizabeth McDOUGALL** |
| | Name: | Elizabeth McDOUGALL |
| | Gender: | Female |
| | Birth: | 23 Jan 1843 in Edinburgh, Scotland |
| | Death: | 15 Jun 1920 in Mudgee NSW |
| | Father: | |
| | Mother: | |

**Children:**

| | | |
|---|---|---|
| 1 | Name: | Charles TEMPLETON |
| M | Gender: | Male |
| | Birth: | 15 Jul 1864 in Hartley NSW |
| | Death: | 16 Jan 1923 in Sydney NSW |
| | Marriage: | 01 Feb 1889 in Little Hartley, NSW |
| | Spouses: | Hannah ENFIELD (b: 04 Mar 1872) |
| 2 | Name: | Matilda Sophia TEMPLETON |
| F | Gender: | Female |
| | Birth: | 04 Sep 1868 in Hartley NSW |
| | Death: | 09 Nov 1870 |
| | Spouses: | |
| 3 | Name: | Anna Jane TEMPLETON |
| F | Gender: | Female |
| | Birth: | 06 Apr 1872 in Hartley NSW |
| | Death: | 02 Feb 1933 in Sydney NSW |
| | Marriage: | 15 Jun 1893 in Bathurst NSW |
| | Spouses: | Joseph MEADER |
| 4 | Name: | John James TEMPLETON |
| M | Gender: | Male |
| | Birth: | 04 Nov 1875 in Bathurst NSW |
| | Death: | 04 Mar 1923 in Melbourne Vic |
| | Marriage: | 12 Dec 1885 in Melbourne Vic |
| | Spouses: | Amelia Frances KING (b: 04 Feb 1870) |

**Notes**

**Sources**

1    [no sources]

**Figure 9-4:**
A family
group sheet
in Family
Tree Maker.

**Kinship Report for John Josiah TEMPLETON**

Kinship of John Josiah TEMPLETON

| Name: | Birth Date: | Relationship: |
| --- | --- | --- |
| CONNOLLY, Eliza | 03 Apr 1809 | Great Grandmother |
| ENFIELD, Hannah | 04 Mar 1872 | Mother |
| HARPER, Louisa Maude | Abt. 1903 | Wife |
| KING, Amelia Frances | 04 Feb 1870 | Aunt In Law |
| McDOUGALL, Elizabeth | 23 Jan 1843 | Grandmother |
| MEADER, Joseph | | Uncle In Law |
| TEMPLETON, Anna Jane | 06 Apr 1872 | Aunt |
| TEMPLETON, Charles | 15 Jul 1864 | Father |
| TEMPLETON, Isabella Maude | 20 Apr 1938 | Daughter |
| TEMPLETON, John James | 04 Nov 1875 | Uncle |
| TEMPLETON, John Josiah | 04 May 1898 | Self |
| TEMPLETON, Josiah | 13 Mar 1800 | Great Grandfather |
| TEMPLETON, Mary Louisa | 23 Jun 1893 | Sister |
| TEMPLETON, Matilda Sophia | 04 Sep 1868 | Aunt |
| TEMPLETON, Robert Charles | 08 Oct 1837 | Grandfather |

**Figure 9-5:**
An example
of a kinship
report in
Family Tree
Maker.

## Formatting and customising charts and reports

Keep in mind that you can control exactly what to include in each of these charts or reports by telling Family Tree Maker how many generations to include, to exclude particular ancestors, to change the types of information to include or to customise the appearance (borders and fonts). Other genealogical software programs enable you to manipulate your charts and reports in a similar manner.

## Additional reports

Other reports that may be useful to you include

- *Source lists*, which detail all the sources you've looked at and which individuals you found in each of those sources
- *Task lists*, which allow you to generate a 'to do' list of research you wish to carry out on a specific individual or family

The beauty of using genealogical software is that after you enter your family history information into the program, you can quickly generate any of these reports and see them on the screen.

# Understanding Which Hardware Options Are Your Genealogical Best Friends

As you grow more accustomed to using your software program, you may want to consider adding electronic images of some of the photographs and original documents that you have in your paper filing system. Perhaps you want to include a recording you made of your grandmother reminiscing about her childhood, or a video of your grandchild greeting people at a family reunion. As you find important documents like certificates and shipping lists, you may want to add images of them to your main database. So what kind of hardware or equipment do you need in order to include images and other enhancements in your genealogical database?

The most obvious pieces of equipment are a scanner and digital camera, to help you to record material in digital format. And if you're going to be out and about interviewing relatives, an MP3 player or similar recording equipment may be handy. You should also consider how you keep back-up copies of all the information you compile, so a writable CD-ROM or DVD drive, an external hard drive and a mini USB drive may all be useful additions.

You may already own some of this equipment, but if you don't the good news is that most of it's becoming increasingly affordable.

## Scanners

Scanners are one of the most popular computer peripherals for genealogists. Most family historians like to include some family photos with their genealogy and many prefer to preserve precious documents electronically. And with the cost of scanners decreasing, adding a scanner to your equipment collection can make your genealogical research more colourful and more efficient without making a big dent in your wallet.

Scanners work like photocopiers, but instead of copying a document, the scanner converts it into a graphics image in your computer. From there, you can modify the image, save it to disk, add it to a document or send it off as an email attachment.

A variety of scanners are available, and these days many come packaged as a multi-function centre (MFC) with a printer, photocopier and/or fax machine, which can save valuable desk space. Here are a few important points to remember when shopping for a scanner:

- **Flatbed scanners:** These are best for photographs because photos are laid on the scanner's glass rather than being fed through the device. With a flatbed scanner you lift the top of the scanner and place your document or photograph on the bed, close the lid and tell the scanner (through software) to capture the image.

  Some of the higher-priced flatbed scanners include options such as transparency adaptors (for scanning slides or negatives) and sheet feeders (for people who need to scan in large quantities of text), so consider whether these options are important to you before making your purchase.

- **Multi-function centre scanners:** Make sure that you receive easy-to-use scanning software as part of the bundle. Pay attention to the ink cartridge requirements too: It can cost more to refill or replace the ink cartridges than it does to buy the equipment! If you intend to print out many copies of your photographs and documents (to distribute to family members, for example), buy a unit with individual ink cartridges. Although these units may be more expensive initially, they can be more economical to run in the longer term.

- **Portable scanners:** You can find some very cheap portable scanners on the market that quite readily fit into your suitcase or the boot of your car. If you're visiting a relative you've never met before who turns out to be the family repository of photographs spanning the last 150 years, chances are you won't be allowed to borrow the photos to take home and scan if the person has only just met you. However, he or she may have no objection to you hooking up a small flatbed scanner to your laptop and instantly making copies of those sepia prints. In fact, your relative may be especially appreciative if you offer to leave an electronic copy of the photo collection that you burn there and then onto a CD or DVD.

Scanners are judged by their resolution, which is measured by the number of dots-per-inch (dpi) the scanner can read. The higher the dpi resolution, the better the scanned image.

## Digital cameras

Over the past couple of years, family historians have embraced digital cameras. Being able to take photographs with a camera that downloads the images directly to your computer — so that they can be easily imported into your genealogical database — is a great time saver and can be a very cost-effective way of gathering genealogical information.

A digital camera comes into its own when you're doing research away from home: You can store the images on your camera's memory card so that you don't have to carry paper copies around in your bag for the remainder of your trip.

Many libraries and record repositories permit you to use your digital camera to copy items from their collections. Most ban the use of flash photography because of concerns about exposing frail documents to sudden sharp light — as well as the annoyance the constant use of a flash can cause to others in the library. Having a digital camera on hand allows you to quickly and economically obtain a copy of an original certificate or document with relatively little fuss. In addition, you can often use your digital camera in conjunction with microfilm and microfiche machines to capture screen shots of items that you then email to other family contacts or add to your database.

Many libraries and archives can loan you a tripod or have an area set aside where you can use your digital camera to best effect. However, if you have you own small portable tripod in your camera bag, you can still take the best possible photographs if a tripod isn't available to borrow.

Imagine: You arrive home after a research trip and realise that you've got 350 photos from the archive you just visited, but no record of what the documents were that you photographed! To avoid such a scenario, before you start taking images of a file's contents, take a quick shot of the order slip you used to call up the document or the covering page of the file. You can delete these shots later when you download and identify the images that relate to each specific file.

As with every other computer peripheral, if you're considering purchasing a digital camera, carefully read the package and software requirements to make sure that the camera meets your expectations.

In general, the greater the number of pixels a digital camera can produce, the better quality your images (that is, the higher the resolution). Prices for digital cameras continue to come down, but the general rule applies that the higher the camera's resolution, the more costly it is to buy.

In addition, the software you use to manipulate the photographs after you store them on your computer is an important consideration. You may prefer to take very high-resolution images, but you won't want to email them to genealogical contacts around the world, as they are slow to transmit and quickly eat into your recipients' megabyte download limits. So you need software that can condense the images for you, ready to send as email attachments.

## Digital voice recorders

If you're going to be out and about visiting and interviewing relatives, you may like to use a digital voice recorder. The recorder connects to your computer via a USB port, allowing you to quickly transfer new audio files to your computer and also to make a back-up copy of each one. In addition, it's light to carry and isn't obtrusive sitting on a table in front of you recording your conversation as you talk about the family history with Aunty Flo. For example, say you have 20 photographs that you want Aunty Flo to help you identify. If she agrees to let you record your conversation while she looks at the photos, you'll find it much easier later on to listen to the recording and transcribe the information she was able to give you than to be hurriedly writing down everything she says while at the same time directing the discussion. And at the end of the day you also have her voice on record, which can become a lovely addition to your family memorabilia.

Begin any recording session by giving a short introduction containing the names of those involved in the recording and the date and place where the recording is taking place. If more than two people are being interviewed, ask them to state their names and introduce themselves at the beginning, so that later listeners can identify which voice belongs to which person.

When you record your relatives' stories and conversations, remember to respect their wishes about what they say to you. Explain how you intend to use the audio files and get their permission to do so. Aunty Flo may be comfortable telling you that the lady in the front row of the Sunday School photograph ran off with the husband of the pretty woman standing next to her, causing a major scandal in their home town in 1948. However, she won't necessarily want you to divulge what she really thought of them for all the world to hear through the audio file you load to your website, especially if she still lives in that same town today.

# Back-up tools

All computer users should back up their vital data, and genealogists working with multimedia usually discover they need extra storage beyond their hard drive sooner rather than later. A variety of handy tools are available for storing data and multimedia files, and these are getting cheaper by the week while being able to accommodate more and more data:

- ✔ **CD or DVD reader/burner:** Most new PCs are packaged with a CD or DVD reader/burner, which lets you 'burn' your own CDs or DVDs — all you need is a set of the appropriate blank disks. CDs are cheaper than DVDs but hold less data — about 800 megabytes for CDs compared with 5 gigabytes for DVDs — but CDs are a very affordable way of distributing information to other family members and researchers. Cheaper disks cannot be reused: After you fill a disk to its capacity, you cannot delete the data and reuse the disk.

- ✔ **Mini USB drive:** Also known as a flash drive or thumb drive, this is a great tool for family historians. You can take this portable drive anywhere and use it in any compatible computer that has a spare USB slot — you simply plug it into the USB port for instant access. Mini USB drives can even be 'locked' for security and the data stored on them can be encrypted, so that if you lose your mini drive no-one can access your personal information. Mini USB drives are a terrific way of transporting data from one computer to another and making an instantaneous back-up of the file or database you're working on.

- ✔ **Portable external hard drive:** This is a more robust way of backing up and storing data. The drive is about the size of a small paperback book and connects via a USB socket. It is a great way of making a more permanent back-up of your computer files, and can be programmed to perform a back-up at a specified time each day or week if you wish.

With the hardware required to back up your files getting more and more portable, as well as more and more affordable, you have no excuse for not making regular back-ups. Your computer will fail one day, and it would be horrible to lose years of work when it does. Use a combination of the previously mentioned technologies to ensure that when your computer has a bad day, you don't lose all your hard work.

# Carrying Your Genealogy Files on the Run

Whether you head off to a family reunion, travel a couple of hundred kilometres to research in a particular town or go on a genealogical holiday interstate or overseas, chances are you may eventually want to take your show on the road. If you're just testing the waters to see whether buying a computer for genealogical purposes is worth your time and money, you may want to consider getting a laptop or notebook computer instead of a desktop system. Portable computers give you the flexibility to take your genealogical database with you wherever you go, as well as some presentation possibilities that desktop systems don't allow because of their size.

If you wish to buy a portable computer to take with you on your travels, you may like to consider a *netbook*, which is specifically designed to be transportable. Netbooks are light to carry, quite small to pack into a briefcase or bag and very cheap. In addition to basic word-processing and database capabilities, netbooks usually come packaged with wireless internet and webcam. Bear in mind, however, that the compromise for making these computers so portable is usually reflected in the small keyboard and screen. Practise typing on a system before you buy it, and if you're likely to be storing a lot of text, check out a sample of text on the screen so you can decide how comfortable you feel using the device.

Suppose you already own a desktop system and aren't in the market to buy a netbook? Don't worry! Earlier in this chapter we discussed other means for storing and transporting your data and reports without spending money on a second computer. Of course, the drawback to taking your genealogy records on, say, a mini USB drive to a family reunion is that you need a computer at the other end that can not only handle your USB drive but also allow you to access the information contained on it. So, before you take a mini USB drive or DVD with all your family information to that reunion at Aunty Elsie's, make sure that Aunty Elsie's computer has a USB port or DVD drive and any necessary software to open the contents of your disk.

You're wasting your time taking along a copy of your family history files from a program like Family Tree Maker if the computer of the person you're visiting doesn't have the same software: You won't be able to readily open your files on that computer. And if you've just met the other person, he probably won't want you to import GEDCOM files into his computer.

If you plan to carry out research on your travels, bear in mind that many libraries are set up for researchers using notebook computers and can provide you with desk space and access to electricity. However, try to have a fully charged battery on hand in case you're not able to sit near a power outlet.

The library or archive you're visiting may permit you to download its electronic images and records directly to an external storage device: Check whether you're allowed to use your own flash drive or have to purchase a CD-ROM and then burn the image straight to that medium yourself. Some repositories charge a small fee for using your own digital equipment to compensate them for the loss of photocopying revenue, while others simply require you to fill out an appropriate copyright release form.

# Hit the Road, Jack! Planning Your Genealogy Travels Using the Web

At no time are you likely to find the internet so useful as when you're planning to venture away from home to visit new-found relatives (or long-lost ones) or to research at a distant repository. Whether you're going to the next town, interstate or overseas, the internet is an invaluable research tool.

We don't need to tell you that you can plan your travel experience without leaving your lounge room if you wish. Airfares, train and bus trips, accommodation and all sorts of other essential travel information can be obtained and arrangements made online.

If your visit involves going to a records office, library or genealogical society, you need to spend time online visiting the organisation's website and checking out the following:

- ✔ The location of the building
- ✔ The organisation's opening hours (days as well as times — and be mindful of local public holidays, especially if you're travelling overseas)
- ✔ Whether you need to book or make an appointment to see someone
- ✔ Whether you need to take any special identification with you

Planning is crucial: Imagine travelling across the world and only allocating Tuesday to visit a specific repository, simply to find out when you get there that this is the one day of the week it isn't open to researchers!

Additionally, the internet can offer you so much more as a researcher. Here are two examples:

✔ **Google doc account:** Need to keep to an itinerary while travelling but don't want to take reams of paper with you? Have some specific checklists of research you need to do, and places you need to visit, but worried you may misplace these lists on your travels? By registering with Google and setting up a free Google doc account, you can upload files and create online documents in your account, and then access them from anywhere in the world — as long as you have internet access. Google doc accounts have quite generous storage allowances. So, for example, you can store the key dates of ancestors' lives, or the names of all their children and when they were born. Then, when you're overseas conducting more research, even if you don't have your notebook computer with you and you can't access your genealogical database on your flash drive, you can go online, open your Google doc account and read (and alter) your documents.

You can use your account to keep in contact with others too, because you can share your account and password details with trusted friends and relatives and invite them to collaborate with you online. For example, you may like to load a document into the account and ask two or three relatives to make additions and corrections — whenever they choose and wherever they are.

✔ **Webmail:** If you have an email account, you should be able to set up a webmail feature with your internet service provider so that you can access and send emails using your normal email address while you're on the road. Again, all you need is internet access. Check with your provider to see whether it offers this feature. If not, you can register for a free email account through companies like Google and Yahoo! In fact, when you're travelling you may prefer to set up a temporary email address using one of these free services.

Don't have a laptop or notebook to take on your travels? No problem. Competition for internet access is so fierce, you can probably find a reasonably priced internet cafe during your travels where you can pay for access while you check your emails and files.

Many repositories and local libraries provide free internet access to visitors. In addition, if you have a laptop with wireless internet capabilities, remember that an increasing number of hotels, cafes and libraries around the world now offer free wireless internet — from five-star hotel lobbies to McDonald's restaurants!

# Part IV
# Share and Share Alike

*'I've just downloaded three hundred new relatives in two minutes. Now that's what I call quality family time!'*

## In this part ...

The chapters in this part show you how to maximise your online research by effectively using as many resources as possible and by sharing your information with others. This part addresses sharing information using reports, GEDCOM and web pages that you create yourself, as well as how to coordinate research efforts. Along the way, you also find out about the best way to respect others' privacy and copyright.

# Chapter 10

# Coordinating Your Attack: Getting Help from Other Researchers

· · · · · · · · · · · · · · · · · · · · · · · · · · · · · · · · · · · · · · ·

· · · · · · · · · · · · · · · · · · · · · · · · · · · · · · · · · · · · · · ·

*T*hink of genealogical research as a long journey. You may begin the journey by yourself, but before long, you discover that time goes a lot faster when someone else is along for the ride. In your genealogical journey, these travel partners may appear in the form of individuals researching the same family, a research group searching for several branches of a family in which you're interested, or a genealogical society that coordinates the efforts of several individuals researching different families.

In this chapter, we explore ways of finding (and keeping) research partners, as well as ways that research groups and genealogical societies can help you to meet your research goals.

## Finding Others to Share Your Journey

Don't put all your eggs in one basket — so the old saying goes. A variation of this adage applies to genealogical research — don't try to do all the research yourself. As you'll discover, an awful lot of people out there are researching family trees, and it would be a shame for you not to take advantage of the work that they have done, and vice versa.

## *Avoiding the shotgun approach*

You're probably wondering how to find individuals to share your information with. Well, you could start by going through telephone books and ringing everyone with the surname that you're researching. But given how some people feel about telemarketers, we don't recommend this as a strategy.

Similarly, you can send mass emails to anyone that you find with your surname through one of the online *White Pages* sites. We refer to this mass email strategy as the *shotgun approach*. Although you may find one or two people who answer you in a positive way, a lot of people can find your unsolicited email irritating or downright intrusive.

Instead of incurring the wrath of hundreds of people, go to a site focusing on genealogy to find the names of researchers who're interested in your surname — this is a much better way to go about finding others with the same interests as you.

We aren't saying that email directories and online telephone listings don't have a function in genealogy. Email directories can be a good place to find an email address that you've lost or an address of a relative who may be interested in your research. You can also use online telephone directories to check the distribution of your surname in a specific area, state or country, which may help you to track down living descendants. We like Infobel World (www.infobel.com), which lets you find anyone, anywhere in the world (see Figure 10-1).

## *Making (and keeping) friends online*

The best place to begin your search for others doing similar research to you is Genes Reunited (www.genesreunited.com). You need to register to use the site and to use its full features you need to become a subscriber (currently this costs $19.95 for six months), but the site has more than nine million members, so you may very well find others who're doing the same research as you. When you register, you're encouraged to load some of your own family history information onto the site.

After you register at Genes Reunited, you can find out whether others are researching the same family members as you. Here's how.

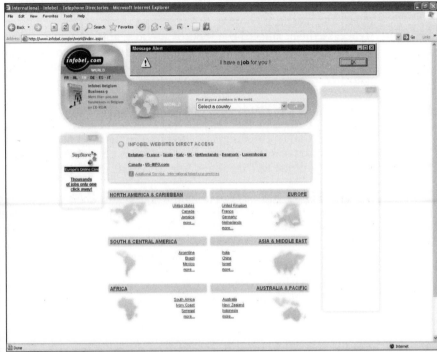

**Figure 10-1:**
Infobel
World links
to online
telephone
directories
around the
globe.

1. **Go to** www.genesreunited.com.

2. **Type the name and location of one of the relatives you're trying to trace in the Find Your Family box and click on the Search button.**

   For example, enter the details for one of your grandparents.

3. **Click on the View Tree Matches link.**

   If anyone else has registered that same person, you see a listing showing those 'hits' together with the first name of the person who submitted the information.

4. **To make contact with someone on the listing, click on the Find Out More button.**

   This sets up an automated email, which you send to the person via your ISP.

The beauty of using Genes Reunited is that you don't have to reveal your email address or details to others: All initial contact is made through the site.

Genes Reunited also offers access to parts of the English census and birth, death and marriage records, but you have to pay a higher subscription fee to access them. Since these records are available on a variety of other sites (see Chapter 7 for more details), we recommend that you concentrate on using Genes Reunited for the purpose of trying to find other researchers who share common ancestors with you.

Another source of data is the RootsWeb Surname List (`rsl.rootsweb.ancestry.com`), a page from which is shown in Figure 10-2 for the surname Kelly. The RootsWeb Surname List is part of the Ancestry.com stable and currently contains information on more than 1.2 million surnames being searched worldwide. The site is free to search.

A search shows you a list of individuals, the surnames they're researching and the geographic locations and date ranges where those surnames are of interest to them. This is another great way to quickly check whether someone else out there is doing research on the same family and in the same area as you. (For more info on using the RootsWeb Surname List, see Chapter 3.)

Unlike Genes Reunited, RootsWeb gives you the email addresses of those who've submitted entries to the site so that you can contact them directly.

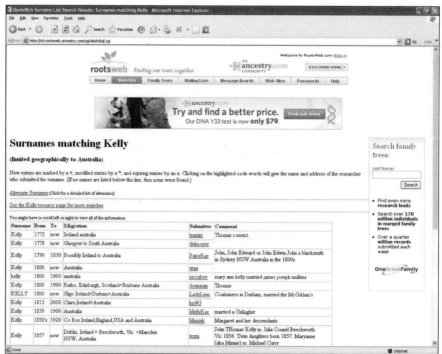

**Figure 10-2:**
Entries for the surname 'Kelly' in Australia on the RootsWeb Surname List.

Advertising your own research interests is also an excellent way to ensure that others get to know about the families you're tracing. You can participate in mailing lists (if you need a refresher on using these or other surname resources, check out Chapter 3), register your details with online directories and use any printed sources you can find to publicise your interests. (See Chapter 3 for more information on research methods.)

The *Genealogical Research Directory*, or GRD, was published annually from 1979 until 2007. Each year it contained thousands of entries placed by researchers from around the globe, particularly Australia. The directory is available on CD-ROM and in book form in many libraries, and is well worth checking as a means of tracking down people who may already have done work on the family lines you're tracing. Alternatively, you can still buy back issues through the online bookshop of Gould Genealogy (www.gould.com.au) or the Society of Australian Genealogists (www.sag.org.au).

After you identify some potential online friends, you can send them email messages introducing yourself, briefly explaining your purpose for contacting them and giving the names of the ancestors you're researching — but hold off sending anything until you read the following tips.

Before you contact people, we want to give you a few pieces of advice:

- ✔ **Before sending a message to a website maintainer (or owner), make sure that the person can use or respond to information on the surname you're researching:** Don't send a message if the website displays a notice stating that it doesn't personally answer research questions. In such cases, these sites are facilitators, helping individual researchers to communicate with each other: The sites can't help you with your individual research.

- ✔ **Don't disclose personal information that could violate a person's privacy:** Information such as address details and birth dates for living persons is considered private and shouldn't be freely shared with other researchers you've just met on the internet. (See Chapter 11 for more on privacy issues.)

- ✔ **Ensure that your message has enough detail for the recipients to decide whether the information relates to their research:** Include names, dates and places as appropriate.

- ✔ **Get permission before forwarding messages from other researchers:** Sometimes a researcher may provide information that he or she doesn't want made available to the general public. Asking permission before forwarding a message to a third party eliminates any potential problems that could violate the trust of your fellow researchers.

- ✔ **Make your message brief and to the point:** An email message that runs to five or six pages can overwhelm some people. If the person you send the message to is interested in your information, you can send a more-detailed message at a future date.

✔ **Use net etiquette, or** *netiquette*, **when you create your messages:** Remember, email can be an impersonal medium. Although you may mean one thing, someone who doesn't know you may mistakenly misinterpret your message. (For more on netiquette, see the sidebar 'Netiquette: Communicating politely on the internet'.)

# Netiquette: Communicating politely on the internet

Part of becoming a member of the online genealogy community is learning to communicate effectively and politely on the internet. Online communication is often hampered by the fact that you can't see the people with whom you're corresponding — and you can't hear the intonation of their voices to determine what emotions they're expressing. To avoid misunderstandings, follow some simple guidelines — called *netiquette* — when writing messages online:

✔ Be careful when you respond to messages. Instead of replying to an individual, you may be replying to an entire group of people. Check the To line before you press the Send button.

✔ Don't send a message that you wouldn't want posted on a noticeboard at work. Expect that every email you send is potentially public.

✔ If you participate in a mailing list or newsgroup, and you want to reply with a message that interests only one person, consider sending that person a message individually rather than emailing the list or group as a whole.

✔ If you receive a *flame* (a heated message usually sent to provoke a response), try to ignore it. Usually, no good comes from responding to a flame.

✔ Make sure that you don't violate any copyright laws by sending large portions of written/published works through email. (For more information on copyright, see Chapter 11.)

✔ Use mixed case when writing email messages. USING ALL UPPERCASE LETTERS INDICATES SHOUTING! The exception to this is when you send a query and place your surname in all uppercase letters, such as George HAMMOND.

✔ When joking, use smileys or type <grins> or <g>. A *smiley* is an emoticon that looks like :-). (Turn the book on its right side if you can't see the face.) *Emoticons* are graphics created by combinations of keys on the keyboard to express an emotion within an email. Here are a few emoticons that you may run into:

:-) Happy, smiling

;-) Wink, ironic

:-> Sarcastic

:-( Sad, unhappy

:-< Disappointed

:-o Frightened, surprised

We can't emphasise enough the benefits of sharing genealogical data. Sharing is the foundation on which the genealogical community is built. In fact, you're probably not the only person interested in your particular family line. Even at this moment, another distant family historian somewhere else in the world may be trying to track down the arrival of your family's first immigrant ancestor into Australia, or looking for that pre-1700 baptism of an ancestor in Hertfordshire.

By tapping into what other researchers are pursuing, you can coordinate with them not only to share information you've already collected, but also to work together towards your common goal. Maybe you live near a government archive centre and can check shipping records of common ancestors, while a distant cousin who's also researching the family tree lives closer to a cemetery where some descendants are buried. Rather than duplicating efforts to collect information, you can divide the workload and share the results over the internet or through traditional mail. Many lifelong genealogical friendships are formed in this way, and you can share the highs and lows — and costs — of the research as you go.

# Forming Research Groups

Are your relatives tired of hearing about your genealogy research trips or the information that you found on your grandmother's 37 first cousins, but you still want to share your triumphs with someone? Then you may be ready to join a research group. *Research groups* consist of any number of people who coordinate their research and share resources to achieve success. These groups may conduct research based on a surname, family branch or geographic location. Individuals who live geographically close to each other may make up a research group, or the group may consist of people who've never personally met each other. Research groups may have a variety of goals and may have a formal or an informal structure. They are quite flexible organisationally and depend entirely on the membership of the group.

Members of informal research groups contribute the results of their own personal research that may be of use to others. As a whole, the group may sponsor research by a professional genealogist in another country to help everyone in the group to get more information on common ancestors. Such a cooperative venture is not only fun, but also cost-effective.

An example of a more formal research group is the DASHPER family website (www.dashper.net.nz), shown in Figure 10-3, which aims to coordinate research on the surname Dashper throughout the world — especially its origins in the United Kingdom. The site offers online access to records collected from a variety of sources, such as census data, and acts as a hub for those researching the name to share their work, pictures and research queries.

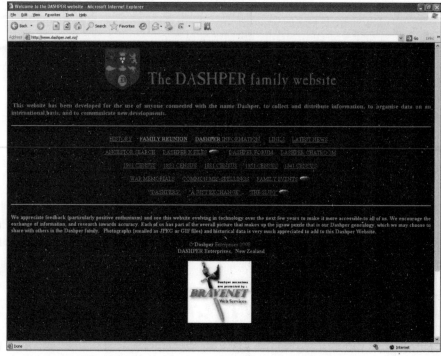

Figure 10-3:
The
research
group for
the Dashper
family
name.

One of the easiest ways to track down individuals interested in the same surname as you is to visit websites specifically created for that surname. The Registry of Websites at RootsWeb (www.rootsweb.ancestry.com/~websites) is one of your best stops for finding these sites. Simply choose a letter from the alphabet and then scroll through the list to see whether a site is registered for the name you're interest in. Sometimes you find a number of sites registered for one surname.

Become familiar with different sites on the internet that relate to names you're researching — even those you initially find to be of no use. While a vast majority of these sites are probably US-based, their researchers are no doubt ultimately hoping to trace their ancestry back to Ireland or England (or some such region), just as you are. Although you may not be interested in their immediate ancestry in Virginia or Kentucky, you may link back into the same family in Wicklow or Manchester. You may even be able to contribute to their research — your findings on the surname in Australia may involve descendants of the family who came to this part of the world that your American counterparts know nothing about.

In addition to using comprehensive genealogy websites and specialised surname sites, you can use other strategies to identify possible research groups. One option for finding research groups pertaining to surnames is to visit a one-name studies index. The Guild of One-Name Studies website (www.one-name.org) has a searchable listing of one-name studies sites. Such sites are more than just web-based listings of research interests: Each site represents an organisation of researchers committed to researching all occurrences of a specific surname anywhere in the world.

If you can't find an established online group that fits your interests, why not start one yourself? If you're interested in researching a particular topic, chances are others are interested too. In fact, maybe the time has come for you to coordinate efforts and begin working with others towards your common research goals. Starting an online research group can be relatively easy — just post a message stating your interest in starting a group at some key locations, such as RootsWeb. You can also set up a web page to serve as the central resource for anyone researching a particular topic, area or family. (See Chapter 12 for details on setting up your own web page.) Soon (hopefully) others will visit your site, and you can begin to coordinate your efforts with them.

# Becoming a Solid Member of (Genealogical) Society

Genealogical societies can be great places to discover family history records and to get help in finetuning your research methods. Many societies run regular lectures or courses that can help you to further your knowledge on aspects of research, and nearly all are operated by volunteers who are experienced researchers ready and willing to share their knowledge and give advice. In addition, many volunteers have excellent knowledge of the local community in which their society is based.

## Searching out geographically based genealogical societies

A *geographically based genealogical society* can be a group that helps you to discover resources in a particular area in which your ancestors lived or a group in your town that helps you to discover how to research effectively. A local genealogical society can also provide a service to its members by sponsoring projects that coordinate the local research efforts of its members.

To locate a geographically based society, consult a genealogical gateway site such as GENUKI (www.genuki.org.uk) or Coraweb (www.coraweb.com.au). Alternatively, check out the website of a family history federation in the country of interest to you. For example:

✔ **Australia:** The Australasian Federation of Family History Organisations at www.affho.org

✔ **United Kingdom:** The Federation of Family History Societies at www.ffhs.org.uk

✔ **United States:** The Federation of Genealogical Societies' Society Hall at www.familyhistory.com/societyhall

More sources for locating geographical societies are listed in Chapter 4.

Locate a genealogical society in an area where you have research interests and check out the projects currently underway (these are often listed on the society's website). For example, the society may be preparing a biographical register of all the pioneers who lived in that area, focusing on an historic event (see Figure 10-4) or perhaps transcribing the local cemetery records.

Smaller groups of members sometimes work on projects in addition to the society's official projects. For example, as a member of a local genealogical society, you may decide to hook up with a few other members to write a history on the pioneers of a particular township within the district.

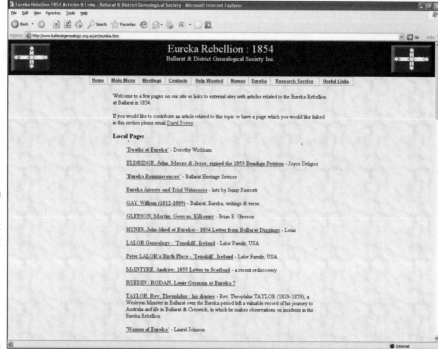

**Figure 10-4:**
The Ballarat & District Genea-logical Society's Eureka Rebellion project.

Even if you don't live locally, you may be able to become involved in the work of the society, helping with data entry, checking information or contributing your own research. The point is, when members share the fruits of their research, they can cover three or four times more ground than they can by going it alone.

## Finding family and surname associations

Groups that are tied to particular names or family groups are known as *family associations* or *surname associations*. Family associations also frequently sponsor projects that coordinate the efforts of several researchers regarding a particular surname or family group. These projects may focus on the family or surname in a specific geographical area or point in time, or they may attempt to collect information about every individual possessing the surname throughout time and then place the information in a shared database.

You can find family and surname associations through websites specialising in associations, such as RootsWeb (`www.rootsweb.ancestry.com/~websites`).

If a family or surname association isn't currently working on a project that interests you, by all means suggest a project that does interest you (as long as the project is relevant to the association as a whole). Family associations are also covered in Chapter 3.

# Increasing Your Social Network

You'd have to be living on a desert island to avoid hearing about the popularity of what's generally called *online social networking*. These days, social networking isn't just about teenagers being on the phone all night while they organise parties with friends when they're meant to be doing their homework. Certainly that happens, but social networking is now a regular part of daily life for many Australians — and not just those still at school. Online networking is changing the way people communicate with their friends, work colleagues, family and probably even strangers!

*Facebook* is the best known social networking website. The Facebook website consists of individuals who load their own profiles to the website and then invite their friends to connect to them and join their Facebook group.

Here's an example. Tom Smith of Melbourne invites his old school friend Peter Turner of Perth to be his friend on Facebook. Tom leaves messages about what he's been doing since they were both at school together (this is known as leaving a posting *on the wall*). After Peter becomes Tom's friend on Facebook, Peter can reply to these postings and add details about what he's been doing. Of course, since Peter moved to Perth he's found a whole new circle of friends and colleagues, so he invites all of them to join him on Facebook. One of Peter's friends is Brian Morton, and before long Tom begins interacting with Brian while chatting with Peter on Facebook. And so through Facebook Peter finds a new friend called Brian who lives on the other side of the country and whom he has never met — and possibly never will. The friends can chat live online, leave messages on the wall, load pictures, videos and much more — all for free.

Bear in mind that 'friends' is a bit of a loose term and simply means someone you know or who you've met through Facebook who's linked their page to yours. Some people only have a couple of friends on Facebook, while others have heaps — Barack Obama's friends on Facebook number in the millions, and you can bet he's never personally met the vast majority of them!

Facebook is a very public forum, so it isn't the place to gossip about another mutual friend or give away secrets.

To find out more about Facebook, check out www.facebook.com. You'll be prompted to register and load your own profile before you can start looking around.

When you subscribe to Facebook, you're introducing yourself to an online community of millions of other subscribers, so you may not want to answer all the questions you'll be asked. You must provide your date of birth to register, so we'd suggest you initially record just your name, sex, date of birth and country of residence. After you subscribe and enter the site, you have the opportunity to view and change your profile. You can either remove your date of birth from your public profile or simply record the year of your birth and not your full birth date: We suggest you select one of these options straight away.

The opportunity for finding out more about your family history on Facebook is huge. Facebook has many features, including the following:

- ✓ **Group section:** Although this feature wasn't designed specifically to help family historians, you can certainly use it as yet another source of online contacts for those with an interest in the same name as you are researching. For example, many clubs and societies have pages. The Society of Australian Genealogists has a page where members can go online and chat with other participants.

You can also find family historians with an online forum for their research interests. For example, the Timmerman family has a group on Facebook — people with that surname join the group, and others with an interest in that name can find them using a simple Facebook search. Similarly, you can find groups formed around a specific research interest, such as German research.

✔ **We're Related:** This is one of the fastest growing areas on the site and it's based on family history. The idea is that you load a basic family tree about your family so that others who find your profile can determine whether they're connected to you genealogically. This becomes an interactive project for families to share and develop together. Many young people are using Facebook to keep in contact with their aunts, uncles and grandparents, and the We're Related feature gives them an opportunity to share family history information that they may otherwise never discuss with each other — especially if they don't see each other very often. This isn't designed to be the main application in which you develop your online family history presence, but it's a great way to get family members interested in your family history and encourage them to contribute their own details.

At last count, more than 150 million people around the world were signed up for Facebook. If you haven't already explored the website, we suggest it's another place where you're sure to find people with an interest in your family's name and history.

# Examining Your DNA: Where Do You Really Come From?

One of the most exciting developments in genealogy in recent years is the progress that's been made in deoxyribonucleic acid (DNA) testing. DNA molecules in the human body are responsible for transferring genetic characteristics, and DNA testing can provide clues about your origins, for example, or help determine whether two people are related to each other.

If some media reports and television police dramas are to be believed, to find out who you really are, all you need is to run a DNA test on a strand of your hair or a small sample of your saliva and presto, your lineage is instantly identifiable, enabling you to trace your family tree back more generations than you ever dreamed is possible.

Not surprisingly, of course, the science isn't that simple. DNA is a complex subject. It's also an area of science that's developing very quickly. Within a few years, genealogists who wish to utilise DNA in their research will no doubt have more opportunities than they have today.

Without getting bogged down in the science, two types of DNA test exist:

- ✔ *Mitochondrial DNA (or mtDNA) testing*, which looks at the female line. Both men and women possess mtDNA, but only women can pass it on to their children. However, male members of the family, such as cousins and brothers, can take an mtDNA test.

- ✔ *Y chromosome testing*, which looks at the male line. The Y chromosome is carried only by males, so for this test you must find a brother, cousin or father who's willing to provide a DNA sample. The Y chromosome test is used more regularly by genealogists, because the male line usually carries the surname and so has been embraced by many one-name groups, clans and surname studies.

All DNA testing is done by collecting a saliva swab from inside the mouth. So you can reassure any reluctant family members who don't like needles and think you want a blood sample!

mtDNA is probably best seen as 'deep genealogy'. One of the best-known projects researching deep genealogy is the Genographic Project run by the National Geographic Society. For more details, check out www.genographic. nationalgeographic.com/genographic/index.html. You may also have heard of Bryan Sykes' deep genealogy work, *The Seven Daughters of Eve*, where he established that everyone of European origin is descended from one of seven women who lived between 10,000 and 45,000 years ago. Having an mtDNA test tells you which one of these seven women you're most likely descended from. However, although this information may be of general interest, it isn't going to advance your family history research a great deal.

A Y chromosome test may be useful if you can find enough males who share the same surname and who are likely to have had their origins in the same area — for example, an Australian and an American who share the same surname and who both believe they are descended from a common family in the same small village in Wiltshire in the United Kingdom.

The result you get from a DNA test won't mean much to the average person, because it's shown as a series of numbers or 'markers'. The more expensive the test, the more markers it checks and hence the more defined the results. Current recommendations are that you undertake a test that checks at least 20 markers (out of a total 43). If our example American and Australian have very few matching markers, they aren't descended from the same man who lived in the Wiltshire village. Conversely, the more markers that match, the more likely it is that the two men have a connection.

Notice that we said the *more likely* they have a connection, not that they definitely have a connection. The reason for this is that DNA testing is not an exact science — it simply shows the probability (or likelihood) that something is true.

If you don't want to test your own DNA, or are just curious, you can check out a number of websites to see what names have already been tested. In some cases these sites allow you to view family trees of those tested to determine whether the surname is 'yours' or not. One example is the Sorenson Molecular Genealogy Foundation (www.smgf.org), which collected samples from a number of Australian genealogists a few years ago (see Figure 10-5).

DNA testing is still quite expensive and you need to understand the limitations of any test you undertake. Check out the following websites for more information about the tests available, how much they cost and the results you receive:

- Ancestry.com (dna.ancestry.com)
- DNA Heritage (www.dnaheritage.com)
- Oxford Ancestors (www.oxfordancestors.com)

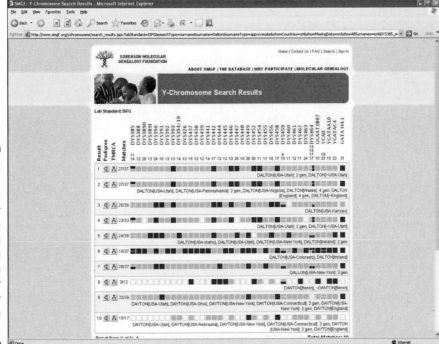

**Figure 10-5:** Y Chromosome results for the name Dalton on the Sorenson Molecular Genealogy Foundation website.

In addition to looking at these websites, you may like to go to the following sites to read more about the role of DNA in genealogy and to see some data results:

- ✔ EthnoAncestry (EthnoAncestry.com)
- ✔ Family Tree DNA (FamilyTreeDNA.com)
- ✔ International Society of Genetic Genealogy (www.isogg.org)
- ✔ RootsWeb DNA mailing list (lists.rootsweb.ancestry.com/index/other/DNA/GENEALOGY-DNA.html)

A word of caution about DNA testing: You may find out something you'd rather not know — for example, that you or other family members are not biologically related to the family from which you think you descend. Although such instances are rare, you do need to be aware of the possibility of such results if you decide to explore your DNA.

# Chapter 11

# Sharing Your Wealth Online

. . . . . . . . . . . . . . . . . . . . . . . . . . . . . . . . . .

## In This Chapter

▶ Understanding why sharing is important

▶ Marketing your research

▶ Exporting your work from your genealogical database

▶ Citing electronic resources

▶ Paying attention to privacy issues

▶ Coping with copyright

. . . . . . . . . . . . . . . . . . . . . . . . . . . . . . . . . .

*A*fter you hit a certain point in your research, you may want to find ways to share the valuable information you've discovered — after all, sharing information is one of the foundations of the genealogical community. When you share information, you often get a lot of information in return from other researchers. For example, when you create your own family-based website, other people with interests in that family are likely to contact you. They may have already managed to scale that genealogical brick wall you're still contemplating and even tell you about lines of the family you didn't know existed.

In this chapter, we focus on methods that you can use to share information (except for placing your information on the World Wide Web, which we cover in Chapter 12) and ways to let other researchers know that you have information to share.

# Why Would Anyone Want Your Stuff?

'Why would anyone want my stuff?' seems like a logical first question when you stop and think about making the many tidbits and treasures that you've collected available to others. Who would want a copy of that old, ratty-looking photograph you have of your great-great-grandmother as a girl sitting in a pile of dirt on a farm in Longreach? Nobody else wanted it in the first place, and that's probably how you ended up with it, right? The picture has sentimental value only to you. Wrong! Some of your great-great-grandmother's other descendants may be looking for information about her. They, too, would love to see a picture of her when she was a little girl — even better, they'd love to have their own electronic copy of that picture!

As you develop more and more online contact with other genealogists, you may find a lot of people who're interested in exchanging information. Some may be interested in your research findings because you share common ancestors, and others may be interested because they're researching in the same geographical area where your ancestors were from. Aren't these the reasons that you're interested in seeing other researchers' stuff? Sharing your information is likely to encourage others to share theirs with you. Exchanging information with others may enable you to fill in some gaps in your own research efforts. Even if the research findings that you receive from others don't directly answer questions about your ancestors, they may give you clues about where to find more information to fill in the blanks.

Also, just because you haven't traced your genealogy back to the Middle Ages doesn't mean that your information isn't valuable. Although you need to be careful about sharing information on living persons, you should feel free to share any facts you do know about deceased ancestors. Just as you may not know your genealogy any further than your great-grandfather, someone else may be in the same boat — and with the same person! Meeting up with that fellow researcher can lead to a mutual research relationship that can produce a lot more information in a shorter amount of time.

# Spreading the Word on What You Have

So you're at the point where you recognise the value in sharing your genealogical information online. How do you begin to let people know what you have? Well, the first thing you need to do is to come up with a marketing plan for your information — much like a business does when it decides to sell a product.

## Masterminding a surname marketing plan

A *surname marketing plan* is simply a checklist of places and people to contact to effectively inform the right individuals about the information that you have to contribute to the genealogy community. As you devise your plan, ask yourself the following questions:

- ✔ **What surname sites are interested in my information?** To find surname sites, see Chapter 3.

- ✔ **What geographical sites are interested in my information?** For geographical sites, see Chapter 4.

- ✔ **What association sites (both family and geographical) are interested in my information?** See Chapters 3 and 4 for association sites.

Use all available internet resources to let people know about your information, including mailing lists, newsgroups and websites.

For example, you may have collected information on the Sleep family. You know that they came from Truro in Cornwall and that descendants settled in South Australia. To identify sites where you could post this information, you could look for one-name study pages on the surname Sleep, personal pages that have connections to the Sleep family and any mailing lists dedicated to discussing the family. Look for sites and mailing lists that relate to Cornwall and more specifically to Truro. Contact the Cornwall Family History Society and any other historical groups with interests in that county in the United Kingdom. Finally, general query sites (places where you can post genealogical questions to get help from other researchers) and GEDCOM repositories may accept your information on the Sleep family of Truro in Cornwall.

## Contacting your target audience

After you collect the names and addresses of websites that probably attract an audience that you want to target, you need to notify them. Create a brief but detailed email message to make your announcement. When you submit your message, look at the format required by each resource that you're contacting. Some query sites also have specific formats, so you may need to modify your message for each site. (For more information about newsgroups and query sites, and posting messages or queries, see Chapter 3.)

Here's a sample message to give you some ideas:

```
SLEEP, 1750-1830 CON, UK

I have information on the family of Richard Sleep
of Truro. Richard was born 1783, married Elizabeth
JENKINS in February 1810 and emigrated to NSW in
1826. They had the following children: Richard,
Elizabeth, Mary, Sarah, Robert, Bathsheba and
Joseph.
```

Most people understand that you're willing to share information on the family if you post something to a site, so you probably don't need to say that within your message. Remember, people are more likely to read your message if it has a short, descriptive subject line, is brief and to the point, and contains enough detail for readers to determine whether your information can help them (or whether they have information that can assist you).

# Exporting Your Information

Suppose you contact others who're interested in your information. What's the best way to share your information with them? Certainly, you can type everything up, print it and send it to them. Or you can export a copy of your genealogy database file that the recipients can import into their databases and then run as many reports as they want — and save a few trees in the process.

## GEDCOM files

Most genealogical databases subscribe to a common standard for exporting their information called *Genealogical Data Communication*, or *GEDCOM*. (Beware that some genealogical databases deviate from the standard a little — making things somewhat confusing.) A GEDCOM file is a text file that contains your genealogical information with a set of tags that tells the genealogical database importing the information where to place it within its structure. Figure 11-1 shows an example of a GEDCOM file.

So why is GEDCOM important? It saves you a lot of time and energy in the process of sharing information. The next time people ask you to send them some information, you can export your genealogy data into a GEDCOM file and send it to them instead of typing it up or saving your entire database.

```
□ TEMPLETON GEDCOM.ged - WordPad                              _ □ ✕

File   Edit   View   Insert   Format   Help

 □ ☞ 🖫   🖨 🖺 🗛   ✂ 🖿 🖺 ↻   🖷

 0  HEAD                                                          ⌃
 1  SOUR FTM
 2  VERS Family Tree Maker (17.0.0.965)
 2  NAME Family Tree Maker for Windows
 2  CORP The Generations Network
 3  ADDR 360 W 4800 N
 4  CONT Provo, UT 84604
 3  PHON (801) 705-7000
 1  DEST FTM
 1  DATE 14 APR 2009
 1  CHAR ANSI
 1  FILE C:\Documents and Settings\User\Desktop\TEMPLETON GEDCOM.ged
 1  SUBM @SUBM@
 1  GEDC
 2  VERS 5.5
 2  FORM LINEAGE-LINKED
 0  @SUBM@ SUBM
 0  @I000001@ INDI
 1  NAME Charles /TEMPLETON/
 1  SEX M
 1  BIRT
 2  DATE 15 JUL 1864
 2  PLAC Hartley NSW
 1  DEAT
 2  DATE 16 JAN 1923
 2  PLAC Sydney NSW
 1  FAMS @F00005@
 1  FAMC @F00001@
 0  @I00005@ INDI
 1  NAME Eliza /CONNOLLY/
 1  SEX F
 1  BIRT
 2  DATE 03 APR 1809
 2  PLAC Stepney London
 1  DEAT
 2  DATE 04 DEC 1873
 2  PLAC Kelso NSW
 1  FAMS @F00002@
 0  @I00011@ INDI
 1  NAME Hannah /ENFIELD/
 1  SEX F
 1  BIRT
 2  DATE 04 MAR 1872
 2  PLAC Donegal, Ireland
 1  DEAT
 2  DATE 23 DEC 1939
 2  PLAC Artarmon, Sydney, NSW
 1  FAMS @F00005@
 0  @I00014@ INDI
 1  NAME Louisa Maude /HARPER/                                   ⌄

For Help, press F1                                         NUM
```

**Figure 11-1:**
A typical
GEDCOM
file
displayed in
WordPad.

Making a GEDCOM file using genealogy software is easy. For example, to export information to GEDCOM using the Family Tree Maker genealogy program, follow these steps:

1. **Open your Family Tree Maker software.**

   Usually, you can open your software by double-clicking the icon for that program or by going to the Programs menu from the Start button (in Windows) and selecting the particular program.

2. **Use the default database that appears, or choose File ⇨ Open Family File to open another database.**

3. **After you open the database for which you want to create a GEDCOM file, choose File ⇨ Export.**

   The new Export File dialogue box appears. This dialogue box enables you to choose whether to export the entire file or only details of a specific individual.

   You also have the option to save the information as a Family Tree Maker file or a GEDCOM file (version 5.5). Obviously, if you're sharing your research with another Family Tree Maker user you can provide the data in the Family Tree Maker format.

4. **Type the new name for your GEDCOM file in the File Name field, choose the location into which you want to save the file and click on OK.**

   The Export to GEDCOM dialogue box appears, as shown in Figure 11-2. This dialogue box enables you to set up the GEDCOM file in a specific format.

   When you click on OK, a bar appears across the screen showing the progress of the export. When the export is complete you receive a message telling you the export has been successful.

You may notice that when you set up a GEDCOM file for export, Family Tree Maker allows you to select the option 'Privatise Living People'. If you select this option, people who don't have a death date recorded against their names in your database and so are likely to still be alive are automatically shown in the GEDCOM file as 'LIVING' without any identifying information being provided. This is common genealogical practice and ensures that the privacy of living relatives isn't violated.

If you promised Aunty Peggy that you wouldn't divulge her personal details to anyone else, you'll break your promise if you include her in a GEDCOM file that you send to a new-found research friend you met through Genes Reunited or Ancestry.com.

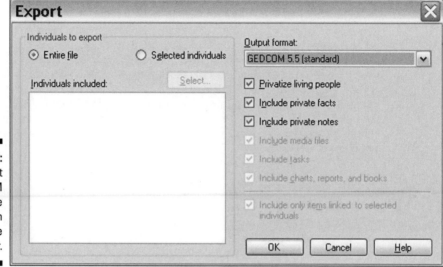

**Figure 11-2:**
The Export
to GEDCOM
dialogue
box in
Family Tree
Maker.

If you share your family history information with other researchers via GEDCOM, you lose control of your files, since other researchers can load your research into their own software and 'claim' it as part of their own research. Of course, most family historians are honest and give credit where credit is due. But occasionally we hear stories whereby a well-meaning researcher shared his or her hard-won family history research files with another researcher met via the internet, only to discover later that these files had then been loaded onto the other researcher's website, with no word of acknowledgement or credit for the person who spent so long compiling the data.

Genealogy is based on sharing, and we're certainly not suggesting that you shouldn't share your data with other researchers. But you may want to be cautious at first, sharing only one branch of your family tree or basic information on one line of your family. Then, as you build up a relationship with another researcher, you can provide that person with more details.

## *Reports*

GEDCOM is a great option when two individuals have genealogical software that supports the standard. But what about all the people who are new to genealogy and haven't invested in software yet? How do you send them information that they can use?

One option is to generate reports through your genealogical software and save them as PDF (portable document format) files. Using Adobe's Acrobat Reader software (which is downloadable for free from www.adobe.com) you can save material as a PDF file and read any PDF file. The advantage is that any report you export as a PDF file retains its 'look', which can be very useful when you're exporting charts and reports. However, the downside is that the person receiving the PDF file can't readily merge your data into his or her own records. Sometimes you may not want people to merge your data with theirs, but if you're nurturing a new genealogical friendship, then sending a ten-page report that the receiver can't readily access may not seem very friendly.

If the person you're sending the report to doesn't have access to a full suite of word-processing and spreadsheet software, suggest that he or she visits the OpenOffice website (www.openoffice.org) and downloads free software that has similar features but without the associated costs.

The CD-ROM accompanying this book has a copy of Adobe Acrobat Reader that you can download and try out.

## If you post it, they will come

Instead of sending information to several different individuals, consider placing your information at a site where people can access it at their convenience. You could post your information on a website (see Chapter 12 for more information). But you have some other options if you're not ready to take the web-designing plunge:

- ✔ Find others who're working on the same surnames or geographical areas and who already have web pages, and then ask them to post your information on their sites. Don't be offended if they decline — most internet accounts have specific storage limits and they may not have room for your information.

- ✔ Submit your information to a general site that collects GEDCOM files. Examples of these sites include

  - Ancestry World Tree (www.ancestry.com/share/awt/main.htm)

  - GenServ (www.genserv.com)

If you're using Family Tree Maker software and are an Ancestry.com subscriber, you can automatically upload your data to the Ancestry World Tree website. Only people who're also subscribers to Ancestry.com can view your entry in full and merge specific lines you've provided into their own family history files. Non-subscribers can't view your tree, but the names of deceased individuals in your tree and their birth dates and birthplaces may appear in the Ancestry.com search index. Ancestry.com members searching for these individuals can then contact you anonymously through Ancestry.com's connection service to request more information. Go to ftm.custhelp.com to read more about this feature of the Family Tree Maker software.

# Citing Your Sources

We can't stress enough the importance of citing your sources when sharing information — either online or through traditional means. Including references that reflect where you obtained your information is just as important when you share information as it is when you research the information. Not only does referencing provide the other person with leads to possible additional information, but it also gives you a place to return to so that you can double-check your facts if someone challenges the information. Sometimes, after exchanging information with another researcher, you both notice that you have conflicting details about a particular ancestor. Knowing where to turn to double-check the facts and hopefully find out whose information is correct can save you time and embarrassment.

Here are some examples of ways to cite online sources of information:

- **Email messages:** Sarah Gardner [<sgardner5@bigpond.com> or PO Box 2834, Armidale, NSW 2350], 'Looking for Francis Gardner', Message to John Smithers, 14 February 2008. [Message cites headstone details from Armidale cemetery in Sarah Gardner's possession.]

- **Newsgroups:** Sarah Gardner [<sgardner5@bigpond.com> or PO Box 2834, Armidale, NSW 2350], 'Armidale cemetery records' in www.rootsweb.ancestry.com. Armidale, 12 February 2008.

- **Websites:** Sarah Gardner [<sgardner5@bigpond.com> or PO Box 2834, Armidale NSW 2350], 'The Gardner Family of New South Wales' <www.gardnernsw.org>. [Site contains information on the descendants of Robert and Sarah Gardner in NSW, including headstone inscriptions from Armidale cemetery where most early family members are buried.]

Although most genealogical software programs now enable you to store source information and citations along with your data, many still don't export the source information automatically. For that reason, double-check any reports or GEDCOMs you generate to see whether your source information is included before sharing them with other researchers. If the information isn't included, create a new GEDCOM file that includes sources.

# Respecting Privacy Rights

We couldn't sleep at night if we didn't give you the mandatory lecture on maintaining the privacy of living individuals when sharing your genealogical information.

In the rush to get genealogical information posted on the internet, people sometimes forget that portions of the information in their databases, and thus in their GEDCOM files, are considered private. It may be one thing for family members to share with you the details of the births, deaths and marriages of their close relations, but quite another for this information to suddenly appear on the internet for all the world to see — and possibly abuse. Remember that information gathered by genealogists can be misused by criminals trying to assume false identities, gain government benefits they aren't entitled to or even access people's bank accounts. In addition, you could cause a great deal of heartache if you broadcast to the world that your 65-year-old grandmother had a baby before she married, especially if she never quite got around to actually telling her husband or five other children about it, and they're all still living.

The rights of individuals to ensure that their personal information remains confidential is a hotly debated topic today and governments are moving to ensure that these rights are protected. The genealogical community has adopted specific conventions and does *not* support researchers including details of living people on websites, in mailing lists and in GEDCOM files that are transferred between researchers.

To avoid any legal problems, and to make sure that you're not disowned by your whole family, always clean out (exclude) any information on living individuals from your GEDCOM files before you give them to anyone.

A number of programs have been designed to clean out information on living individuals from GEDCOM files. One such program, GEDClean, is available on the CD-ROM that accompanies this book, as well as from www.gedclean.com. Even if you use software to clean a file, always double-check the data in the file to ensure that the software catches everything and you don't end up sharing any information on living people.

# *Understanding How Copyright Affects You*

Copyright is a very complex issue and we could take most of this book to cover the many aspects of copyright law. We don't want to bog you down with legalities, but you do need to be aware of your rights and responsibilities with regard to copyright. Keep the following points in mind:

- ✔ **Birth, death and marriage certificates, along with downloads of census images and online maps and images, may require special permission if you want to reproduce them.** Check with the original source of such items before you make further use of them. Just because you purchased your grandmother's birth certificate from the relevant state registry, you don't automatically have the right to reproduce it on a website.

- ✔ **Don't be fooled into thinking that because no copyright symbol (©) appears on something you've been given, you're free to use it.** Copyright is automatic and free: It doesn't have to be registered.

- ✔ **Even if an item is old, it may still be in copyright.** Say a researcher provides you with a transcript of a shipboard diary kept by your ancestor when he sailed to Western Australia in 1850. Certainly, the person who kept the diary (your ancestor) is now long dead, but the person who made the transcript no doubt put a great deal of time and effort into preserving the contents of the diary for others by laboriously transcribing it. Just because this person generously sent you an electronic copy doesn't mean you can put the work on the Web. He or she has put *intellectual property* into the transcript and if you use this work without permission, you're breaking the law.

- ✔ **Information given to you in good faith by another researcher shouldn't be included in your submission to an online database without the other person's permission.** Always acknowledge the source of family information, especially historical information provided to you by other family members or researchers.

- ✔ **Libraries and other repositories are permitted by law to provide a certain amount of information to you under 'fair dealing'.** For example, such organisations can allow you to photocopy up to 10 per cent of a book, or one article in a magazine. However, this does *not* give you the right to then reproduce that work (for example, by scanning it and putting it online) without the permission of the copyright owner.

✔ **The time that copyright lasts depends on the item.** As a general rule, copyright lasts for 70 years after the death of the person who created the item. So if Aunty Maude wrote her biography as a young girl in 1920 but lived until 1987, she (and her estate) holds the copyright in that item until 2057. However, any photographs taken before 1955 are out of copyright, regardless of whether the person who took the photograph is still alive.

The Australian Copyright Council provides excellent free advice for family historians through a series of brochures that can be viewed online. Go to www.copyright.org.au and search under Publications.

# Copyright

Copyright is the controlling right that a person or corporation has over the duplication and distribution of a work that the person or corporation created. Although facts themselves can't be copyrighted, works in which facts are contained can be. Although the fact that your grandmother was born on 1 January 1900 can't be copyrighted by anyone, a report that contains this information and was created by Aunty Elsie may be. If you intend to include a significant portion of Aunty Elsie's report in your own report, you need to secure permission from her to use the information.

With regard to copyright and the internet, remember that just because you found some information on a website (or other internet resource) does not mean that it's not copyrighted. If the website contains original material along with facts, it is copyrighted to the person who created it — regardless of whether or not the site has a copyright notice or symbol on it!

To protect yourself from infringing on someone's copyright and possibly ending up in a legal battle, you should do the following:

✔ Never copy another person's web page, email or other internet creation (such as graphics) without his or her written consent.

✔ Never assume that a resource is not copyrighted.

✔ Never print an article, story, report or other material to share with your family, friends, genealogical or historical society, class or anyone else without the creator's written consent.

✔ Always cite sources of the information in your genealogy and on your web pages.

✔ Always link to other web pages rather than copying their content on your own website.

# Chapter 12

# From Your Computer to the World

So you've loaded your genealogical database with information about your relatives and ancestors, and you've shared data with others by email. Now you're ready to create and post your own website. In this chapter, we explore the basics on creating a website.

This chapter covers only the very essentials about website design to get you started. If you're looking for more detailed information about creating a full-blown and fancy website, we recommend you check out the following great books:

✔ *Creating Family Websites For Dummies*, by Janine C Warner (Wiley Publishing Inc.)

✔ *Creating Web Pages For Dummies*, 9th Edition, by Bud Smith (Wiley Publishing Inc.)

✔ *The Internet For Dummies*, 4th Australian Edition, adapted by Paul Wallbank (Wiley Publishing Australia Pty Ltd)

## Home Sweet Home

Before you can build your home page on your website, you need to find a home (or a *host*, if you prefer) for your website. Although you can design your home page on your own computer using a word processor, others won't be able to see it until you put the page on a web server on the internet. A *web server* is a computer that's connected directly to the internet and that serves up web pages when you request them using your computer's web browser.

## Commercial internet service providers

If you subscribe to a national *internet service provider (ISP)* like Telstra BigPond or OzEmail, or a local provider, you most likely already have a home for your web pages — whether you realise it or not. Most commercial ISPs include in their membership agreements a specific web space allocation for user home pages, as well as access to (or information about) some tools to help you build your website. You may as well take advantage of this service if you're already paying for it!

Check your membership agreement to see how much free space your ISP offers, and follow your ISP's instructions for creating your website and uploading your web pages from your computer to the ISP's server.

If you no longer have a copy of your membership agreement, don't fret. Your ISP should have an information page setting out membership benefits that you can access from its home page.

If your particular membership level doesn't include web space, but your ISP has other membership levels that do, you may find it economical to stay with that ISP and simply upgrade your membership. However, before you commit to a new deal, compare your current ISP's service with that offered by other ISPs to make sure that you get the best deal around. To compare services, you can use a search engine such as Google or Yahoo! and limit the results to Australia.

## Free web-hosting services

Various websites give you free space for your home page provided that you agree to their rules and restrictions. We can safely bet that you won't have any problems using one of these freebies, because the terms (such as no pornography, nudity or explicit language allowed) are genealogist-friendly. Using that picture of Uncle Bob in his birthday suit on New Year's Eve would be in poor taste, anyway.

For listings and reviews of websites that offer free web space, check out the following:

- 100 Best Free Web Space Providers (www.100best-free-web-space.com)
- FreeWebspace.net (www.freewebspace.net)

If you follow the free web space route, remember that the companies providing the space must pay their bills. Often, they're able to make web space available free to you by charging advertisers for banners and other advertisements that sit right there on your home page. If you don't like the idea of an advertisement on your home page, or if you have strong objections to one of the companies that advertises with the hosting site, you can ask whether you can upgrade to a fee-based web-hosting membership level that excludes advertising.

## Commercial web-hosting services

The market for commercial web-hosting services is extremely competitive and you'll quickly discover just how many companies want your business. So how do you find the service that's right for you? Try the following:

- Chat with other online genealogists and ask them for their recommendations.
- Search online using a term such as 'website hosting'.

We can't stress enough how competitive the web-hosting market is and the huge number of companies that are vying for your business. Do your research carefully: Don't sign up with the first web-hosting service that you find.

Compare different web-hosting services by checking their fees, the disk space they offer and their advertised bandwidth speed — the higher the bandwidth, the quicker a page on your website downloads. People setting up a family history site for the first time generally have pretty modest needs, so you can start at the lower end of the range and then upgrade later. The level of service offered is also important, which is why getting recommendations from other genealogists can be helpful.

The internet is a global market: Some of the best deals around may come from companies that are based in the United States or Europe.

One advantage of using a commercial web-hosting service is that you can register your own *domain name*, which is the name by which your website is found on the internet. So, if you're a member of the Butler family, for example, you can register a domain name like `www.butlerfamily.org.au`. Having a domain name gives your website a strong identity and helps users to remember your site. In addition, when a researcher enters a term such as 'Butler family' into a search engine, the search engine picks your site as one of the first it finds. Thus, an easily identifiable domain name helps more people to find your website.

Before you can register your domain name, you need to check whether it's available. You can check out the available domain names using a domain registration company such as Australian Domain Registration Services (`www.domainregistration.com.au`). If the domain name you require is available, you can then search online for the company that offers the best domain registration fee. Again, this is a highly competitive market, but you should be able to register a domain name to be used for non-commercial purposes for less than $10.00 per year.

Look for special deals that offer both domain name registration and website hosting: these options are sometimes offered as a package, which can represent good value.

## User pages from software companies

Some software companies offer free websites to customers who use their products. A few of the genealogical software manufacturers allow software users to upload web pages created with the software directly to their servers. One example is Family Tree Maker. Chapter 11 briefly covers uploading your family tree to the Family Tree Maker website. If you use a different program, we recommend that you check the user's manual that comes with your software for more information about creating and posting web pages using that software.

# Understanding How Websites Are Created

How the Web works is probably a bit of a mystery to most people. *Hypertext Markup Language* (or HTML) is the language of the Web and is a code in which text documents are written so that web browsers can read and interpret those documents, converting them into graphical images and text that you can see through your web browser.

You'll be relieved to know, however, that you don't have to learn HTML to create your own great-looking website — you can build your website using web-page building software. This software allows you to write and set up your pages in plain English while in the background the program creates all the HTML tags needed for the pages to function properly when they're loaded onto the Web. You may see this kind of software referred to as a *WYSIWYG editor* — standing for What You See Is What You Get. In other words, you type the words exactly as you want them to appear on your website, and the program does the rest for you.

Here are a few web-page building software programs to explore:

- **Arachnophilia** (www.arachnoid.com/arachnophilia): This free program has a built-in facility that enables you to create a web page and load it to your website without the need for a second software program. The program also has a spell-checker and an internal browser that allows you to see the changes you make as you type.

- **Dreamweaver** (www.adobe.com/products/dreamweaver/): This is one of the many professional web-page editing programs that you can purchase. It is designed for professional web-builders who are creating detailed websites, so it comes with a pretty hefty price tag. However, you can download a trial version valid for 30 days before you buy.

- **Page Breeze** (www.pagebreeze.com): This free program is designed for private or educational use, and allows you to switch between visual (WYSIWYG) pages and HTML format at any time.

# Knowing What to Include on Your Website

Before you design your home page, you need to decide exactly *what* you want your website to contain. Ideally, your site should include a summary of your family's history on its home page, so that new visitors can quickly decide whether or not your site relates to the family or surname they're researching. Other items you may want to include on your site are

- Genealogical information about family members
- Maps of the areas in which your ancestors lived
- Photographs of your ancestors

If you want to include genealogical information, you don't have to retype all those birth, death and marriage details you've collected. Use your family history software package to export this information using GEDCOM.

Chapter 11 details how to share your GEDCOM data with other researchers and place your GEDCOM file on specialised genealogy websites. In this section, we explain how to prepare your GEDCOM file for sharing on the Web. (For more information about GEDCOM, see Chapter 9.)

First and foremost, make sure that your GEDCOM file is ready to share with others. By this, we mean that it's free from any information that could land you in the doghouse with any of your relatives — close or distant! For more about the importance of ensuring that your GEDCOM file has no information about living individuals, see Chapter 11.

While most genealogical software programs on the market today allow you to remove living relatives from your GEDCOM file before you load it onto the internet, some programs don't allow you to do this. So, a fellow genealogist has developed a helpful little program called GEDClean that you can use to ensure that your GEDCOM file is ready to be shared with the rest of the online world.

GEDClean is a freeware utility that searches through your GEDCOM file and removes any information about living persons. The utility then saves the cleaned GEDCOM file for you to use with other genealogical utilities designed to help you put your information on the Web.

We include GEDClean on the CD-ROM that accompanies this book.

Here's how to use the GEDClean utility:

1. **Install and open the GEDClean program from the CD.**

   A window pops up with the three steps for GEDClean.

2. **Click on Step 1: Select the Name of Your GEDCOM File.**

   You see a dialogue box asking you to specify the GEDCOM file that you want to use GEDClean on.

3. **Choose the GEDCOM file that you created in Chapter 10 or another GEDCOM file that you have readily available. Click on OK.**

   This step brings you back to the first window, and the name and directory path of your GEDCOM file should appear under Step 1.

4. **Click on Step 2: Select Individuals to Exclude from Your GEDCOM File.**

   A dialogue box appears asking what you want to do to exclude living individuals from your GEDCOM. You have three options:

   • **Option 1:** You can use an existing file that identifies all living persons whose data are in your GEDCOM file.

- **Option 2:** GEDClean can scan your GEDCOM file looking for anyone with a specific note that indicates that they are alive.

- **Option 3:** GEDClean can scan your entire GEDCOM file and look for anyone who may possibly be alive.

Unless you have an existing file that states who should be excluded or you've somehow marked your GEDCOM file to reflect living individuals, we suggest that you choose Option 3 and have GEDClean scan the whole GEDCOM file looking for people who may be alive.

5. **Click on your preferred option and then click on OK.**

For each person that GEDClean finds with no vital information (primarily birth date or death date), you get an Unknown Status window asking what you want to do with that person.

6. **If GEDClean prompts you with an Unknown Status window, type either** living **(details are excluded in the cleaned GEDCOM) or** not living **(details are included).**

Be forewarned that if you have a lot of people in your database and thus in your GEDCOM file, the process of responding to each Unknown Status window can be a little time-consuming. However, making sure that you exclude information on any living relatives is well worth the effort!

7. **Click on Step 3: Clean the GEDCOM File.**

GEDClean runs through the GEDCOM file and removes information on those people that you indicated as alive. The utility then saves your original GEDCOM file under a new name (with the extension .old) and saves the cleaned GEDCOM file under your original GEDCOM filename.

8. **Choose File ➪ Exit to exit GEDClean.**

After your GEDCOM file is free of information about any living persons, you're ready to prepare the file for the Web. Unfortunately, the web-page building software you use to create your website can't handle GEDCOM files: GEDCOM is just a standard format developed so that genealogical data can be easily shared between different family history software programs. So, in order for visitors to your website to be able to read the family history information in your GEDCOM file, you need to convert your GEDCOM file into HTML first. You can choose from several programs to help you with this conversion.

GED2HTML is probably the most commonly known GEDCOM-to-HTML converter available, and guess what — we include it on the CD-ROM that accompanies this book.

## Privacy

Sometimes, genealogists get so caught up in dealing with the records of deceased persons that they forget that much of the information they've collected and put in their databases pertains to living individuals. In their haste to share their information with others online, they create GEDCOM files and reports and ship them off to recipients without thinking twice about whether they may offend someone or invade someone's privacy by including personal information.

Why shouldn't you include everything that you know about your relatives?

✓ You may invade someone's right to privacy: Your relatives may not want you to share personal information about themselves with others, and they may not have given you permission to do so.

✓ Genealogists aren't the only people who visit genealogical internet sites: For example, private detectives are known to lurk about, watching for information that may help their cases. Estranged spouses may visit sites looking for a way to track down their former partners. People with less-than-honourable intentions may also visit a genealogical website looking for potential scam or abuse victims. And some information, such as your mother's maiden name, may help the unscrupulous carry out fraud.

Your safest bet when sharing genealogical information is to include only data that pertains to people who have long been deceased — unless you have written consent from living persons to share information about them. By long been deceased, we mean deceased for more than ten years — although the time frame could be longer depending on the sensitivity of the information.

# Adding Photos and Other Features to Your Website

Although the content of genealogical web pages with a lot of textual information about ancestors or geographic areas may be very helpful, all-text pages won't attract the attention of your visitors. People get tired of sorting through and reading narratives on websites; they like to see things that personalise a website and are fun to look at. Graphics, icons and photographs are ideal for this purpose. A couple of nice-looking, strategically placed photos of ancestors make a site feel like a home. Likewise, you can enhance interest in your website by including a blog to regularly update visitors on your research progress. In this section we give you some points to consider if you want to incorporate photos or add a blog to your website.

## Uncle Ed for all to see: Uploading photos and other images

If you have photos that have been scanned and saved as JPEG or TIFF images, you can post these images on your website. Just make sure that a copy of each JPEG or TIFF file is uploaded to your web host's server in a directory that you can point to, so that browsers pick up each image or photograph. Your web host should advise you how to upload the files. Be sure to type the filename for each image exactly as it appears on your hard drive or other resource.

Take care when selecting photographs to upload to your website. You may be happy opening a large 2–3 megabyte high-resolution image on your personal computer, but once the image is on your website it may take a long time to download, making visits to your site very tedious for others — especially for those using a dial-up connection or with a very low download limit.

Spend some time editing your photos into a standardised format and size. Check out the following websites for more help and advice:

- **NetMechanic GIFBOT (www.netmechanic.com/accelerate.htm):** This graphics optimiser can help you to shrink the size of the photos and graphics on your website.

- **Picasa (picasa.google.com):** One of Google's add-on features, this program can help you to manage your photographic collection and select, edit and prepare photos to include on your website.

- **Picnik (www.picnik.com):** This free online photo editing service also works with sites such as Facebook and Flickr.

Just as you should be careful about posting factual information about living relatives on your website, be careful about posting photos of them too. If you want to use an image that has living relatives in it, you need to obtain their permission before doing so. Some people are very sensitive about having their pictures posted on the Web. Also, use commonsense and taste in selecting pictures for your page. Although a photo of little Susie at age 3 wearing a lampshade and dancing around in a tutu may be cute, a photo of Uncle Ed at age 63 doing the same thing may not be so endearing!

In addition to including family history files and photos, you may like to add copies of some of the most important documents you've discovered about your family. (Don't forget to ensure that you aren't infringing copyright by including them — see Chapter 11 for guidance.) For example, you can include an image of your ancestor's arrival record in Australia, or a map showing exactly where in Brewarrina your family's farm is situated.

## *Adding a blog*

Many family historians are adding blogs to their websites. A *blog* is short for 'web log' and is a web page made up of short statements, comments and articles posted on a random but regular basis on a specific topic.

Some family historians use blogs to document their family history research — which may be of limited appeal to others. How many people will be interested in knowing you caught the 321 bus to the archives on Friday morning to search shipping records? But family members may be interested if you use your blog to announce significant research discoveries, such as the fact that after three months of searching, you finally found Uncle Tom's shipping arrival details when you visited the archives on Friday.

To explore more about blogs, you can find thousands of examples at `www.google.com.au` by choosing the Blog option from the More tab at the top of the page. A good example is one created for the Davern family at `davern.blogspot.com`. Or you can try entering a name you're researching to determine whether a blog for that name already exists.

For more details on how to include a blog on your website, check out `www.blogger.com`, which has a video tutorial you can view online.

# Part V
# The Part of Tens

*'It's kind of humbling to think it took all of these people to make me.'*

# In this part ...

**A**h, The Part of Tens — a staple of the *For Dummies*
books. Use these chapters as quick references
when you're looking for the following:

- ✔ Online databases to search for records and information
- ✔ Websites to visit when you're getting started in your genealogical pursuits
- ✔ Tips for making the most of your research
- ✔ Some things to ponder when designing your own genealogical web pages

# Chapter 13

# Ten Handy Databases

*T*hroughout the book, we talk about the different online databases available. In this chapter, we list some of the databases that we think you may find useful in your research. For each one we include a brief description of the data that it contains and how you may use it to further your research goals.

## RootsWeb

www.rootsweb.ancestry.com

RootsWeb is a massive website that's ideal for finding people who're researching the same family name as you are. You can search the RootsWeb Surname List and also the names in family trees at WorldConnect. In addition, RootsWeb hosts thousands of mailing lists and message boards that you can use to keep in contact with researchers who have an interest in the same family name, place or subject that you do.

RootsWeb is ideal for beginners and veterans alike — it's one of those sites you opt to revisit every time you discover a new line in your family tree.

## Ancestry.com

www.ancestry.com

Tracing your family history online you're bound to come across Ancestry. com, since it has massive market exposure around the online world. A number of its subsites are dedicated to records from specific geographical regions, such as Ancestry.com.au, which deals with Australian records, and

Ancestry.co.uk, which deals with records from England, Wales, Scotland and Ireland. You can find census records; records of births, deaths and marriages; and printed book and historical databases. Searches are free, but to view complete records you need to subscribe or use 'pay to view' vouchers, which you pre-purchase.

Look for Ancestry.com's regular promotions and trial periods, which give you free access for a nominated period of time.

# The National Archives

www.nationalarchives.gov.uk

The National Archives website has loads of guidance, data and fun areas to explore. The site has catalogues of the holdings of the UK's main archive, as well as online databases to many records, including surviving World War I army papers, probate records and Royal Marine service records. Through its Documents On Line service you can download a copy of an original record for a small fee.

The site has useful information for beginners and includes tutorials on topics such as how to read old handwriting.

# Find My Past

www.findmypast.com

Find My Past, a UK-based site, has an excellent reputation for providing very accurate transcriptions of the full range of English census records, and it recently added the 1911 British Census to its stable. In addition, Find My Past is working with many family history societies to add data to its site, which means you may often find quirky items on the site, such as shareholder lists for the Great Western Railway or registers of passport applications for British people wanting to travel abroad. Searches of the site are free, but to view complete records you need to be a subscriber.

# World Vital Records

www.worldvitalrecords.com

Although World Vital Records is a US-based site, it has a very strong connection with Australian genealogists and has begun to place online some very valuable records for local research, including entries from the Government Gazette and the Police Gazette, post office directories and electoral rolls. World Vital Records is also working in partnership with The Church of Jesus Christ of Latter-day Saints to provide a number of new resources online.

The site is subscription based but offers free searches. New datasets are normally free for the first few weeks they're placed online: If you register with the site, you can be advised about new records as they're loaded.

# UK Archives Network

www.nationalarchives.gov.uk/a2a

The UK Archives Network brings together online catalogues from more than 250 of England's main record offices, archives and libraries. You can work your way through everything catalogued, or you can search by surname, or surname and given name, and even confine your search to a specific region in England or to a particular record repository. The indexes are so detailed that with patience you're likely to dig up previously unknown information about ancestors tucked away in eighteenth century land records, Poor Law documents or wills. Specific reference details are shown with each entry, and many entries contain abridged transcripts of the original record.

To search the network, start by simply entering a surname of interest in the Quick Search box. The results screen shows the number of entries found for that name. If too many results appear, you can refine your search by selecting the specific repository in which you'd like to search.

Although this website is no longer adding new databases, it's still one that you should explore.

# FreeBMD

www.freebmd.org.uk

The UK's FreeBMD site is one of the biggest cooperative projects among family historians on the Web and draws on a large pool of volunteer transcribers to enter index records into its database. This free service lets you search birth, marriage and death indexes for England and Wales from 1837 onwards and the coverage is growing all the time — for example, at the time of writing the website had good coverage for all three indexes up to almost 1930.

What makes this site so useful is that you can search several years in one go — which is quite different from ploughing through microfiche versions of the records, where each event is separately indexed and divided into quarters for each year.

The site also has some useful additional features, such as the ability to tag a record with a 'Postem' to show that it's of interest to you or you have further information about the entry: Others interested in the same registered event can then make contact with you.

# Ryerson Index

www.ryersonindex.org

The Ryerson Index is a fabulous volunteer-run project providing access to recent death notices from many Australian newspapers, especially the *Sydney Morning Herald*. You can use this site not only to search for the death notices of family members but also to find living relatives, since newspaper notices often give the names of surviving spouses or children and grandchildren, who you can then track down.

# Commonwealth War Graves Commission

www.cwgc.org

The Commonwealth War Graves Commission maintains the records of almost 1.7 million known grave sites of service men and women, commemorating members who served in the armed forces in the United Kingdom, Australia, New Zealand, India and South Africa in World War I and World War II. Searching by surname and given name provides details of where the person is buried (including exact burial place and plaque or grave number), as well as the person's service number and regiment, age, date of death, nationality and next of kin.

If you're planning to visit a war grave, especially in France or Belgium, this site can give you specific directions on how to get there.

# ScotlandsPeople

www.scotlandspeople.gov.uk

The Scottish government has embraced the World Wide Web and made available online all the country's publicly available birth, marriage and death indexes, as well as its census and will indexes. You can search baptisms, marriages and burials in old parish registers from 1538 to 1854, and births, deaths and marriages in statutory registers from 1855 onwards. All census data from 1841 to 1901 are also available on this site.

Although the website is subscription based and you have to pay to carry out a detailed search, when you find a record of interest you can download the relevant certificate electronically there and then for a very reasonable price.

# Chapter 14

# Ten Websites for Genealogy Beginners

**D**o census records make you feel senseless? Do you panic at the idea of ploughing uselessly through online archives? Are you just plain confused about where to start? These ten websites may relieve some of the anxiety you feel towards researching your genealogy.

## Society of Australian Genealogists

www.sag.org.au

Never lose sight of the fact that many established family history societies have been in the business of helping people to trace their family trees since way before the internet came along — and those years of experience can be very helpful to you. Besides focusing on building family history resources in a particular region, these groups specialise in the best methods for finding information about people who once lived in their area. And this is good news for genealogy beginners.

For example, the website for the Society of Australian Genealogists maintains a series of research guides that overview the range of topics of particular interest to Australians embarking on researching their family history — whether it be shipping records, convict records or old business directories. Each guide summarises the main records available, where to find them and links you to other websites that can help. The Society also posts online details of the family history courses and lectures it runs nationwide and has an online shop for software, CDs and books.

To keep up-to-date with what's happening in family history in Australia and overseas, you can subscribe (for free) to the Society's monthly *SAG-E newsletter*.

# Coraweb

www.coraweb.com.au

Cora Num's *Web Sites for Genealogists* — better known as Coraweb — is ideal for Australians new to genealogy because it's so high in local content. The site is a directory that concisely groups its main categories of links on its home page, covering everything from mailing lists to maps, cemeteries to surname searching, and researching Irish, English and Aboriginal and Torres Strait Islander resources.

Cora Num also produces a print edition of *Web Sites for Genealogists*, along with other titles that focus on finding immigration and convict records. Coraweb is the best Australian gateway site around, and can quickly help you to locate an Australian family history website of interest.

# GENUKI: UK & Ireland Genealogy

www.genuki.org.uk

One of the most well-known websites for tracing English, Irish, Scottish, Welsh, Channel Islands and Isle of Man genealogy, GENUKI provides great paths into all kinds of interesting sites relating to family history in the British Isles. The website has a hierarchical structure, which means you search for information at different levels — by country, by county or by place. Allow yourself time to see how this works, because a search at one level doesn't usually unearth information at another level. For example, if you search for England ⇨ Church Records, GENUKI returns sites of general interest; if you search for Somerset ⇨ Church Records, GENUKI takes you to sites with county coverage; and if you search by a specific town or parish in the county of Somerset (for example, Taunton ⇨ Church Records), GENUKI takes you to online transcriptions of church registers for that town or parish. Knowing which level to use for a specific search ensures you go straight to the information you need — and, no doubt about it, you can find plenty here.

# FamilySearch

www.familysearch.org

FamilySearch is maintained by The Church of Jesus Christ of Latter-day Saints and is one of the largest and oldest of the free genealogical database sites on the Web. It draws together records collected worldwide through its own microfilming projects and information submitted by church members, genealogical societies and family historians. It also provides access to the Church's Family History Library catalogue, which contains records on more than 2.2 million reels of microfilm. These can be ordered for viewing at the Church's Family History Centres around the world, including in Australia.

The site tracks millions of different names in many different databases, and the Church is working to make many of the original records to which these relate available online as digital images.

# Cyndi's List

www.cyndislist.com

Cyndi's List is the most famous of all genealogical gateways and is the one to visit when you can't readily find the information you want anywhere else. Want to know what records exist for births in Barbados, or how to reach a family history society in the Netherlands or whether 10 April 1843 was a Saturday? This site has the answers! It links thousands of genealogy sites across the Web and is growing steadily by the day. You can either search Cyndi's List for specific information or browse through the alphabetical listings of topics.

# State Records Authority of NSW

www.records.nsw.gov.au

If your ancestors had dealings with the New South Wales government, especially in the nineteenth century or early twentieth century, the archives held by the first colony to be settled in Australia is a great place to start your research. The State Records Authority of NSW website provides Archives in Brief guides on all kinds of records, covering shipping arrivals, convicts, bankruptcy, gaols, occupation of Crown Land, cemeteries, and

Italian migration and settlement to name just a few. You can also access Archives Investigator, the catalogue of holdings of State Records.

Using the Fast Find feature you can search across a number of the site's online indexes simultaneously: This is a great way to get a lead on your family's activities in colonial New South Wales.

# *National Archives of Australia*

www.naa.gov.au

At Federation in 1901 when Australia's former colonies came together under the Commonwealth government, many records previously maintained by each state were handed over to the Commonwealth and subsequently became part of the collection of the National Archives of Australia (NAA). But the NAA's main collection focuses on records created after 1901 and an ambitious project is now underway to digitise many records and place them on the NAA's website. This includes the service records of World War I personnel — a fabulous resource if anyone in your family served in the Great War.

You can use the RecordSearch feature to find descriptions of millions of records created by Commonwealth agencies, and the PhotoSearch feature to find or browse through thousands of captions and images online. The NAA holds many twentieth century shipping records and some records for arrivals into Western Australia can be searched through the Passenger Index Search feature.

This website is particularly useful if you're interested in service records for either world war or for post-World War II immigration to Australia.

The NAA's website has many fact sheets for genealogists detailing how to get information about a specific family history topic — online or off.

# *World War 2 Nominal Roll Call*

www.ww2roll.gov.au

At the World War 2 Nominal Roll Call website, maintained by the Department of Veterans' Affairs, you can search the service records of more than one million soldiers, army and navy personnel who served in World War II. Search results list details such as the service person's date of birth, date of enlistment, next of kin at time of enlistment, rank, service number, date of discharge or death, decorations and so on. You can search by surname, or surname and given name, as well as by service number or place of enlistment or birth date, making the site not only useful for family historians, but also for local history research.

# New South Wales Registry of Births, Deaths and Marriages

www.bdm.nsw.gov.au

Want a quick way to check the coverage of a surname in New South Wales — or better still, to track down ancestors who lived in the state? The website of the New South Wales Registry of Births, Deaths and Marriages has a free online index to births (1856–1908), baptisms (1788–1856), deaths (1856–1978), burials (1788–1856) and marriages (1788–1958). Baptism and burial records were kept before official civil registrations began in March 1856. You can search by surname, given name, year or place of registration. Search results list the name of the person found, the registration number and year of the event, where the event was recorded and, if shown on the original record, other details such as the spouse's name or parents' names. You can use the online ordering service to order certificates via the website, paying by credit card.

This site also offers information on the system of registration in New South Wales and links to other registries and sites of interest around Australia.

# Picture Australia

www.pictureaustralia.org

You want your ancestors to be more than just a name, and finding photos of what they looked like or the places where they lived add interest to your research. You can use Picture Australia to search the photographic collections of many archival repositories and libraries around Australia and then view a copy of any images found that match your search criteria. Access conditions to the images found vary according to the institution that has provided them: In some cases you can use an image for free, but in others you need to approach the relevant repository to purchase a good-quality copy.

# Chapter 15

# Ten Tips for Genealogical Smooth Sailing

*In This Chapter*

▶ Enhancing your genealogical research

▶ Avoiding pitfalls

*Y*ou want to make optimal use of your time when researching your genealogy — online and off. Being time-efficient means planning well and keeping organised notes so that bad leads don't distract you. Making the most of your time also means staying motivated if a bad lead does distract you. Family history research is sometimes frustrating and at other times just plain hard work, but never give up!

In this chapter we offer some tips to help you plan, organise and execute your research.

## Start with What You Know

Sure, this concept seems basic, but it's worth repeating: When you begin researching your genealogy, start with what you know — information about yourself and your immediate family. Then work your way back in time using information from relatives and records that you acquire. Putting together the puzzle is much easier if you have some pieces first. If you start directly with your great-grandad and all you know about him is his name, you're going to get frustrated very early in the process — especially if great-grandad has a relatively common name like John Roberts or William Martin. Can you imagine trying to track down records on all the John Roberts or William Martins that turn up in one year's census? (We believe in thoroughly covering the basics, so if you want to hear this again, go to Chapter 1.)

# Get Organised

The better organised you are, the more success you're likely to have with your research efforts. If you know ahead of time where you stand in researching your family lines, you can identify rather quickly which records or other materials you need to find about a particular surname, location or time frame. This strategy enables you to get right down to the nitty-gritty of researching instead of spending the first hour or two of your research rehashing where you left off last time.

To help yourself get organised, keep a research log recording when and where you searched for information. For example, if you ran a search on the surname McSwain on the National Archives of Australia website on 31 October 2008 and found three entries that you wanted to follow up, record that in your research log. Also record when you looked at those entries and whether they provided any useful information. That way, next time you're online researching your McSwain ancestors, you know that you've already run a particular search and visited the resulting pages, so you don't need to do it again. (Of course, you may want to check back in the future and run the search again to see whether any new McSwain-related items turn up. And again, your research log can come in handy because it can remind you which sites you've already visited.)

You can find samples of research logs online and modify one for your own purposes, if necessary. The FamilySearch website (www.familysearch.org) has a beginners' section that includes a large number of charts and forms you can print out — click on Research Help on the home page and then select 'R' for research log. You can also create your own log using an ordinary notebook or set up a spreadsheet on your computer. If you use genealogical software, a research log may come built in.

# Gather Your Evidence

Don't trust everything you hear from other people, or read in their books, reports, web pages or any other written documents. Always be a little sceptical about second-hand information and seek to get your own proof of an event. We're not saying that if your Aunty Irene gives you a copy of your great-grandmother's birth certificate you still need to get your own copy from the original source. However, if Aunty Irene merely tells you that your great-grandmother was born in Tamworth, New South Wales, and that she knows this because another relative said so, you do need to get a copy of your great-grandmother's birth certificate or some other primary record that verifies this information.

If you assume that everything you hear or read is true, you're likely to get frequently distracted by bad leads. Jumping to conclusions and leaping back a few generations without proof is also a recipe for disaster. You could end up tracing an entire branch of a family that you're not even related to. And just think of all the lost time that you could have spent working on your own family line!

# Always Cite Your Sources

We can't say this enough — *always* cite your sources. Make sure that you know where, when and how you obtained a particular piece of information about your ancestors just in case you ever need to verify the information or get another copy of the record. Doing so saves you a lot of grief.

In addition, by stating where your information came from, others with whom you share your research can verify the data too. If Cousin Jill has spent the last ten years trying to establish the date of death of your great-great-grandfather, she'll want to know where you found that information if you suddenly include it on the family tree chart you send her. And she won't be very impressed with your research if you can't tell her! Citing your sources brings you greater respect from others for your efforts.

# Focus, Focus, Focus

If you're trying to remember all your ancestors in all your family lines and research them all at the same time, you're bound to get confused and burn out. Focus on one or two branches at a time. Even better — concentrate on one or two people within a branch at a time. By maintaining a tight focus, you can still find information on other relatives in that branch of the family and collect records and data that pertain to them — but you're able to do so without driving yourself crazy.

# Share Your Information

One of the best ways to get others to share their family history with you is to offer them some information first. Although most genealogists are rather generous people to begin with, some still believe in protecting their discoveries like closely guarded treasures — it's 'every man for himself' in their minds. However, after they realise that you want to give information as well as receive it, some of them lighten up and are much more willing to share with you. By sharing information, you can save each other time and energy, as well as begin to coordinate your research in a manner that benefits both of you.

Sharing information is one area where the internet has proven to be an invaluable resource for genealogists, since it provides easy access and a forum for unconditional and conditional sharing of information:

✔ Those of you who're willing to share your knowledge can go online and post information to your heart's content. And in return, you can simply ask the researchers who benefit from your site to share their interesting information with you.

✔ Those of you who're a little more apprehensive about sharing your knowledge can post messages describing what you're looking for and state that you're willing to share what you have with anyone who can help you. Then you can gradually divulge information to other researchers when you've established that they have a genuine interest in your family and are willing to share their research with you.

You have many different options to share your information online. You can share your research in one-on-one email messages, mailing lists and newsgroups (covered in Chapter 3), or you can load your family history files via GEDCOM to many of the major websites that host this information on your behalf (refer to Chapter 11). Alternatively, you can also set up your own website devoted to your family history research (see Chapters 12 and 16 for more information).

# *Join a Society or Research Group*

You've probably heard the phrase 'Two heads are better than one', right? Well, this theory holds true for genealogy. Joining a society or a research group enables you to combine research efforts with others who're interested in a particular surname or geographic location, so that together you save time and energy obtaining documents that benefit everyone. A society or research group also provides you with a support network to which you can turn when you begin to get discouraged or whenever you want to share a triumph.

You can find genealogical societies and research groups in several ways:

✔ Check out Cora Num's Genealogy Gateway site (www.coraweb.com.au) and click on the Family History and Historical Societies link on the home page.

✔ Go to Cyndi's List (www.cyndislist.com), select your region's name on the home page and follow the links.

✔ To find societies just in the United Kingdom and Ireland, visit GENUKI's website (www.genuki.org.uk) and select the country of interest, such as England, and the subheading Societies.

# *Head to a Conference or Workshop*

Conferences and workshops that are hosted by genealogical societies can be a great resource: They can help you get organised, learn how to research a particular place or look for specific records, and motivate you to keep plugging along with your research even if you have days when you feel like you haven't accomplished a thing. Conferences and workshops also enable you to meet other researchers with whom you have something in common, whether it's researching a specific surname or geographic location, or just research in general. Being in the company of people with whom you can share your genealogical successes and failures is always great.

Typically, conferences and workshops offer sessions that instruct you on various traditional researching topics like the following:

- Finding and using land records
- Making the most of census records
- Using birth, death and marriage records
- Using local libraries and archives
- Writing and publishing your family history

More and more workshops offer computer-based sessions such as:

- Creating your own genealogical website
- Joining online societies and mailing lists
- Using genealogical software
- Utilising genealogical websites

You can use your trusty computer and internet connection to find out about many genealogical events and educational activities in Australia. Look for genealogical events listings on major genealogy websites like Gould Genealogy (www.gould.com.au), and check the websites of the larger family history societies to see what they're advertising. The Society of Australian Genealogists (www.sag.org.au) has a comprehensive series of educational activities running regularly and most local groups present guest speakers about once a month.

# Attend a Family Reunion

Family reunions enable you to visit relatives that you haven't seen in a long time and to meet new relatives you never would have known! Reunions are a wonderful opportunity to build your genealogical base by just chatting with relatives about old family stories, ancestors and the like. Although a reunion doesn't feel like a formal interview, it can give you much of the same information that you'd receive if you sat down and formally interviewed each of the people in attendance.

Taking along a digital voice recorder or video camera is a good idea because you don't have to worry about writing down everything your relatives say right at that moment — you can just sit back and enjoy talking with your family. Plus, your genealogy records are greatly enhanced by audio or video. Just make sure that you have the permission of the relatives you plan to record.

Family reunions also offer you the opportunity to share what you know about the family and exchange genealogical records and reports. If you know ahead of time that several of your relatives are also into genealogical research, you can better plan with them what records, pictures, reports and other resources to take along. If you're not sure whether any of your relatives are into genealogical research, we recommend that you take a notebook — paper or electronic — along with some printed reports and maybe a written family history or some biographical notes (if you've already compiled these). Remember, your work doesn't have to be complete (in fact, it probably won't be) or grammatically perfect for others to enjoy seeing what you've collected.

# Don't Give Up

You're going to have days where you spend hours at the library or archives or on the internet with no research success whatsoever (or so you may think). Don't let those days get you down, and certainly don't give up! Instead of thinking about what you didn't learn about your ancestors on such days, think in terms of what you did learn — that your ancestors were not in that record for that particular place at that particular time. By checking that record, you eliminated one more item on your to-do list. So the next time you get ready to research, you know exactly where *not* to look for more information.

Researching your family history requires a slow and methodical approach. The successes may seem few and far between, but those 'eureka' moments you experience when you find that little fact you've been searching for are worth all the work — and always inspire you to carry on.

# Chapter 16

# Ten Things to Remember When You Design Your Genealogical Website

## In This Chapter

▶ Generating an original website

▶ Making sure your website is useful for others

Y ou've probably seen them: websites that look like the creators simply plugged their surnames in specified spots and maybe changed the background colour of the page. Such pages don't contain much information of value to anyone — they simply offer a list of surnames with no context and possibly links to some of the better-known genealogical websites. Clones! That's what they are.

You don't want your genealogical website to look just like everyone else's and neither do you want it to contain almost exactly the same information. You want yours to be unique and useful to other genealogists so that a lot of people visit your site — and recommend it to others. So what can you do to avoid the genealogical website rut that many genealogists find themselves in? In this chapter we offer a few ideas and places to get help.

## Be Unique — Don't Copy Other Websites

Okay. So you want your home page to look different from all the other genealogical sites on the Web! You don't really have to be told not to copy other sites, right? But when you design your site, the pressure's on, and sometimes coming up with ideas for textual and graphic content can be pretty hard. We understand that this pressure can make it awfully tempting for you to take ideas from other websites that you like. Although you can certainly look to other sites for ideas on formatting and types of content, don't copy them! Websites are copyrighted by the people who created them — even if the sites don't contain a copyright notice — and you can get in trouble for copying them. (See Chapter 11 for more information about copyright.)

The other reason you shouldn't copy websites is that you want your page to attract as many visitors as possible and, in order to do this, you need to offer something unique that makes it worth people's time to stop by. After all, if your site has the same old information as another site that already exists, people have no need to visit your page. For example, because several good gateway sites already exist, setting up a website that merely has links to other genealogical pages doesn't make much sense.

Be creative. Look around and see what other genealogical websites offer and then seek to fill the void — pick a unique topic, name or location that doesn't have much coverage (or better yet, one that doesn't have any coverage at all). If you really want to post a surname site, think about making a site for your surname that covers a particular state or country, especially if a number of sites already exist relating to the same surname. Or think about posting some transcribed records that would benefit genealogists who're researching ancestors from a particular area or region.

# Include the Surnames You're Researching and Provide Your Contact Information

If the purpose of your website is not only to share your collection of genealogical information but also to get information from others, then be sure to include a list of the names that you're researching on your home page. And don't be stingy with information: Share at least a little detail about your ancestors with those surnames. Just a list of surnames alone isn't going to be very helpful to visitors to your site. An online version of the information contained in your GEDCOM file (see Chapter 11 for more information) is fine because it includes an index of surnames that people can look through as well as information about your ancestors with those surnames.

Remember to include your name and email address on your website so that people can get in touch with you to share data. If you're comfortable doing so, you can also include your address and phone number so that people have alternative ways to contact you. Or, if you're not comfortable providing such personal information, you can rent a post office box and use this as your contact address so that people can write to you about family history. Likewise, you can set up a new, free web-based email account — with, say, Hotmail (www.hotmail.com) or Yahoo! Mail (www.yahoo.com.au) — just for genealogy-related email and post this alternative address on your website.

# Use Caution When Applying Colours and Graphics

Choose your colours and graphics wisely. Although using some colour and graphics (including photographs) helps your website stand out and makes it more personal, be careful about using too much colour or too many graphics. By too much colour, we mean backgrounds that are so bright that you blind your visitors or backgrounds that drown out the colours of your links. You want your site to be appealing to others as well as to you, so before using neon pink or lime green, stop and think about how others may react.

The more graphics you use and the larger they are, the longer the viewer's computer takes to load them. (And animated graphics are even worse: Not only can they take a long time to load, but they can also make your visitors dizzy and disoriented if you have several graphics moving in different directions at the same time.) Waiting for a page to load that has more graphics than useful text content is frustrating. You can pretty much bet that people won't wait around, so concentrate on making your page as user-friendly as possible from the beginning. Use graphics tastefully and sparingly.

If you have a large number of family photos that you really want to share on your website, make sure that you compress the photos so they're quick to load. Nothing discourages visitors to your site more than waiting for ages while large files download. See Chapter 12 for information on how to make your photographs suitable for inclusion on your website.

# Be Careful What You Post

Be careful and thoughtful when designing your website. Don't post any information that could hurt or offend someone. Respect the privacy of others and post information only on people who've been deceased for many years. (Ten years is a good conservative figure to use when in doubt.) Even then, be cautious about telling old family stories that may affect people who're still alive. (For more information about privacy, see Chapter 11.)

# *Remember to Cite Your Sources*

We can't stress this enough! Always cite your sources when you put genealogical narrative on your website, or when you post information from records that you've collected or people you've interviewed. That way, people who visit your site and get data from it know exactly where you got the information and can follow up on it if they need or want to.

Also, by citing your sources, you keep yourself out of trouble because others may have provided the information to you and they deserve the credit for their research.

# *Not All Web Browsers Are Created Equal*

Web browsers interpret HTML documents differently depending on who created the software. So, although you may create a website that looks great using Microsoft Internet Explorer, it may look off-centre or somewhat different when using another web browser such as Netscape Navigator or Mozilla Firefox. Thus we recommend that you test your page in several browsers before posting it for public access.

Better yet, use a testing service that allows the 'experts' to look at your page and give you feedback. The Yahoo! HTML Validation and Checkers page at dir.yahoo.com/Computers_and_internet/Data_Formats/HTML/ Validation_and_Checkers provides a list of programs that check your website for you.

# *Check and Recheck Your Links*

If you include links on your home page to other websites that you've designed or sites maintained by someone else, double-check the links when you post your pages. Make sure that the links work properly so that visitors to your site don't have problems navigating around sites that you recommend or that support your home page.

Many genealogical websites tend to be transient — the maintainers move them for one reason or another, or take them down entirely — so check back periodically (once a month or so) to make sure that any links you provide on your site still work.

Try to encourage another member of the family to take an interest in your genealogy website. That way, if you go away for a while or have a prolonged absence from your genealogy project because of work or health reasons, you can put someone in place to periodically check the site and keep it up-to-date. After broken links, nothing turns off visitors more than to discover a website that was last updated four years ago. Plan ahead and consider who could maintain the site sometime in the future if you become sidetracked by other commitments.

If you have a lot of links on your website and you don't have the time to check every single one yourself (which is a common scenario), look to the Yahoo! HTML Validation and Checkers page noted in the section 'Not All Web Browsers Are Created Equal'.

# Market Your Genealogical Website

After you put together your website and post it on your internet provider's server, you need to let people know that your site exists so they can stop by and visit. How do you do this? You can follow some of the same tips in Chapter 3 for marketing the research that you've done on your surnames (using mailing lists if the site deals with particular surnames or geographic areas). In addition:

✔ Check out the major search engines, because some have links to pages within their sites that enable you to submit your URL. For example, if you've created a website devoted to the Davenport family, by submitting your URL to the major search engines, your website will be listed as one of the 'hits' found when people type the word 'Davenport' into their search engine.

✔ To save time, try Submit Express (www.submitexpress.com) or AddPro (www.addpro.com), both of which offer a variety of announcement services, including submitting your URL to search engines for free.

# Helping Others Is Its Own Reward

Post your genealogical home page with the intent of helping other genealogists and encouraging a sharing genealogical community — not to get a pat on the back. If your site manages to pick up merits or an award from magazines, societies or other places on the Web, don't flaunt it to the detriment of the other information on your home page. Let it be known that you've been successful, but don't go overboard — your bragging may turn visitors away, which defeats your purpose in getting them to visit your site in the first place.

Now, we're not saying that you shouldn't acknowledge the merits or awards that your site receives if it has interesting and sound genealogical content. We recognise that it's good business to give a little traffic back to the sites, magazines, societies or other sources that send visitors your way by awarding your page some honour. We're simply saying that you can acknowledge the feedback you receive in a tasteful and humble manner. Set up a separate web page to cover merits, awards and feedback, and provide a link from your home page so that interested visitors can go to that page.

# *Where to Go for Help*

If you want to learn more about how to do fancier things with your website, check out the courses offered by TAFE colleges and evening schools in your area, or the workshops offered by genealogical societies, since many societies now offer courses on how to create your own website.

If the thought of attending a structured class gives you hives or makes you roll your eyes, you can learn more about website design online. The following websites have free tools to help you to design and maintain your own website:

- ✔ download.cnet.com/windows/web-site-tools
- ✔ www.thefreecountry.com/webmaster

You need to devote considerable time to keeping your website up-to-date. If you think you'll need months to learn the intricacies of setting up your own website, you probably won't progress your family history research much during that time! Starting with a simple, no-fuss website is best; then, as you develop more confidence and learn about maintaining and developing the site, you can add to it.

If you don't want to put in the time and effort to maintain your own website, you may prefer to use the various file-sharing sites discussed in Chapter 11, such as Ancestry World Tree (www.ancestry.com/share/awt/main.htm) or GenServ (www.genserv.com), whereby you supply a GEDCOM file of some or all of your family history research and let others maintain its online presence.

# Appendix A

# What Does This Mean? (A Glossary of Terms)

**Abstract:** A brief overview or summary of what a document or website contains.

**Administration:** The handling of the estate of a person who died *intestate*.

**AFFHO:** Australasian Federation of Family History Organisations.

**Ahnentafel:** A genealogical numbering system. Ahnentafel is a method of numbering that has a mathematical relationship between parents and children. The word itself means ancestor and table in German; also referred to as the Sosa-Stradonitz System of numbering.

**Albumen print:** A type of photograph that was produced on a thin piece of paper coated with albumen and silver nitrate and usually mounted on cardboard; typically taken between 1858 and 1905.

**Ambrotype:** A type of photograph that was printed on thin glass and usually had a black backing; typically taken between 1858 and 1866.

**Ancestor:** A person from whom you are descended.

**Ancestor chart:** A chart that runs horizontally across a page and identifies a primary person (including that person's name, date and place of birth, date and place of marriage, and date and place of death), his/her parents and then the parents' parents and so on for a number of generations. Sometimes called a *pedigree chart*.

**Ancestral File:** A database created and maintained by The Church of Jesus Christ of Latter-day Saints with millions of names available in family group sheets and pedigree charts. See also *Family History Centre* and *Family History Library*.

**Archive:** A physical location where historical documents and records are stored.

**Assisted immigrant:** See *Bounty immigrant*.

**Asylum:** Historically, a place of refuge for the socially disadvantaged or an institution where insane people were housed.

**Automoderator:** A computer program that determines whether a post to a newsgroup is appropriate; if the post is appropriate, the program posts it to the newsgroup.

**Bandwidth:** The capacity that a particular phone line or other networking cable has to carry traffic to and from the internet or computer network.

**Banns:** See *Marriage banns*.

**Baptismal certificate:** A certificate issued by a church at the time of a person's baptism; sometimes used to approximate a person's date of birth in the absence of a birth certificate.

**Bibliography:** A list of books or other materials that were used in research; also a list of books or other materials available on a particular topic.

**Biographical sketch:** A brief written account of a person's life.

**Biography:** A detailed written account of a person's life.

**Birth certificate:** A legal record stating when and where a person was born.

**Bookmark:** A method for saving links to your favourite websites within your web browser so that you can return to the sites quickly and easily.

**Bounce:** When an email doesn't reach the intended party for whatever reason and is returned to the sender.

**Bounty immigrant:** A person whose passage to Australia was paid for, or partly funded by, government authorities. Often called an *assisted immigrant*.

**Browser:** See *Web browser*.

**Cabinet card:** A larger version of the *carte-de-visite* photograph; typically taken between 1866 and 1905.

**Cache:** A directory on your computer where your web browser stores information about web pages and images that it has downloaded. This enables the browser to load these pages faster if you visit the website again within a specified period of time.

**Canon code:** A code that explains a bloodline relationship in legal terms by identifying how many degrees of separation (or steps) exist between two people related by blood. Canon law counts only the number of steps from the nearest common ancestor of both relatives.

**Carte-de-visite:** A type of photograph that was a small paper print mounted on a card; collections were often bound together in photo albums. Typically taken between 1859 and 1891.

**CD-ROM (or CD):** Compact Disk-Read Only Memory; a computer disk that stores large amounts of information (including multimedia) that can be retrieved by your computer.

**Census:** The counting of a population undertaken by a government.

**Census index:** A listing of people who are included in particular census records, along with references indicating where you can find the actual census records.

**Census return:** The record/form on which census information is collected. Also called a *census schedule*.

**Census schedule:** Another term for a census return.

**Certificate of Freedom:** A certificate indicating that a convict had served out his term and was now free. Many convicts never bothered to obtain their certificate.

**Charter:** A formal or informal document that defines the scope of a newsgroup.

**Chat room:** An internet site where you can log in and participate in real-time conversations.

**Cite:** To name the source of some information and provide reference to the original source.

**Civil code:** A code that explains a bloodline relationship in legal terms by identifying how many degrees of separation (or steps) exist between two people related by blood; civil law counts each step between two relatives as a degree.

**Civil registration:** A primary record of a vital event in life (birth, death or marriage); for the most part, originals are kept by state governments. Also called *vital records*.

**Copyright:** The exclusive right of a creator to reproduce, prepare derivative works, distribute, perform, display, sell, lend or rent his or her creations.

**Cyberspace:** A slang term for the internet.

**Daguerreotype:** A type of photograph that required a long exposure time and was taken on silver-plated copper; typically taken between 1839 and 1860.

**Database:** A collection of information that is entered, organised, stored and used on a computer.

**Death certificate:** A legal record stating when and where a person died.

**Deed:** A document that records the transfer of ownership of a piece of property or land.

**Descendant:** A person who is descended from a particular ancestor.

**Descendant chart:** A chart that contains information about an ancestor and spouse (or particular spouses if there were more than one), their children and their spouses, grandchildren and spouses, and so on down the family line; usually formatted vertically on a page like a list.

**Digest mode:** An option for receiving postings to some mailing lists in which several messages are batched together and sent to you instead of each message being sent separately.

**Digital camera:** A camera that captures images to memory instead of to film; you can then download the images to your computer.

**Digitised record:** A copy or image of a record that has been made using electronic means.

**Directory:** A collection of information about individuals who live in a particular place.

**Domain name:** A name registered by the owner of a website so that the site can be found by search engines. For example, the Baker family might register the domain name www.bakerfamilyhistory.org.

**Download:** Getting a file (information or a program) to your computer from another computer or the internet.

**Electronic mail (or email):** Messages that are sent from one person to another electronically over the internet.

**Emigrant:** A person who leaves or moves away from one country to settle in another country.

**Emoticons:** Graphics created by combinations of keys on the keyboard to express an emotion within a message.

**Enumeration district:** The area assigned to a particular enumerator or collector of the census.

**Enumerator:** A person who collected details on individuals during a census.

**Estate:** The assets and liabilities of a person who dies.

**Facebook:** A social networking website that allows individuals to meet up online, to chat and share photos and videos with their friends and family in a free environment.

**Family association:** An organised group of individuals who're researching the same family.

**Family association site:** A website that's designed and posted by an organisation devoted to researching a particular family.

**Family group sheet:** A summary of a particular family, including biographical information about a husband and wife and their children.

**Family history:** The written account of a family's existence over time.

**Family History Centre:** Local branches of The Church of Jesus Christ of Latter-day Saints' worldwide Family History Library.

**Family History Library:** The Church of Jesus Christ of Latter-day Saints' main library in Salt Lake City, Utah. The Library has the world's largest collection of genealogical holdings, including print sources and microfilmed records, as well as records and other information shared by genealogical researchers worldwide.

**Family History Library catalogue:** A listing of records (books, films, microfiche, CDs, cassette tapes, videos, microfilms and databases) available at the Family History Library in Salt Lake City, Utah and online. Also part of the FamilySearch website.

**Family history software:** Software in which you enter, store and use information about ancestors, descendants and others relevant to your genealogy.

**Family outline report:** A list of the descendants of a particular ancestor.

**FamilySearch:** A collection of information compiled by The Church of Jesus Christ of Latter-day Saints; it includes Ancestral File, the Family History Library catalogue, International Genealogical Index, census records and the US Social Security Death Index.

**FAQs:** Frequently Asked Questions.

**File Transfer Protocol (or FTP):** A way to transfer files from your computer to another, or vice versa, over the internet.

**Flame:** A verbal (written) attack online, sometimes occurring on mailing lists and in newsgroups.

**Forum:** A subject-specific area where members post messages and files.

**Freeware:** Software that you usually obtain and use for free by downloading it off the internet.

**Frequently Asked Questions (or FAQs):** A web page or message posted to a mailing list or newsgroup that explains answers to the most-asked questions to the particular website, mailing list or newsgroup. Usually serves as a starting point for people new to a site or resource.

**FTP:** File Transfer Protocol.

**Gazetteer:** Geographical dictionary that provides information about places.

**GEDCOM:** GEnealogical Data COMmunication; see *Genealogical Data Communication.*

**Genealogical database:** Software in which you enter, store and use information about ancestors, descendants and others relevant to your genealogy. Usually referred to as *family history software.*

**Genealogical Data Communication (or GEDCOM):** The standard file format for exporting and importing information between genealogical databases; intended to make data translatable between different genealogical software programs so that you can share your family information easily.

**Genealogical gateway site:** A website that identifies genealogical websites containing information on families, locations or other genealogically related subjects.

**Genealogical research directory (or GRD):** A listing that was published every year containing the research interests of contributors.

**Genealogical society:** An organised group that promotes the tracing of families in its region and helps its members to research their ancestors. Many societies also work to preserve documents and records relating to their locality.

**Genealogy:** The study of ancestors, descendants and family origins.

**Geographic-specific website:** A website that has information pertaining to a particular locality (town, county, state, country or other area).

**Glass plate negative:** A type of photograph made from light-sensitive silver bromide immersed in gelatine; typically taken between 1848 and 1930.

**Henry System:** A widely used and accepted genealogical numbering system, which assigns a particular sequence of numbers to the children of the progenitor and subsequent generations.

**Historical society:** An organised group that researches, collects and preserves documents and history for the area in which the society is located.

**Home page:** The entry point for a website.

**IGI:** International Genealogical Index.

**Immigrant:** A person who moves into or settles in a country.

**Immigration record:** A record of the entry of a person into a specific country where he or she wasn't born or naturalised.

**Index:** A list of some sort, such as a list of websites, types of records and so on.

**Interface:** An online form or page.

**Interlibrary loan:** A system in which one library loans a book or other material to another library for a person to borrow or use.

**International Genealogical Index (or IGI):** A list of baptisms and marriages of deceased individuals reflected in records collected by The Church of Jesus Christ of Latter-day Saints. The International Genealogical Index is part of the FamilySearch database, which is accessible online and at local Family History Centres.

**Internet:** A global network of interconnected computers that enables users to share information along multiple channels.

**Internet service provider (or ISP):** A company or other organisation that provides people with access to the internet through a direct connection or dial-up connection.

**Intestate:** A person who died without leaving a valid will.

**ISP:** Internet Service Provider.

**Kinship report:** A list of family members and how they relate directly to one particular individual in your database; usually kinship reports include the civil code and canon code for the relationship to the individual.

**Land grant:** Land that is either given freely or for an agreed sum, sometimes in exchange for military service, civic duty or at the expiration of a convict sentence.

**Land record:** A document recording the sale or exchange of land.

**Lurking:** Reading messages that others post to a mailing list or newsgroup without posting any messages of your own.

**Maiden name:** A woman's surname prior to marriage; sometimes reflected as 'née' on records and documents.

**Mail mode:** The method for mailing lists in which each message is sent to you separately as it's posted.

**Mailing list:** An email exchange forum that consists of a group of people who share common interests; email messages posted to the list come directly to your email in full-format (mail mode) or digest mode. The list consists of the names of everyone who joins the group; when you want to send a message to the group, you post it to a single email address that subsequently delivers the message to everyone on the list.

**Marriage banns:** An announcement read out in front of a congregation for three successive Sundays, expressing an intention for two individuals to marry. Usually read in the parish of both the bride and bridegroom if they come from different parishes.

**Marriage bond:** A financial contract guaranteeing that a marriage was going to take place; usually posted by the groom and another person (often the father or brother of the bride).

**Marriage certificate:** A legal document certifying the union of two individuals.

**Marriage licence:** A document granting permission to marry from a civil or ecclesiastical authority.

**Maternal:** Relating to the mother's side of the family.

**Microfiche:** A clear sheet that contains tiny images of documents, records, books and so on; you must read it with a microfiche reader.

**Microfilm:** A roll of clear film that contains tiny images of documents, records, books and so forth; you must read it with a microfilm reader.

**Modem:** A piece of equipment that allows your computer to talk to other computers through a telephone or cable line; modems can be internal (inside your computer) or external (plugged into one of your computer's serial ports).

**Moderator:** A person who determines whether a post to a newsgroup or mailing list is appropriate, and if so, posts it.

**Monumental inscription:** Extraction of information contained on a headstone or plaque in a cemetery or crematorium.

**Muster:** Similar to a census record, but referring to the counting of a group of individuals after they were required to meet at a specific place and time in order to have their personal details recorded by the authorities.

**Naturalisation:** The process of becoming a citizen or subject of a particular country in a manner other than birth in that country.

**Naturalisation record:** The legal document proving that a person is a naturalised citizen.

**Netiquette:** Simple guidelines for communicating effectively and politely on the internet.

**Newsgroup:** A place to post messages of a particular focus so that groups of people at large can read the messages online; messages are posted to a news server which, in turn, copies the messages to other news servers.

**Obituary:** An account of a deceased person's death that usually appears in a newspaper or other type of media.

**One-name study:** Research that focuses on one particular surname and its variants regardless of the geographic location in which it appears. Many websites are based on one-name studies.

**Orphan:** A child whose parents are both deceased. In colonial times a child could be considered an orphan if one parent was deceased and the other was incapable of supporting the child.

**Passenger list:** Listing of the names of passengers who travelled from one place to another on a particular ship.

**Paternal:** Relating to the father's side of the family.

**'Pay to view':** A website that requires you to first subscribe or pay a specific fee in order to view or download information from the site.

**'Pay to view' voucher:** A prepaid voucher that can be used to access a specific website in lieu of taking out a subscription to that site.

**Pedigree chart:** A chart that runs horizontally across a page, identifying a primary person (including that person's name, date and place of birth, date and place of marriage, and date and place of death), his/her parents and the parents' parents and so on until the chart runs off the page. Also called an *ancestor chart*.

**Pension record:** A type of military record reflecting the amount of pension that the government paid to an individual who served in the military; pension records also showed the amount of pension paid to the widow or orphan(s) of such an individual.

**Permission to marry:** A document relating to the convict period that signified that a convict's request to be allowed to marry had been granted.

**Platinum print:** A type of photograph with a matt surface that appeared to be embedded in the paper. Images were often highlighted with artistic chalk, giving the photo a hand-drawn quality; typically taken between 1890 and 1930.

**Poor Law:** The rules guiding the provision of relief to the poor or infirm of a parish, especially in England between the 1600s and 1800s.

**Portable document format (pdf):** A file format used for document exchange between computers; it can be opened and read by another computer regardless of that computer's operating system and software.

**Primary source:** A document, oral account, photograph or any other item that was created at the time a certain event occurred; information for the record was supplied by a witness to the event.

**Probate:** Settlement of a person's estate after death.

**Probate records:** Types of court records that deal with the settling of an estate upon a person's death. Probate records include contested wills and will readings; often the file contains testimonies and the ruling.

**Professional researcher:** A person who researches your genealogy — particular family lines — or obtains copies of documents for you for a fee.

**Progenitor:** The farthest-back ancestor you know about in a particular family line.

**Query:** A research question that you post to a particular website, mailing list or newsgroup so that other researchers can help you to solve your genealogical research problems/challenges.

**Research groups:** A group of people who coordinate their research and share resources to achieve success.

**Robot:** A program that travels throughout the internet looking for search engines and collects information about sites and resources that it comes across. Also called a *spider.*

**Roots Surname List (or RSL):** A list of surnames, their associated dates and locations accompanied by the contact information for persons researching those surnames.

**Scanner:** A device that captures digital images of photographs and documents into your computer.

**Search engine:** A program that searches either a large index of information generated by robots or a particular website.

**Secondary source:** A document, oral account or any other record that was created after an event took place or for which information was supplied by someone who was not an eyewitness to the event.

**Sentence:** The number of years a convict had to serve. This was greater according to the severity of the crime for which the person had been found guilty — usually seven years, 14 years or life.

**Server:** A computer that makes information available for access by other computers.

**Service record:** A type of military record that chronicles the military career of an individual.

**Shareware:** Software that you can try before you pay to license and use it permanently; usually you download shareware off the internet.

**Signature file:** A file that you can create and attach to the bottom of your email messages that gives your name, contact information, surnames that you're researching or anything else you want to convey to others.

**Social networking website:** A site that allows individuals to meet up online, to chat and share photos and videos in a free environment. Facebook is one of the best known examples of a social networking website.

**Social Security Death Index:** An index of those persons for whom Social Security death claims were filed with the US government. The Social Security Death Index is part of the FamilySearch database.

**Soundex:** A system commonly used as the basis for computer searches in many genealogical databases. Soundex places names that sound the same but are spelled differently into groups to help researchers locate entries they may otherwise overlook.

**Source:** Any person or material (book, document, record, periodical and so on) that provides information for your research.

**Spam:** Unsolicited junk email that tries to sell you something or offers a service.

**Spider:** A program that travels throughout the internet looking for a search engine and collects information about sites and resources it comes across. Also called a *robot*.

**Stereographic card:** A type of photograph that was curved and rendered a three-dimensional effect when used with a viewer; developed in the 1850s.

**Subscribe:** Pay a fee in order to access specific information or to join a mailing group for which there is no charge.

**Surname:** A last name or family name.

**Survey:** A detailed drawing and legal description of the boundaries of a land parcel.

**Thread:** A group of messages with a common subject on a newsgroup.

**Ticket of Leave:** A certificate signifying that a convict had the right to work for himself/herself for a certain numbers of hours per week.

**Tintype:** A type of photograph that was made on a metal sheet; the image was often coated with a varnish; typically taken between 1880 and 1890.

**Tiny tafel:** A compact way to show the relationships within a family database. Tiny tafel provides a Soundex code for a surname and the dates and locations where that surname may be found according to the database.

**Transcription:** A copy of a record that has been duplicated word for word.

**Uniform Resource Locator (or URL):** A way of addressing resources on the Web.

**Victualling list:** A list drawn up by the colony's authorities to note everyone who was eligible for government rations.

**Vital record:** A primary record of a vital event in life (birth, death or marriage); for the most part, originals are kept by state governments. Often called *civil registrations*.

**Web browser:** Software that enables you to view multimedia documents on the internet.

**Webmaster:** A person responsible for creating and maintaining a particular website.

**Web page:** A multimedia document that is viewable on the internet with the use of a web browser.

**Website:** One or more web pages created by an individual or organisation; also called a site.

**Will:** A legal document that explains how a person wishes his or her estate to be settled or distributed upon his or her death.

**Witness:** One who attests that he or she saw an event.

**World Wide Web:** A system for viewing and using multimedia documents on the internet; web documents are read by web browsers.

# Appendix B

# About the CD

$H$ere's some of what you can find on the *Tracing Your Family History Online For Dummies* CD:

- ✔ Demo versions of Ezitree and Relatively Yours — Australian genealogy software products
- ✔ Open Office — a great tool that allows you to write documents, keep spreadsheets and much more
- ✔ The standard version of Legacy Family Tree — genealogy database software

## System Requirements

Make sure that your computer meets the minimum system requirements shown in the following list. If your computer doesn't match up to most of these requirements, you may have problems using the software and files on the CD. For the latest and greatest information, please refer to the ReadMe file located at the root of the CD-ROM.

- ✔ A PC running Microsoft Windows
- ✔ A Macintosh running Apple OS X or later
- ✔ An internet connection
- ✔ A CD-ROM drive

If you need more information on the basics, check out these books: *PCs For Dummies*, 4th Australian Edition, by Dan Gookin and Paul Wallbank (Wiley Publishing Australia); and *Macs For Dummies* by Edward C. Baig, *iMacs For Dummies* by Mark L. Chambers, *Windows XP For Dummies* by Andy Rathbone and *Windows Vista For Dummies* by Andy Rathbone (all Wiley Publishing, Inc.).

# Using the CD

To install the items from the CD to your hard drive, follow these steps.

1. **Insert the CD into your computer's CD-ROM drive.**

   The licence agreement appears.

   ***Note to Windows users:*** The interface won't launch if you have autorun disabled. In that case, choose Start ⇨ Run. (For Windows Vista, choose Start ⇨ All Programs ⇨ Accessories ⇨ Run.) In the dialogue box that appears, type **D:\Start.exe**. (Replace *D* with the proper letter if your CD drive uses a different letter. If you don't know the letter, see how your CD drive is listed under My Computer.) Click on OK.

   ***Note for Mac Users:*** When the CD icon appears on your desktop, double-click the icon to open the CD and double-click the Start icon.

2. **Read through the licence agreement and then click on the Accept button if you want to use the CD.**

   The CD interface appears. The interface allows you to browse the contents and install the programs with just a click of a button (or two).

# What You'll Find on the CD

The following sections are arranged by category and provide a summary of the software and other goodies you'll find on the CD. If you need help with installing the items provided on the CD, refer to the installation instructions in the preceding section.

- ✔ *Freeware programs* are free, copyrighted games, applications and utilities. You can copy them to as many computers as you like — for free — but they offer no technical support.

- ✔ *GNU software* is governed by its own licence, which is included inside the folder of the GNU software. There are no restrictions on distribution of GNU software. See the GNU licence at the root of the CD for more details.

- ✔ *Shareware programs* are fully functional, free, trial versions of copyrighted programs. If you like particular programs, register with their authors for a nominal fee and receive licences, enhanced versions and technical support.

- ✔ *Trial, demo* or *evaluation* versions of software are usually limited either by time or functionality (such as not letting you save a project after you create it).

# Genealogy programs

## Ancestral Quest for Windows, demo version

www.ancquest.com

Produced by Incline Software, Ancestral Quest family tree software is an easy-to-use program suitable for beginners but also offering many features of interest to more advanced researchers, including how to create excellent charts and publish a family history book.

Once installed, the demo version is fully functional for 60 days, after which time most update and export functions will cease to work unless you purchase a registration key (see the website for details), but you can still use the software to view family databases without the key.

## Brother's Keeper for Windows, shareware version

www.bkwin.org

Brother's Keeper genealogical shareware enables you to store information about your family and create charts and reports using that information. The shareware product is the full version; you can also order a copy of the program with a user's manual for a one-off fee via the publisher's website.

## Ezitree Plus for Windows, demo version

www.ezitree.com.au

Ezitree is an Australian product, popular with many researchers who like the comfort of having local support. This version has been completely revised and enables you to enter, manage, search and publish your family history.

The demo version contains most features and allows you to enter up to 100 individuals. You can purchase a fully registered version via the website and add to it the data you entered in the demo version.

## Family Historian for Windows, demo version

www.family-historian.co.uk

Family Historian has won a number of awards for being the best family history software on the market. Using the software you can link photos to each individual in your database and load sound and video files as well.

The demo version runs for 30 days; to use the software after this trial period you must purchase a licence and obtain a registration key (see the website for more details).

### Legacy Family Tree for Windows, full standard version

www.legacyfamilytree.com

Legacy software has a strong following in Australia. The CD has the full standard edition of the program. At the company's website you can purchase the deluxe edition, which has 98 additional features such as wall charts and mapping features.

### Heredis Mac X.2 for Mac, trial version

www.myheredis.com

Using the trial version of Heredis you can enter data on 50 individuals and import as many people as you wish using a GEDCOM file. A full version of the software can be purchased and downloaded from the website.

### MacFamilyTree, trial version

www.synium.de

Synium Software's MacFamilyTree version 5.4 has a database that's readily configurable to suit individual needs and can produce a wide range of charts and reports. The CD contains a trial version; visit the website to purchase the fully registered version to begin utilising the software's full potential.

### Relatively Yours for Windows, trial version

www.relativelyyours.com

Relatively Yours is an events-based recording and tracking tool that allows you to list multiple sources against events and allows you to enter unlimited narratives. The trial version of the full program is limited only by the number of individuals you can enter; otherwise it has full functionality. You can purchase the full registered version through the website.

### Reunion for Mac, demo version

www.leisterpro.com

The demo version of this popular genealogical program allows you to enter data on 50 individuals, but you cannot export data or save charts. The full registered version, which you can purchase through the website, has these features.

# GEDCOM transfers

## GED2HTML for Windows, shareware version

www.starkeffect.com/ged2html/3.6a

This shareware program converts your GEDCOM file into an HTML file so that you can post data contained within the file on the Web. You must register if you decide to keep the program after the trial period of 14 days is over and pay a US$20 fee. The GED2HTML website provides additional information about the program.

## GEDClean for Windows, freeware version

www.raynorshyn.com/GEDClean/Default.asp

Using the GEDClean freeware you can strip out information about living persons from your GEDCOM file so that you can share your file with others and/or load it onto the internet. The CD contains the freeware 16-bit basic version; you can pay a small registration fee to download the 32-bit version, which has more features, via the website www.gedclean.com.

# Internet tools

## Internet Explorer 7.0 for Windows, full version

www.microsoft.com

Internet Explorer 7 is part of the Microsoft suite of software, and one of the most popular web browsers on the market. A full version is available on the CD, but you can learn more about the browser or check for updated versions by visiting the Microsoft website.

## Mozilla Firefox 3.0 for Windows, full version

www.mozilla.com

This web browser has developed a huge following, largely because of its flexibility and the many additional features you can add to personalise your browser. For example, you can customise Firefox not only to look how you want but also to add features such as organisation tools for photographs and videos.

## Anti-virus software

### AVG Free Version 8.5 for Windows, home version

free.avg.com

AVG is a well-respected anti-virus software program that provides anti-virus and anti-spyware protection. The copy of AVG Free included on the CD can be used for home and non-commercial use. If you want to obtain the full program, which has a number of additional features such as identity protection, a firewall and anti-spam software, you can download the program from the website.

## Useful utilities

### Abiword 2.6.8 for Windows, full version

www.abisource.com

If you don't need the full range of documents like spreadsheets and databases that are included in Microsoft Office, but want to be able to type a few letters, Abiword is a good program to try. It's simple to learn and offers a basic but useful word-processing package.

### Acrobat Reader for Windows, full version

www.adobe.com

Acrobat Reader 9 is a free program that lets you view and print PDF (Portable Document Format) files. The PDF format is widely used as it's readily transferable between different computers without losing content, style or format.

### Cute FTP for Windows, evaluation version

www.cuteFTP.com

Cute FTP (File Transfer Protocol) by GlobalSCAPE® allows you to transfer large numbers of files between your computer and other computers with internet access anywhere in the world. FTP is especially useful if you're building a website or downloading large files. After using the 30-day trial version, you can upgrade to a registered product through the website.

### Open Office 3.0 for Windows, full version

www.openoffice.org

If your budget doesn't stretch to buying a full version of Microsoft Office, you may like to consider using Open Office instead. With Open Office you can do word processing, make spreadsheets, create graphics, give presentations and much more.

You can use the full version that comes on the CD on any computer, without restriction. You may want to visit download.openoffice.org to check whether a newer edition is available for download. If you have any problems using the software, you can contact the software's community support forum at user.services.openoffice.org.

### Paint.NET 3.3.6 for Windows, full version

www.getpaint.net

This free image and photo-editing software program enables you to insert special effects into your photos as well as to edit them.

### WinZip for Windows, evaluation version

www.winzip.com

WinZip 12.0 is an invaluable file compression and decompression program. Many files that you find on the internet are compressed — or shrunken in size via special programming tricks — to save storage space and to cut down on the amount of time that they require to be downloaded. After you have saved a compressed file on your hard drive, you can use WinZip to decompress it and make it useable again.

After the 30-day evaluation period is up you can purchase the full version of WinZip Pro through the website.

# Using the Directory Links

The *Tracing Your Family History Online* Internet Directory in Appendix C provides many URLs for sites that we recommend you visit to get an idea of what's available in various categories. Rather than making you flip page by page through the directory to find these URLs, we thought we'd save you some time by putting links to all of the sites identified in the directory on the CD. Isn't that convenient? To access the Directory links, click on the Links button within the CD interface and then on the URL you wish to visit.

# Troubleshooting

We tried our best to select programs that work on most computers with the minimum system requirements. Alas, your computer may differ, and some programs may not work properly for some reason.

The two likeliest problems are that you don't have enough memory (RAM) for the programs you want to use, or you have other programs running that are affecting installation or running of a program. If you get an error message such as Not enough memory or Setup cannot continue, try one or more of the following suggestions and then try using the software again:

 ✔ **Turn off any antivirus software running on your computer.** Installation programs sometimes mimic virus activity and may make your computer incorrectly believe that it's being infected by a virus.

 ✔ **Close all running programs.** The more programs you have running, the less memory is available to other programs. Installation programs typically update files and programs; so if you keep other programs running, installation may not work properly.

 ✔ **Have your local computer store add more RAM to your computer.** This is, admittedly, a drastic and somewhat expensive step. However, adding more memory can really help the speed of your computer and allow more programs to run at the same time.

# Customer Care

If you have trouble with the CD-ROM, please call Wiley Product Technical Support in the United States on 317-572-3993. You can also contact Wiley Product Technical Support at http://support.wiley.com. Wiley Publishing will provide technical support only for installation and other general quality control items. For technical support on the applications themselves, consult the program's vendor or author.

# Appendix C

# Internet Directory

• • • • • • • • • • • • • • • • • • • • • • • • • • • • • • • • • • •

*L*ook no further for an overview of the types of sites that you can find online. The *Tracing Your Family History Online* Internet Directory lists sites and abstracts of what you find at each site. We've also provided some descriptive narratives telling you why these types of sites are useful to you. Among our examples are search engines, genealogical gateways and resources that are surname-related, government-sponsored, geographic-specific or commercial in nature. More specifically, this directory has information to help you find the following:

- ✔ Cemetery records
- ✔ Commercial genealogy sites and databases
- ✔ Elusive records
- ✔ Family associations
- ✔ Family history societies gateways
- ✔ Genealogical gateways
- ✔ Genealogical software and utilities
- ✔ General search engines
- ✔ Government repositories (in Australia and overseas)
- ✔ Local and family history societies
- ✔ One-name studies
- ✔ Online bookshops
- ✔ Professional researchers
- ✔ Records of births, deaths and marriages (in Australia and overseas)

# About Those Micons

For each site, we provide the name of the site, the URL (web address) and a brief description of what you can find there. Also, the mini icons (micons, as we like to call 'em) tell you at first glance what kinds of resources the site offers. Here's a list of the micons and what each one means:

**Book:** Using this software you can put together your own genealogical book containing charts, forms, photographs and reports that you generate using the data you enter into the software.

**$ Charge for services:** You'll be charged for some services and records detailed on this site.

**Download documents:** You can download copies of original documents from this site.

**Download software:** You can download software from this site.

**Electronic newsletter:** This site offers a regular electronic newsletter (sometimes only for members).

**FAQs:** This site includes a section with Frequently Asked Questions and their answers about a particular aspect of genealogical research, guides on specific records and topics in family history.

**GEDCOM:** This software supports GEDCOM, the standard for sharing data between genealogical programs.

**Index:** This site includes a section listing genealogical resources, guides and links to other genealogical sites.

**Members only section:** Access to parts of this site is restricted to members or subscribers.

**Multimedia:** This site includes photographs and sound or video files.

**Online database:** This site includes an online database of genealogical information.

**Online ordering:** You can place online orders at this site.

**Online records:** Here you find transcribed and/or digitised records with genealogical value. The information at this site is either in the form of transcriptions from actual records (such as vital records, census returns and so on) or digitised (scanned) copies of actual records.

**On the CD:** A version of this software is included on the CD-ROM that accompanies this book.

**$ 'Pay to view' site:** Access to parts of this site is available only on payment of a charge or as part of a membership or subscription.

**'Pay to view' vouchers:** You can purchase 'pay to view' vouchers for use on this site so that you don't have to provide your credit card details online.

**Queries:** At this site, you can post genealogical questions pertaining to surnames, geographic locations or research in general; read and respond to queries left by other researchers; or participate in a forum.

 **Registration:** This site requires you to register some personal details and to obtain a user name/ password before you can fully use the features on the site.

 **Searchable:** This site has a search engine you can use to look for keywords and/or surnames.

# Cemetery Records

Cemetery records are a very important source of family history information for genealogists. Luckily, many volunteers have helped place cemetery transcriptions online and cemetery authorities are beginning to offer online searching of their records.

## Australian Cemeteries

www.ozgenonline.com/aust_cemeteries

This is a good starting point for Australian cemetery research, since it points you to online databases, transcripts and volunteer search services. You can select a state or territory and then a specific cemetery by name, or simply browse the list of cemeteries for your chosen state or territory.

## Australian Cemeteries Index

cemindex.arkangles.com

This site has excellent coverage of cemetery inscriptions in regional New South Wales and parts of Queensland, and includes transcriptions, photographs of headstones, location maps and additional information to help you establish who administers a particular cemetery today. You can search by surname across the whole database or by specific cemetery.

## Brisbane City Council's cemeteries database

www.brisbane.qld.gov.au

Brisbane City Council's cemeteries database searches across 12 cemeteries and three crematoriums in the Brisbane area. To access the database, from the Council's home page click on Cemeteries and then do a Grave Location Search, using a surname and at least one initial for the given name. Search results cover burial information (including whether anyone else is buried in the grave) and a map showing the grave's location.

## Metropolitan Cemeteries Board of Western Australia

www.mcb.wa.gov.au/default.php

The Metropolitan Cemeteries Board website provides online access to burial records held by five of the six cemeteries the Board operates in the Perth region. In addition to burial information the site has maps and downloadable brochures on historical walks and tours where available.

This is one of the first cemetery authorities to offer webcasting of funeral services for the benefit of those unable to attend services for their family and friends.

### Rookwood Independent Cemetery

www.rookwoodindependent.com.au

Rookwood Independent Cemetery near Sydney covers the Methodist, Wesleyan, Uniting, Lutheran and Presbyterian sections of Rookwood Cemetery, the largest cemetery in the southern hemisphere. You can access all burial and cremation records administered by the Independent Cemetery and use its mapping facility to locate a specific grave within the main cemetery.

# Commercial Genealogy Sites and Databases

The following are some of the major commercial companies offering genealogical material. Although each website allows you to conduct a limited search for free, you need to subscribe to the site or purchase 'pay to view' vouchers to view the full records and/ or download a copy of an indexed document.

### Ancestry.com

www.ancestry.com

Ancestry.com has various sister sites, including www.ancestry.com.au for Australia and www.ancestry.co.uk for the British Isles, as well as sites for Canada, Germany, Italy, France, Sweden and China. Australian databases include convict records, shipping material, electoral rolls and post office directories, to name just a few. Ancestry.com is a subscription-based service that offers limited index searches. Occasionally the site has special offers giving you a free trial of its full database for a limited period.

### FamilySearch

www.familysearch.org

The FamilySearch website is maintained by the Genealogical Society of Utah (GSU), which is part of The Church of Jesus Christ of Latter-day Saints. If you undertake a surname search the site looks for all occurrences of the name in a number of databases, including the International Genealogical Index (largely baptism and marriage records extracted from parish records around the world), the Ancestral File (records submitted to the Church by its members), the US Social Security Death Index, the Vital Records Index and the Pedigree Resource file. You can also search the census records for 1880 (United States) and 1881 (England and Canada). In addition, the site provides access to the Church's Family History Library catalogue, which contains records on more than 2.2 million reels of microfilm. These can be ordered for viewing at Family History Centres around the world, including in Australia. The GSU has begun a project to place digitised images of many of its records online.

### Find My Past

www.findmypast.com

Find My Past is one of the key commercial genealogical websites and has a range of online databases that you can search by subscription or on a 'pay to view' basis, including many English census records, BDM indexes, London parish burials and Great Western Railway shareholder records for the period 1835–1910. Recently Find My Past has taken on a number of records formerly offered by the Federation of Family History Societies, including the National Burial Index for the UK for the years 1538–2005.

In partnership with the National Archives, Find My Past has available on its partner site, at www.ancestorsonboard.com, a database of more than 30 million passengers who left England between 1890 and 1960. And you can find the 1911 English census at www.1911census.co.uk, although this database will eventually be incorporated into the Find My Past website.

### Origins Network

www.origins.net

The Origins Network is a great website to remember after you've gone beyond the basics, because it provides access to many smaller databases like pre-1858

wills, London burials and emigration records you won't find online anywhere else. Origins Network incorporates three separate sites, each relating to English, Irish or Scottish research. You can subscribe to each site independently or take out a 'total access' subscription.

### RootsWeb

www.rootsweb.ancestry.com

RootsWeb is part of the Ancestry.com stable but its content is free. You can search more than 480 million names in family trees included in WorldConnect and join any of the 30,000 genealogical Mailing Lists it hosts.

## Elusive Records

Websites containing unique records and resources can be of great value to you in your genealogical pursuits. Some sites pertain to a particular group of people, while others cover records that are otherwise hard to find. Here are some examples of websites that fit the bill.

### AIATSIS Family History Unit

www.aiatsis.gov.au/library/family_history_tracing

The website of the Australian Institute of Aboriginal and Torres Strait Islander Studies (AIATSIS) features a Family History Unit that provides online guides to help Aboriginal and Torres Strait Islanders to track down their ancestors and establish links with lost family members. Fact sheets explain the types of records available to family history researchers, along with how to access them, and links provide pathways to other genealogy resources.

## Australian Society of Archivists

www.archivists.org.au

At this website you can quickly locate the more unusual archival repositories held by private collectors, businesses, church groups and government agencies across Australia. Details include where each archive is located, the type of records the repository holds, hours of opening and access conditions.

## Commonwealth War Graves Commission

www.cwgc.org

The Commonwealth War Graves website details the records of 1.7 million known grave sites of service men and women, commemorating members who served in the British, Australian, New Zealand, Indian and South African forces in both World War I and World War II. In addition to searching the Debt of Honour Register to find an ancestor's final resting place, burial and next of kin details, you can download photographs of many of the cemeteries as well as maps to help you locate a grave should you be planning a visit.

## Families in British India Society

www.fibis.org

The Families in British India (FIBIS) website aims to bring together resources and guidance for those seeking to follow their ancestral ties with countries such as India, Burma, Pakistan and Bangladesh. The site offers a searchable database of records as well as a feature called FiBiWiKi, which is a collection of information to assist researchers.

## Picture Australia

www.pictureaustralia.org

Hosted by the National Library of Australia, the Picture Australia website gives you access to the pictorial collections of libraries, museums, galleries, archives and cultural institutions throughout the country. You can search for an image by name, subject or location.

## The Proceedings of the Old Bailey

www.oldbaileyonline.org

If you have an ancestor who was tried at the Central Criminal Court in London (known as the Old Bailey), you can read his or her trial details on this site, which indexes more than 197,745 trials that took place between 1674 and 1913. Don't forget that some of your ancestors may have been victims or witnesses in trials, so they may appear in the database for that reason too.

## The Statue of Liberty–Ellis Island Foundation, Inc.

www.ellisisland.org

This website features an online index to the arrival details of the 22 million people who immigrated to the United States through Ellis Island between 1892 and 1924. The index provides details of passenger name, place of origin, year of arrival and age. Once you locate the name you're researching in the database, you can register (for free) to see the full passenger record.

## World War 2 Nominal Roll

www.ww2roll.gov.au

The Department of Veterans' Affairs provides this online database of all Australian service personnel who served in World War II. You can search the database by name, service number and/or place. The database records place of enlistment, date of death or return to Australia, if relevant, next of kin and much more. It contains more than one million entries.

# Family Associations

Sometimes, distinguishing between one-name studies and family association sites is difficult because their content is often similar (see 'One-Name Studies' in this directory). Usually a family association has an underlying organisation, whereas one-name studies do not. A formal family association may focus on a surname as a whole or on a particular branch of a family and, as a result, the association's website focuses on the same.

## Entwistle Family History Association

www.entwistlefamily.org.uk

Dating back to the 1000s in Lancashire, England, Entwistle descendants now live in every part of the English-speaking world — including the United Kingdom, the United States, Australia, Canada, New Zealand, Ireland and South Africa. The Entwistle Family History Association website provides historical information about branches of this ancient family, including variations of the surname, family members of repute, heraldry (coats of arms) and much more. The site has in-depth articles, books, the *Twissle Times* quarterly online newsletter, an online forum, FAQs and membership information. A Members Only section contains databases of relevant family history information.

## Peacock Family Association of the South

www.peacockfamily.org

Membership of the Peacock Family Association is open to all people interested in the surname Peacock, regardless of whether they have links to the American south. The website identifies resources available from the Association, including information about reunions and membership, photographs, GEDCOM files pertaining to Peacocks and information on the Peacock DNA project.

### The Rutledge Family Association

www.rootsweb.ancestry.
com/~rutledge

The Rutledge Family Association website has a real-time chat facility where researchers can share their research results and discuss their genealogical challenges, as well as pages with FAQs, a glossary, online Family Group Sheets submitted by other Rutledge researchers containing details of more than 20,000 individuals and links to other websites of interest to Rutledge researchers.

# Family History Societies Gateways

Use the following websites to find directories of family history societies that may be able to help you with your genealogical research. When you identify a society of interest, you can check its website to establish what guidance it can give you and what records it holds.

### Australasian Federation of Family History Organisations

www.affho.org

The Australasian Federation of Family History Organisations website has links to many Australian family history societies. You can search the site by the society's name or by region.

### Federation of Family History Societies

www.ffhs.org.uk

The Federation of Family History Societies website lists all its member societies, giving you a quick link to most English, Welsh and Irish family history societies.

### Federation of Eastern European Family History Societies

www.feefhs.org

The Federation of Eastern European Family History Societies exists to advance genealogical societies in eastern and central Europe. Its online Map Room can help you locate historical maps of the region.

# Genealogical Gateways

A genealogical gateway site is one that identifies a large number of other sites of interest to genealogists. Most gateway sites are set up as directories — they have the names and URLs categorised (or indexed) with individual sites sorted by subject or geographical categories.

Most gateway sites are relatively easy to navigate — so as long as you know the topic that you're looking for, you can glance through the listing and see whether anything is available. For example, if you're looking for cemetery records for the state of Tasmania, you can visit a gateway site and look in its sections pertaining to Tasmania and/or cemetery records.

Some gateway sites make searching even easier by providing a search facility. Rather than clicking your way through the hierarchy of categories and subcategories to find links pertaining to the topic in which you're interested, you can enter a keyword into a form and let the search facility do the work for you. Typically, the search returns a list of possible matches to your keyword, and you can pick sites you wish to visit from this list.

Here are a few of the best-known genealogical gateway sites.

### Coraweb

www.coraweb.com.au

This is the best Australian gateway site around: It can quickly help you locate more than 1,600 links of interest in more than 45 categories. The site covers everything from mailing lists to maps, and cemeteries to surname searching and researching Irish, English and Aboriginal and Torres Strait Islander resources.

### Cyndi's List of Genealogy Sites on the Internet

www.cyndislist.com

This popular site, by Cyndi Howells, has more than 260,000 links indexed and cross-indexed by topic in more than 180 categories. The categories are based on ethnic groups, religious groups, geographic locations, products (such as books and software), types of records, learning resources (like beginner information, how-to and writing a family history) and other interests (for example, adoption, reunions, royalty and travel). Although Cyndi Howells is based in the United States and the site is primarily designed for American researchers, it provides global coverage and includes many Australian resources.

### GENUKI: UK & Ireland Genealogy

www.genuki.org.uk

One of the most well-known websites for tracing English, Irish, Scottish, Welsh, Channel Islands and Isle of Man genealogy, GENUKI provides great paths into all kinds of interesting sites relating to family history in the British Isles. The site has a hierarchal structure, which means you search for information at different levels — by country, by county or by place. GENUKI is run by a cooperative of dedicated volunteers across the British Isles and is a great springboard if you're a genealogy beginner or are just looking for further inspiration for your research. It also has a very useful Genealogical Gazetteer feature available from the home page, which allows you to quickly determine the location of a specific place in the British Isles and the sites that link you to records of interest for it.

# Genealogical Software and Utilities

Whether you want to buy your first genealogical software program, upgrade to a later or registered version of the program you currently use or make an enhancement to your genealogical files, you're probably interested in what software is available and what it has to offer you. Here's a list of software sites and a few specialty utility program sites you may want to check out.

## Ancestral Quest

www.ancquest.com

Ancestral Quest is produced by Incline Software and is suitable for beginners, although it also has features for the more advanced researcher. The website offers a product overview, as well as an introductory video tutorial and information on add-on products.

## Brother's Keeper

www.bkwin.org

The Brother's Keeper website offers free downloads of its shareware software plus an online shop where you can purchase the full registered version. The site also has an FAQ section along with sample charts and family group sheet reports that you can download.

## Ezitree

www.ezitree.com.au

Ezitree is an Australian family history software product and through this website you can download a sample version as well as an instruction manual. The site also has an FAQ section and includes testimonials from Ezitree users.

## Family Tree Maker

www.familytreemaker.com

Family Tree Maker is part of the Ancestry.com range of products. The website offers a product overview as well as numerous webinars and tutorials that you can access to find out more about the software and how to make the best use of it.

## Legacy Family Tree

www.legacyfamilytree.com

At the Legacy website you can find out about creating charts, citing sources and much more. This extensive site is designed for both current users of the Legacy software and those yet to decide which software program to use.

## Relatively Yours

www.relativelyyours.com

Relatively Yours is an Australian program, and as well as examining the features of the software the site provides a discussion group and a useful mapping add-on for registered users of the software.

## Reunion 9

www.leisterpro.com

Reunion 9 is one of the few software applications for use on Macintosh computers. The website is divided into two sections: Welcome, for those contemplating using the program; and Welcome Back, for registered users looking for support from the program developers and the opportunity to share in a discussion group with other users.

## The Master Genealogist

www.whollygenes.com

This site offers a guided tour of The Master Genealogist software. You can download a trial version of the software as well as family history add-ons that you can use with other software programs.

# General Search Engines

Although we don't recommend starting your online genealogical research using one of the major search engines (see Chapter 3 for the reasons), a general search engine may give you some leads if you hit a brick wall in your research. Because a search on one name or word

tends to return thousands — if not hundreds of thousands — of results when you use a general search engine, if you want to try using a general search engine for genealogy you should follow its instructions for narrowing your search. Typically, this means using more than one word in your search and avoiding really common words altogether. (For example, you don't want to include 'the', 'a' and 'of' in your search, or you'll get an unmanageable number of results if the search engine doesn't automatically ignore those words.)

## AltaVista

au.altavista.com

Using the main search box on AltaVista you can search the internet worldwide or limit your search to Australia. You can also choose to search Images or News and do an Advanced Search.

## Google Australia

www.google.com.au

The Google search engine is so well known people now talk about 'googling' their ancestors. Using the simple search function you can search within Australia or worldwide, and you can limit your search with the I'm Feeling Lucky feature, whereby Google selects one website that its robots have listed as being the most relevant to your search term. You can do much more than use Google as a general search engine: You can also explore its many other features, such as images, maps and documents.

### Yahoo!

Yahoo.com.au

With the Yahoo! search engine you can search worldwide or narrow your search to just Australia or just New Zealand. You can also limit your search to images or maps: An images search finds relevant videos posted on You Tube.

# Government Repositories

Government officials create many of the records used by family historians, so visiting a government website often rewards you with vital information about your ancestors. Many government departments have committed vast resources to making their records available online.

## In Australia

### Archives Office of Tasmania

www.archives.tas.gov.au

The website of the Archives Office of Tasmania features a Name Index to various databases covering diverse topics such as shipping arrivals and departures, wills, convict marriages, divorce records and inquests. The site also offers access to the Colonial Tasmanian Family Links database, where you can search for information about families living in Tasmania in the nineteenth century, based on records

of births, deaths, marriages and similar events.

### Australian Libraries Gateway

www.nla.gov.au/libraries

The Australian Libraries Gateway — sponsored by the National Library of Australia — is a directory of more than 5,200 Australian libraries, their collections and services. You can search for a specific library by name, by location or by category.

### Australian War Memorial

www.awm.gov.au

The Australian War Memorial website chronicles the role of Australians involved in past conflicts — including the Sudan Contingent in 1885, World War I, World War II and the 1990–1991 Gulf War. The site features online databases detailing personnel records, honours, awards and commemorations, as well as Red Cross Files of the Wounded and Missing.

### National Archives of Australia

www.naa.gov.au

The National Archives of Australia's main collection focuses on records created since 1901, many of which are now being digitised and placed on its website. You can use the RecordSearch feature to find records created by thousands of Commonwealth agencies, and the PhotoSearch feature to find photos and images from its collection. The Name

Search feature covers specific digitised files on topics such as service in World War I, naturalisation, registering of patents and being identified as an 'alien' in times of international conflict. The site has many free downloadable fact sheets that detail how to obtain information about a specific family history topic within the Archives' collections.

## Northern Territory Archives Service

www.nt.gov.au/nreta/ntas

The Northern Territory Archives Service was set up in 1978 when the Northern Territory government was established, and it inherited records from periods of administration by the South Australian government (1863–1910) and the Commonwealth government (1911–1978). The website provides a wealth of information about the records in its collections, including government archives, personal papers (diaries, manuscripts, photographic prints and slides, scrapbooks, maps, letters and personal papers), organisational records and oral history archives.

## Public Record Office Victoria

www.prov.vic.gov.au

Public Record Office Victoria is adding new digital images to its online collection on a regular basis and is well worth exploring if you have Victorian ancestry. The website has indexes to Inward Passenger Lists for the years 1852 to 1899, and has indexed and digitised Victorian probate records for the period 1841 to 1925.

## Queensland State Archives

www.archives.qld.gov.au

At the Queensland State Archives website you can search a wide range of online indexes to records held in the Archives, including those relating to civil servants, criminal depositions, divorce, immigration, inquests, Justices of the Peace, mineral leases, passports, teachers and wills. To find out how to access other records to assist with Queensland research, see the site's extensive FAQs for genealogists.

## State Records Authority of New South Wales

www.records.nsw.gov.au

The State Records Authority of New South Wales provides online guides to many of its records, as well as indexes to a huge variety of records used by family and local historians, including records relating to convicts, immigration and shipping, companies, bankruptcies, the census and the transfer of land.

## State Records of South Australia

www.archives.sa.gov.au

The website of State Records of South Australia documents South Australia's heritage and provides information about the resources the authority holds, the publications it produces on genealogy and how you can access this material.

### State Records Office of Western Australia

www.sro.wa.gov.au

The archives collection held by the State Records Office of Western Australia includes maps, architectural drawings, microfilm and sound recordings. Extensive online guides document records of interest to genealogists, including Aboriginal records, convict records, passenger lists and immigration records, prison and gaol records, court records, local government records and more. These resources can be accessed by following the relevant link from The Collection on the home page.

# Overseas

### Library of Congress

www.loc.gov

Since its foundation in 1800, the Library of Congress has become the library of national significance in the United States. Its website explains its many collections and includes a number of online exhibitions highlighting some of its treasures.

### Library and Archives Canada

www.collectionscanada.gc.ca/index-e.html

The Library and Archives Canada website includes a Canadian Genealogy Centre that can be accessed from its home page. The site offers searches of its online databases — including records relating to births, deaths and marriages, divorce, immigration, census, military service and land ownership — and also has many useful online guides.

### Public Record Office of Northern Ireland

www.proni.gov.uk

The Public Record Office of Northern Ireland (PRONI) is the official repository for Northern Ireland's records of government agencies, courts and other public offices, as well as for records contributed by businesses, institutions, churches and individuals. The website provides general information about its resources and services and has recently added a Names Search database, which offers access to some online indexes, including an index to wills.

### The National Archives and Records Administration

www.archives.gov

The National Archives and Records Administration (NARA) in the United States says that if you laid every piece of paper it holds in its collection end-to-end, they would circle the earth 57 times! Many of these records are of interest to family historians, including census returns, military service records and passenger lists. Most major record sets have been digitised by the large online commercial providers such as Ancestry.com and are available only to their subscribers (or if you personally visit the National Archives in Washington).

Additionally, NARA has some other databases online that you can find by following the links through the Genealogy/Family Historians link on the home page.

## The National Archives of the United Kingdom

www.nationalarchives.gov.uk

Founded in 1838, the National Archives is the major repository for British government and court records. It offers online searching of a number of databases through its DocumentsOnLine service, which also provides digital copies of the relevant records for instant download at a small fee. This includes all the Prerogative Court of Canterbury wills prior to 1858 and some military records. The site has very useful tutorials on topics such as reading old handwriting and an extensive series of podcasts of its lecture series.

## The National Archives of Ireland

www.nationalarchives.ie

The National Archives of Ireland website contains information to help you research its Archives. Select Genealogy from the home page to find guides to Irish research and useful links to other websites. The National Archives has a project underway to offer the 1901 and 1911 census of Ireland online, and the index and images of the first counties to be covered by this project are now available.

## The National Library of Wales

www.llgc.org.uk

If you're just beginning your Welsh family history research, the National Library of Wales website is a great starting point. Services for genealogists include straightforward information about the records the Library holds, and the site has a number of searchable online archival databases, including some pre-1858 wills and Applications for Marriage Licences for the period 1616 to 1837. If you need someone to look up a document or record for you, the site lists independent researchers who can access the collections in person on your behalf.

# Local and Family History Societies

Local and family history societies often have helpful websites that allow you to learn about the records the societies hold and the services they offer. Here are a few examples of various local and family history societies.

## Australian Lebanese Historical Society of Victoria

alhsv.org.au

The website of the Australian Lebanese Historical Society of Victoria is an example of an ethnic group researching and documenting its role in Australian history. The site provides information on resources and research guides to help those tracing their Lebanese family history, as well as featuring stories of prominent members of the Australian Lebanese community.

## New England Historic Genealogical Society

www.newenglandancestors.org

The New England Historic Genealogical Society is the largest genealogical society in the world, and its website offers many benefits for members, including access to more than 2,000 databases. For visitors, the site has research guides and excellent information on the Society's holdings.

## New Zealand Society of Genealogists

www.genealogy.org.nz

Although the New Zealand Society of Genealogists limits access to most of its online databases to members, visitors to its website can benefit from its research guides on New Zealand resources, download charts and learn more about the Society's research facilities.

## Society of Australian Genealogists

www.sag.org.au

  $

The website of the Society of Australian Genealogists offers several online indexes, such as NSW Convict Tickets of Leave 1810–1875, NSW Ships' Muster

index of passengers and crews departing New South Wales between 1816 and 1825, and the Soldiers and Marines index covering the period 1787 to 1830. There are also guides to both Australian and overseas genealogical resources. The library catalogue is available online and can be searched by author, subject, title and keyword.

## The Scottish Genealogy Society

www.scotsgenealogy.com

The Scottish Genealogy Society website offers a series of research guides and articles contributed by its members and relating to the Society's resources and to Scottish research in general. The site also has an online forum and an index to the family histories in its collection. For a comprehensive directory of Scottish genealogy sites, don't miss the Links page.

# One-Name Studies

Unlike personal web pages, which provide you with detailed information about an individual's research and particular branch of a family, one-name studies give you a wide range of information on one particular surname, often with worldwide coverage. One-name studies typically have information that includes histories of the surname (including its origins), variations in spelling, heraldry associated with the name, and databases, narratives and queries submitted by researchers worldwide.

## Chicken Family Histories

freepages.genealogy.rootsweb.
ancestry.com/~chicken

Chicken Family Histories is 'intended
to be a focus for all Chickens and their
descendants across the world'. The
Master Coop tells you about the origins
of the Chicken surname, and the Chicken
Scratchings section has information
about some better-known Chickens. The
various poultry graphics and play-on-
words at this site make it fun to visit
even if you're not a Chicken!

## Drake Family

www.xroyvision.com.au/drake/
drakepage.htm

The Drake Family website has heaps
of information on the surname Drake,
including a 1999–2008 rollcall of
everyone researching the surname
Drake and databases of references to the
name extracted from BDM records and
war records, as well as miscellaneous
references to the name collected from
around the world.

## The Guild of One-Name Studies

www.one-name.org

The Guild of One-Name Studies website
is literally an association of groups
and online sites that have registered as
repositories for information pertaining to
particular surnames, and the Register of
One-Name Studies is searchable online.

The website also provides information
on forming a one-name group and how to
register it with the Guild.

## Thompson One Name Study

www.thompsononename.org.uk

The Thompson One Name Study site
includes a database of all references to
the Thompson surname and its variants
collected to date, as well as details of
the origins of the surname and research
conducted on families of that name.

# Online Bookshops

Sometimes, finding a specific book
about a particular surname, geographic
location or event in history can be
difficult. After all, most local bookstores
and libraries carry only a small range
of genealogical books and supplies.
When you're trying to locate a certain
genealogical or historical title, online
bookstores come in handy. Here we
list some bookstores that specialise in
genealogical titles.

## Family Tree Magazine & Practical Family History

www.family-tree.co.uk

ABM Publishing, the company behind
the UK monthly magazines *Family Tree
Magazine* and *Practical Family History*,
provides an online shop where you can
buy books and other products relating
to genealogy in the United Kingdom and

beyond. The company claims that it has one of the most extensive listings of genealogical titles available online.

### GENfair

www.genfair.co.uk

GENfair is a cooperative venture run by S&N Genealogy for the Federation of Family History Societies in the United Kingdom on behalf of its member groups. On its website you can find thousands of CDs/DVDs, microfiches, books and pamphlets prepared by local history societies.

### Gould Genealogy & History

www.gould.com.au

Gould Genealogy, Australia's largest online specialist genealogical bookshop, offers access to both Australian and overseas publications, including books, CDs and software. Use this website to track down hard-to-find genealogy titles or, if you want to keep up-to-date on new titles and specials, subscribe to the online newsletter.

### Macbeth Genealogical Services

www.macbeth.com.au

Macbeth Genealogical Services is an Australian provider of genealogy titles, including microfiche and CD products. The company produces a number of its own titles, especially those associated with CDs of indexes to birth, death and marriage records, as well as Victorian shipping records.

### S&N Genealogy

www.genealogysupplies.com

S&N Genealogy is a large UK-based publisher that specialises in producing CDs and software. S&N has published many English census records and offers an online newsletter so that its customers can keep up-to-date with new releases.

### Society of Australian Genealogists

www.sag.org.au

The Society of Australian Genealogists website features a shop that stocks books, microfiches, CDs, software, magazines, vouchers for 'pay to view' websites and genealogical stationery for both Australian and overseas researchers. You can buy items online, or by mail, fax or phone. The Society's monthly newsletter, *SAG-E*, highlights titles from the shop in each issue.

# Professional Researchers

At some time, you may need to hire a professional researcher to pursue your genealogy of a particular family line. Perhaps you've exhausted all your leads or no longer have the time to devote to research. Maybe the records you need are in another state or overseas.

Engaging a member of a professional association to do research for you is a good idea because members sign a code of conduct and often have to meet certain criteria in order to join the association, so you know they can be trusted to do a professional job. Most countries have a professional genealogical association that lists details of members on its website.

## Australasian Association of Genealogists and Record Agents

www.aagra.asn.au

The Australasian Association of Genealogists and Record Agents provides an online directory of its members, its code of ethics and fee guidelines for engaging a professional researcher.

## Association of Professional Genealogists

www.apgen.org

You can search the Directory of Members of the Association of Professional Genealogists in the United States by name, by location or by research speciality. The Association has worldwide membership.

## The Association of Genealogists and Researchers in Archives

www.agra.org.uk

The United Kingdom's Association of Genealogists and Researchers in Archives website allows you to locate a researcher by name, by location or by subject.

## The Association of Professional Genealogists in Ireland

www.apgi.ie

The Association of Professional Genealogists in Ireland website provides a directory of its members and their contact details. It also has some good tips on how to select the right research agent to do research work on your behalf.

## The Association of Scottish Genealogists & Researchers in Archives

www.asgra.co.uk

The list of researchers featured on the Association of Scottish Genealogists & Researchers in Archives website includes not only each researcher's name and contact details, but also areas of special interests and expertise.

# Records of Births, Deaths and Marriages

Birth, death and marriage (BDM) records are such an important part of family history research that having databases and indexes available online is tremendously helpful. Here are a few BDM websites to check out for Australia and overseas.

# In Australia

## New South Wales Registry of Births, Deaths and Marriages

www.bdm.nsw.gov.au

At the New South Wales Registry of Births, Deaths and Marriages you can search online indexes of baptisms/births from 1788 to 1908, marriages covering the period 1788 to 1958, and deaths from 1788 to 1978. You can search the indexes for free and then order a certificate online at a discount price when you quote the index number.

## Queensland Births, Deaths & Marriages

www.justice.qld.gov.au

The Queensland registry offers free online indexes for births for the years 1829 to 1914, and for deaths and marriages for the period 1829 to 1929.

## Ryerson Index

www.ryersonindex.org

The Ryerson Index lists more than two million death notices collected from newspapers around Australia (especially New South Wales) and indexed by volunteers from the Dead Persons Society. The site is a terrific resource for tracking down records of more recent deaths, but the large band of volunteers is steadily working backwards from the present day.

The site is a great companion to the New South Wales Registry of Births, Deaths and Marriages website (www.bdm.nsw.gov.au), which stops its online death index at 1978.

## Victorian Births, Deaths & Marriages

online.justice.vic.gov.au/ots/home

At this Victorian site you can search online indexes for baptisms/births for the years 1836 to 1908, marriages for the period 1836 to 1942 and burials/deaths from 1836 to 1985. The site also has a Marine Index of births, deaths and marriages that occurred on ships going to Victoria during the period 1853 to 1920. You need to pay a fee to search the indexes, and you can download a copy of the required certificate immediately upon payment of the prescribed fee.

## Western Australian Births, Deaths & Marriages

www.bdm.dotag.wa.gov.au

This site has free online indexes covering births for the years 1841 to 1932, marriages for the period 1841 to 1932 and deaths between 1841 and 1953.

# Overseas

## FreeBMD (UK)

www.freebmd.org.uk

Use FreeBMD to search for birth, marriage and death indexes for England and Wales from 1837 onwards. FreeBMD draws on a large pool of volunteer transcribers to enter index records into its database, which contains more than 165 million records. FreeBMD is one of the great success stories of online volunteer projects.

## General Register Office (UK)

www.gro.gov.uk/gro/content/
certificates

At the General Register Office website you can order birth, death and marriage certificates for events that took place in England and Wales after 1837. However, the indexes to these records aren't currently available at the site, so first you need to visit a site such as FreeBMD to obtain the reference number for the certificate(s) you require.

## General Register Office for Northern Ireland

www.groni.gov.uk

The General Register Office for Northern Ireland holds records of civil registration births, deaths and marriages and provides an online application service to obtain copies of certificates.

## ScotlandsPeople

www.scotlandspeople.gov.uk

At the ScotlandsPeople website you can search online indexes of Scottish births for the period 1855 to 2006, marriages for the years 1855 to 1933 and deaths from 1855 to 2006. You can also search the ten-yearly census returns from 1841 to 1901 as well as Scotland's Old Parish Registers, which are Church of Scotland registers of baptisms, marriages, deaths and burials covering the period 1553 to 1854.

## The General Register Office (Republic of Ireland)

www.groireland.ie

The Republic doesn't offer an online certificate ordering service or any online indexes; however, at this website you can download the appropriate order form and find out the fees involved in obtaining a certificate for family history purposes.

# Index

# Notes

# FOR DUMMIES®

## Business & Investment

**Starting an Online Business**
0-7314-0991-4
$39.95

**Small Business**
1-74216-853-1
$39.95

**Investing for Australians ALL-IN-ONE**
0-7314-0838-1
$54.95

**Superannuation**
0-7314-0715-6
$39.95

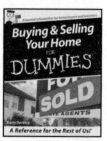

**Buying & Selling Your Home**
1-74031-166-3
$39.95

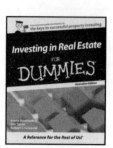

**Investing in Real Estate**
0-7314-0724-5
$39.95

**Online Share Investing**
0-7314-0940-X
$39.95

**Tax for Australians**
1-74216-859-0
$32.95

**Leadership**
0-7314-0787-3
$39.95

**Freelancing for Australians**
0-7314-0762-8
$39.95

**Australian Resumes**
1-74031-091-8
$39.95

**Sorting Out Your Finances**
0-7314-0746-6
$29.95

# FOR DUMMIES®

## Reference

**Work / Life Balance**

0-7314-0723-7
$34.95

**World Poverty**

0-7314-0699-0
$34.95

**Sustainable Living**

1-74031-157-4
$39.95

**Wedding Planning**

0-7314-0721-0
$34.95

**Passing Exams**

1-74216-925-2
$29.95

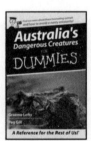

**Australia's Dangerous Creatures**

0-7314-0722-9
$29.95

**Sustainable Australian Travel**

0-7314-0784-9
$34.95

**English Grammar**

0-7314-0752-0
$34.95

## Technology

**The Internet**

0-7314-0985-X
$39.95

**QuickBooks QB**

0-7314-0761-X
$39.95

**MYOB Software**

0-7314-0941-8
$39.95

**eBay**

1-74031-159-0
$39.95

# FOR DUMMIES®

## Health & Fitness

**Breast Cancer** FOR DUMMIES

1-74031-143-4
$39.95

**Menopause** FOR DUMMIES

1-74031-140-X
$39.95

**Food & Nutrition** FOR DUMMIES

0-7314-0596-X
$34.95

**Diabetes** FOR DUMMIES

1-74031-094-2
$39.95

**Fitness** FOR DUMMIES

1-74031-009-8
$39.95

**Living Gluten-Free** FOR DUMMIES

0-7314-0760-1
$34.95

**Yoga** FOR DUMMIES

1-74031-059-4
$39.95

**Pilates** FOR DUMMIES

1-74031-074-8
$39.95

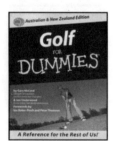

**Golf** FOR DUMMIES

1-74031-011-X
$39.95

**Cricket** FOR DUMMIES

1-74031-173-6
$39.95

**Aussie Rules** FOR DUMMIES

0-7314-0595-1
$34.95

**Sailing** FOR DUMMIES

0-7314-0644-3
$39.95